Volodymyr Paniotto

Sociology in Jokes
An Entertaining Introduction

UKRAINIAN VOICES

Collected by Andreas Umland

54   *Julia Davis*
        In Their Own Words
        How Russian Propagandists Reveal Putin's Intentions
        With a foreword by Timothy Snyder
        ISBN 978-3-8382-1909-7

55   *Sonya Atlantova, Oleksandr Klymenko*
        Icons on Ammo Boxes
        Painting Life on the Remnants of Russia's War in Donbas, 2014-21
        Translated from the Ukrainian by Anastasya Knyazhytska
        ISBN 978-3-8382-1892-2

56   *Leonid Ushkalov*
        Catching an Elusive Bird
        The Life of Hryhorii Skovoroda
        Translated from the Ukrainian by Natalia Komarova
        ISBN 978-3-8382-1894-6

57   *Vakhtang Kipiani*
        Ein Land weiblichen Geschlechts
        Ukrainische Frauenschicksale im 20. und 21. Jahrhundert
        Aus dem Ukrainischen übersetzt von Christian Weise
        ISBN 978-3-8382-1891-5

58   *Petro Rychlo*
        „Zerrissne Saiten einer überlauten Harfe ..."
        Deutschjüdische Dichter der Bukowina
        ISBN 978-3-8382-1893-9

The book series "Ukrainian Voices" publishes English- and German-language monographs, edited volumes, document collections, and anthologies of articles authored and composed by Ukrainian politicians, intellectuals, activists, officials, researchers, and diplomats. The series' aim is to introduce Western and other audiences to Ukrainian explorations, deliberations and interpretations of historic and current, domestic, and international affairs. The purpose of these books is to make non-Ukrainian readers familiar with how some prominent Ukrainians approach, view and assess their country's development and position in the world. The series was founded, and the volumes are collected by Andreas Umland, Dr. phil. (FU Berlin), Ph. D. (Cambridge), Associate Professor of Politics at the Kyiv-Mohyla Academy and an Analyst in the Stockholm Centre for Eastern European Studies at the Swedish Institute of International Affairs.

Volodymyr Paniotto

SOCIOLOGY IN JOKES
An Entertaining Introduction

Bibliographic information published by the Deutsche Nationalbibliothek

Die Deutsche Nationalbibliothek lists this publication in the Deutsche Nationalbibliografie; detailed bibliographic data are available on the Internet at http://dnb.d-nb.de.

Bibliografische Information der Deutschen Nationalbibliothek

Die Deutsche Nationalbibliothek verzeichnet diese Publikation in der Deutschen Nationalbibliografie; detaillierte bibliografische Daten sind im Internet über http://dnb.d-nb.de abrufbar.

Cover picture: © copyright Volodymyr Paniotto, 2024.

ISBN (Print): 978-3-8382-1857-1
ISBN (E-Book [PDF]): 978-3-8382-7857-5
© *ibidem*-Verlag, Hannover • Stuttgart 2024
All rights reserved.

No part of this publication may be reproduced, stored in or introduced into a retrieval system, or transmitted, in any form, or by any means (electronic, mechanical, photocopying, recording or otherwise) without the prior written permission of the publisher. Any person who commits any unauthorized act in relation to this publication may be liable to criminal prosecution and civil claims for damages.

Alle Rechte vorbehalten. Das Werk einschließlich aller seiner Teile ist urheberrechtlich geschützt. Jede Verwertung außerhalb der engen Grenzen des Urheberrechtsgesetzes ist ohne Zustimmung des Verlages unzulässig und strafbar. Dies gilt insbesondere für Vervielfältigungen, Übersetzungen, Mikroverfilmungen und elektronische Speicherformen sowie die Einspeicherung und Verarbeitung in elektronischen Systemen.

Printed in the United States of America

Contents

Preface 7

Part 1. Fundamentals of Sociology

1. What Does Sociology Study? 11

2. Main Theoretical Directions in Modern Sociology 17

3. Culture 21

4. Macrosocial Structures 31

5. Social Differentiation and Stratification 35

6. Socialization 41

7. Social Interaction 51

8. Gender, Sexuality, Marriage and Family 57

9. Religion 75

10. Economic System, Work, Free Time 89

11. Sociology of Crime and Law 103

12. Survey Methodology 119

13. Statistical Data Analysis, Modeling of Social Processes 139

14. Marketing and Advertising 147

Part 2. Results of Some Sociological Research in Ukraine

15. Interethnic Relations in Ukraine (1994–2023) 159

16. Attitudes of the Population of Ukraine Toward Russia and of the Population of Russia Toward Ukraine (2008–2022)... 175

17. Dynamics of the Level of Happiness and Its Determinants in Ukraine (2001–2017).. 187

18. Self-Assessment of Health Status by the Population of Ukraine... 205

19. Dynamics of the Poverty Rate in Ukraine (1994–2020)......... 213

20. Political Orientations of Cat and Dog Owners (2005)........... 223

Application: Anecdotes That Say Something Not Only About Sociology but About Psychology, Philosophy, and More 231

Independent Work

Home Task for Readers 251

Preface

I don't know if anyone reads forewords. I usually look in the preface if there are any questions when reading the book or after reading it. I have sent out the first draft of the manuscript to several colleagues and friends and already there are questions. That is why I am still writing the preface.

From 2011 to 2015, the Kyiv International Institute of Sociology (KIIS)[1] published a newsletter magazine, KIIS Review, and I kept a humor page there (these magazines are available on our website). That is when the idea for this book was born.

The point is that many anecdotes describe social processes very precisely and succinctly. For example, one can talk for a long time about social groups, norms and values, rules of admission to a group, the notions of "we" and "they", and the patterns of transition from one social group to another. If a person has moved from one social group to another, then in the new group, they will be suspected of loyalty to the old group, and they must be "holier than papa", proving loyalty to the new group; they must also demonstrate a negative attitude to the group from which they came. Instead of all this, we can tell a simple anecdote about a crocodile who ate a fisherman, put on his hat and started fishing. Another crocodile swam by; he peeked out of the water and asked, "Well, is it biting?". The crocodile in the hat, with a scornful look, replied: "Swim, swim, green shit!"

From time to time, I wrote down anecdotes that could illustrate some sociological concepts or notions and finally decided to write this book. Unfortunately, I discovered that the collected anecdotes are very unevenly distributed among sociological topics, and it will not be possible to replace a systematic presentation of the basics of sociology with anecdotes. Therefore, I have chosen some topics that show the specificity of the sociological approach to the analysis of society.

---

1 Kyiv International Institute of Sociology is a polling company that my friend Valeriy Khmelko and I created in 1992 and which I still run today

"What is it that you have," friends say, "you have almost no anecdotes for one chapter and dozens for another? And the comments are somehow unevenly distributed". What can I say? Either I collected anecdotes carelessly, or my scientific interests influenced it, or the people who create anecdotes have one picture of the world, and sociologists have another. However, I guess that does not matter. The main thing I want to show is that sociology is interesting and fun. Anecdotes should be used more actively; it is like big data using sociology for creative texts—they have no authorship, they do not cost to create, and they spontaneously arise and spread.

This book was published first in Ukrainian, and I would like to express my gratitude to Ellen Chalyuk for her help in preparing the English edition of the book.

Part 1.
Fundamentals of Sociology

1. What Does Sociology Study?

Maybe I talk too much to journalists and politicians, but I have the impression that by sociology, everyone understands only public opinion. It is also very annoying when people say, "I have done sociology here" (meaning, ordered a sociological survey) or, "a new sociology has arrived," or "I have read sociology here". Other sciences are more fortunate — after reading that the Poincaré problem has been solved, no one will say, "I have read new mathematics" or "I have read physics". Meanwhile, at large sociological congresses, there are more than a hundred sections, and only one is devoted to public opinion. Many people do not know anything about 99% of sociological research issues.

A formal definition can be given. "Sociology is a science that studies society, social relations, social interaction and culture". Nevertheless, it will not become clearer because you need to know what social relations, social interaction, etc., are.

Usually, science has a fundamental part, an applied part and a specific practical application. For example, there is theoretical physics that develops fundamental problems, there are different kinds of applied physics that study applied problems, and there are engineers who use the science of physics to, say, design or repair televisions. Similarly, sociology, as a basic science, explains social phenomena and collects and generalizes information about them (typical problems are social structure, social change, and social inequality). As an applied science, sociology allows predicting and managing social phenomena, in particular, these include ratings of politicians, which are studied through population surveys. There are also political technologists, marketers, and social workers who use the results of sociological research to solve some specific tasks — achieving victory in the electoral struggle, promoting goods on the market, helping vulnerable groups, etc.

Typical questions that have given rise to sociology as a science that attempts to answer them:

Why do people worship different gods?

Why can the lifestyles of different groups differ significantly from each other?

What motivates some people to violate social norms and rules of behavior and others to adhere to these norms and rules?

Why are some people rich while others are poor?

What motivates one group to go to war against another?

What keeps society from disintegrating?

Why are all societies constantly changing? And so on.

In the sphere of social cognition, the scientific method began to be applied much later than in the sphere of cognition of nature. In addition, social systems are much more complex than other living systems, just as living systems are much more complex than non-living systems.

The social sciences, like the natural sciences, are involved in the scientific method, which consists of drawing conclusions based on a careful, systematic analysis of facts. Moreover, these facts can be verified by other researchers. If they do the same research, they should get the same results.

On the other hand, unscientific explanations of events that come only out of so-called common sense or everyday consciousness are based on faith, opinions, and perceptions. The ancient Romans, for example, believed that every day Helios drove the sun across the sky in his chariot, although none of them actually saw it. This is not to say that common sense cannot make correct explanations and predictions. It can and often does. The problem is that, without using the methods of science, there is no way to determine when common sense makes correct conclusions. In the social sphere, even today, many common sense notions are, in fact, myths. Sociology textbooks often cite such examples.

Opinion (overwhelming): members of the lower social classes are more likely to commit crimes than members of the upper class.

Facts: Reliable fact-checking in the United States and Western Europe shows that the percentage of those who commit crimes in the upper social class is the same as in the lower classes. However, the poor are more likely than the rich to commit certain types of crime (for example, petty theft is much more common than grand fraud), and they are also more likely to be arrested and convicted.

An example from family life.

Public opinion: Victims of domestic violence are predominantly women, who are killed by their sexual partners.

Fact: Men also often become victims. For example, of those killed by their partners worldwide in 2020, 58% were women and 42% were men[2]. Although men are usually stronger, women are more likely to resort to dangerous weapons such as kitchen knives.

Public perception: Americans believe that doctors can correctly diagnose most of the patients who see them.

Fact: Surveys of physicians show that in more than half of patients, doctors cannot identify the disease, but they do not want to admit it to their patients.

These are just some examples of the differences between perceptions that are based on the ground of 'common sense' or everyday consciousness and scientific studies of social life.

Unfortunately, the perception of sociological facts is different from the perception of research results in other fields of science. Nowadays, you do not meet people who reject Newton's or Einstein's theories on the basis of their common sense, but this happens all the time with regard to the results of sociological research. Any publication of data from research companies is criticized on the grounds that the results seem implausible to some people and that they do not correspond to their perceptions. These perceptions themselves are formed on the basis of their experiences in their social circle, in their interactions with like-minded people on Facebook and in the 'desirability shift'. The outcome they like (based on their policy preferences) seems plausible, and the one they do not

---

2   Killings of women and girls by their intimate partner or other family members. Global estimates 2020. — DATA MATTERS 3, 11/2021. Report by United Nations Office on Drugs and Crime, 2021. — 34 p. UN_BriefFem_251121.pdf (uno dc.org), https://www.unodc.org/documents/data-and-analysis/statistics/crime/UN_BriefFem_251121.pdf

14   SOCIOLOGY IN JOKES

like seems highly suspect. Therefore, sociologists are accused of having their data bought by the customer or of incorrectly formulating questions (the arrogance of such 'experts' in sociology is astonishing).

Understanding the society in which we live enables us to understand ourselves more fully. The American sociologist Wright Mills called this component of knowledge "the sociological imagination" — the ability to see our lives, concerns, problems, and hopes and their connections to the broad social and historical context in which we live. By studying sociology, we better understand how society is organized, who has power, what beliefs guide our behavior, and how our society came to be the way it is.

* * *

A little boy asks his father: *"Daddy, what is biology?"*
— *"Well ... How can I explain it to you in a simpler way? For example, you look like me. That's biology.*
— *"And 'sociology' is what?"* My son won't stop.
— *"That's. Hmmm ... My neighbor's son also looks like me. That's sociology!"*

By the way, separating biology from sociology is sometimes not as easy as in this anecdote. Much scientific research has been done to understand, for example, which human characteristics are determined by biological heredity and which are determined by the process of socialization and upbringing (see Section 6, Socialization).

* * *

95% of phone conversations are idle chatter, according to the FSB's sociological service[3].

The authors of this anecdote from the Russian Internet hint at the specificity of the FSB's goals and the search for very specific information. However, tapping phones to identify opposition sentiments is not sociological research. The main difference is that

---

3   FSB — the Federal Security Service of Russia — is the main legal successor to the KGB of the USSR

sociologists study the phenomenon, not specific people, and give recommendations not on specific people but on what to do to solve certain problems. Information about each person's answers is strictly confidential; personal data is kept separate from the answers and is never shared with customers. Interestingly, even Nazi sociologists during World War II, who analyzed letters from soldiers at the front, destroyed the envelopes so that their customers would not be tempted to find out who wrote such unreliable things.

* * *

A sociologist rebukes his wife.
— *"Why did you hurt my mom? Why do you talk first and think later?"*
— *"How will I know what I'm thinking until I say it? You're doing the same thing, aren't you?"*
— *"Why is that?"*
— *"I asked you last week why population polls are conducted. And you said that public opinion polls are done so that the public knows what they think."*

"Population surveys are conducted so that the population knows what it thinks" is paradoxically true. In principle, many sociologists, primarily academic sociologists, work not for a specific customer but for society as a whole.

We (KIIS) once had a project—"Mirror of Society." The idea was to conduct regular surveys representative of the Ukrainian population. During this research (unlike 'ordinary' sociological surveys), we asked not about what sociologists are interested in but about what the population is interested in. Therefore, during the survey, we asked what people would like to know about other people and what they would ask respondents about if they were conducting the survey themselves. As a result of analyzing the results of this survey, we find out what questions citizens are most interested in and ask these questions during the next survey. Thus, in each next survey, we get answers to the questions posed by respondents the previous day. The results of the survey must be presented in the mass media (for example, in any of the popular Ukrainian TV channels). Thus, the citizens of Ukraine, with our help and with the help of mass media, asked themselves questions

16   SOCIOLOGY IN JOKES

and answered them themselves; it was like a sociological MIRROR OF SOCIETY.

This anecdote is an example of the work that electoral sociology does. Without data from sociologists, it is virtually impossible to assess the situation and take action.

* * *

Husband asks his wife: *"Honey, have you ever cheated on me?"*
— *"Yes, darling. Three times."*
— *"Well, when?"*
— *"Remember when you wanted to start your own business, no bank wanted to give you a loan, and then suddenly, the president of the bank agreed?"*
— *"Yeah, I remember. Thank you, you helped us get rich. But when was the second time?"*
— *"Remember, you were seriously ill, and no one wanted to operate on you. And then all of a sudden, the chief of surgery himself performed the surgery?"*
— *"Yes, I remember. Thank you, my dear, you saved my life, I'm very grateful to you. But when was the third time?"*
— *"Do you remember that according to the results of sociological research it turned out that you lacked 36 votes from men between 40 and 60 years old?"*

* * *

At a symposium, an American professor asked a Russian colleague:
— *"Does it happen to you that you treat for one disease, but the postmortem shows a completely different one?"*
— *"No, of course not. What we treat for is what they die from."*

This is an illustration of the fact that American doctors often cannot make the right diagnosis, but in post-Soviet countries, this supposedly does not happen.

2. Main Theoretical Directions in Modern Sociology

A. Functionalism

The structural-functionalist or simply functionalist approach was formulated mainly on the ideas of Herbert Spencer and Emile Durkheim. During the 1950s and early 1960s, the functionalist theories of Talcott Parsons (1902–1979) and his disciples became the center of attention in American sociology. In the 1980s, interest in the works of Parsons and other functionalists arose again (in the works of Habermas, Alekzander, Sciuli, Gerstein and others).

Functionalists view society as a kind of system, a combination of parts that make up a whole. Functionalists are trying to do two things: to establish links between parts of society and society as a whole and to establish the connections of each part of society with the others.

Institutions such as family, religion, economy, state, and education are among the most important parts of every society. For example, the main functions of the family are reproduction, socialization, support of children, and self-realization of its members. At the same time, changes in one institution of society create an impact on other institutions and society as a whole. For example, when women were encouraged to work in the economy, they married later and had fewer children. In turn, this led to fewer school-age children and schools in some areas closed. Because of this, the United States military noted a shortage of military personnel to serve in the army in the 1990s.

B. Conflictionism or conflict theory

From the point of view of conflictionism, society looks like an arena of struggles for privileges, prestige, and power, and social groups look like those that resort to coercion — hidden or unconcealed — in order to preserve their advantages. Conflictionist concepts are largely based on the ideas of Karl Marx. I think the ideas of

18   SOCIOLOGY IN JOKES

Marxism are best known to readers. Both functionalism and conflictionism (Marxism in particular) are macrosociological approaches. A significant complement to these macrosociological approaches is microsociological approaches. The main one is the interactionist approach.

C. Interactionism

In addition to those questions addressed in macrosociological concepts, sociologists are concerned with quite a few other questions. For example, "How do individuals and society relate to each other? How can people create, preserve, and change society and, at the same time, be shaped by that society? And how do individuals influence each other? Such questions are the focus of the interactionist approach, also called symbolic interactionism. Its main architect is the famous American sociologist George Herbert Mead (1863–1931). Interactionists argue that our social world is a constructed reality. Society does not exist "out there"; it is constantly being created and reproduced from moment to moment in the processes of our actions with each other. We give it a name: "Ukraine," "France," "United States." And we interact with it as an object.

From an interactionist point of view, societies arise because of this (that we interact with something as an object). We make them real. This also applies to small groups, organizations, and communities. We interact with them as objects on a daily basis. At the same time, each person's everyday interactions with others make them a social being with a certain personality.

* * *

A lecturer in a collective farm[4] club gives a lecture on Marxism. From the audience, a woman asks: *"Tell me, please, is Marxism a science?"*. Then, an older woman beats the lecturer with the answer, *"Manyka, what a fool you are! If it were a science, they would have tried it on rats first."*

---

4   Collective farm (Kolgosp – short for collective farm in Ukrainian) is a form of agricultural enterprise in the territory of the Soviet Union.

The anecdotes I have come across are all about conflictionism, namely, Marxism. In the former Soviet Union, Marxism turned into a dogmatic doctrine resembling religion. This ideology was hammered into everyone at school, at the institute, and in Marxism-Leninism classes at companies. For example, at the mathematics department of Shevchenko University in Kyiv, which I graduated from in 1970, for the first two years, they studied the history of the Communist Party in great detail; then, in the third year, dialectical materialism and historical materialism, and in the fourth year, scientific communism. That was for mathematicians. Moreover, what to say of humanitarian specialties! Here, for example, in the memoirs about the famous pianist Goldenweiser, a professor at the Moscow Conservatory, it is told how an elderly professor was accused of not being in class to study the basics of Marxism-Leninism. Goldenweiser replied: "I myself will soon meet Karl Marx, and he will explain everything well to me." Or here's another:

* * *

— *"Rabinovich, why weren't you at the last Marxism-Leninism class?"*
— *"Oh my goodness, I didn't realize it was the last one. If I had known, I would have loved to attend!"*

Marxism-Leninism has 'annoyed' everyone so much that it has given rise to many jokes. The second reason is the failure to build a successful society based on this theory. Meanwhile, conflictionism (and Marxism) can explain some social phenomena that are not explained by other approaches. It seems that Marxism is now more popular in the USA than in the former USSR.

* * *

— *"What did Germany inherit from Marx?"*
The East replies: *"The Communist Manifesto, the West says, capital."*

* * *

— *What is the difference between math and Marxism?*
— *In math, something is given, and something is required to be proven, while in Marxism, everything is proven, and nothing is given.*

20   SOCIOLOGY IN JOKES

* * *

— What is scarcity from a Marxist point of view?
— It is an objective reality, not given to us by feelings.

* * *

Karl Marx returns to the Earth and comes to Moscow television with a request to allow him to speak. He is refused: *"We already have many programs about Marx every day"*.
Marx insists, asking for permission to say at least a few words. Finally, he concedes but is allowed to say only one single phrase. Marx goes to the microphone and says: *"Proletarians of all countries, forgive me!"*

Unfortunately, I have not found anecdotes dealing with functionalism and interactionism. Maybe the reader will find some.

3. Culture

The word culture is polysemous. In everyday life, this word is most often used to mean (a) Educated, well-read, or intelligent. In this sense, expressions such as "personal culture" or "cultured person" are used. This word also denotes a refined taste for art, literature, and music. It is interesting that, for some reason, our understanding of an educated and cultural person includes only humanitarian knowledge. An absolute ignoramus in mathematics can be considered a cultured person. Is it fair? B) In other meanings, the word "culture" is used in specialized sciences. For example, agrarians say "rice culture" or "grain crops", and archaeologists call culture a community of archaeological monuments of a certain epoch when they speak, for example, of "Tripoli culture". Closest to sociological culture is the understanding of the inherent culture by historians. Most often, they call culture the totality of achievements of a certain people in a certain epoch in their spiritual and material activities (for example, the culture of ancient Egypt, the culture of ancient Greece or Byzantine culture).

In sociological understanding, the concept of culture has a broad meaning — it designates all products of people's creative activity — material (machinery, clothes, houses, cities, books, spaceships) and non-material (values, beliefs, norms, habits, myths, family structure, political organizations). For a sociologist, there is no human being without culture; any ignorant "stooge" from the point of view of sociology is a carrier of culture; the very words "human being" denote a cultural being (as opposed to an animal).

Elements of Culture.

Signs.

The primary component of culture is signs, which enable us to represent objects, events and people to others and ourselves to consider and discuss rules of behavior. However, the rules themselves have no physical existence ("traffic regulations", "rules of behavior during quarantine"). Signs have many forms: gestures (body

22   SOCIOLOGY IN JOKES

postures or movements that have social meaning, flags, emblems, icons, uniforms, and so on. People are beings living in a sign environment.

Language.

The most important sign system is language, perhaps humanity's most complex achievement: a socially structured system of sound patterns. Language makes it possible to express everything from physical needs to spiritual demands, to create culture, to accumulate experience and pass it on to subsequent generations (culture does not exist without language), to perform complex social activities, etc. The more we cognize a phenomenon, the more words we have to designate them. For example, the Arabs have thousands of variations of the word "camel" to designate camels of different qualities. For example, a separate word for a camel between 6 and 20 years old, a separate word for a female riding a camel over five years old ("naki"), and so on. The language of the Hanune people living in the Philippines has 92 names for rice. There are more than 20 names for snow among the Eskimos to denote the slightest differences in snow. According to Benjamin Lee Whorf (1897–1974), speech determines the shape of our thinking and our perception of the world. Speakers of a particular language are forced to interpret the world through the unique vocabulary and grammar that their speech gives them.

Each language provides a different slice of the world, drawing attention to different facets of human experience. According to Whorf, we selectively sift through sensory information in a way that is determined by our language: some things we perceive, others are filtered out by language.

Language allows us in a particular social setting to produce shared understandings about what we can expect from each of us — hopes or expectations (sociologists call them expectations).

Norms.

Examples of social expectations include waiting in line at the store ("the queue will end, and then we will be served"). Expectations about the money we receive for our work — it can be exchanged for goods and services we need (we follow the rule that money is legal tender). Thousands of such shared notions exist in social life. Of course, they take the form of expectations embodied in norms. Norms are social rules or directives that establish what behavior is appropriate and what behavior is inappropriate for a particular situation. Most often, norms are fixed and presented by individuals verbally (by means of language), some of them — in object-significant form (samples of clothes, uniforms, road signs), as well as in the form of symbols (anthems, flags, orders). Violation of these norms has social consequences; society applies certain sanctions. Norms are, above all, the means of our activity by which we orient ourselves in the world of people. They give us instructions on how to behave in order to succeed in common activities. However, norms are also goals. People give norms an independent value and treat them as things of constructed reality. Norms become standards by which people judge each other's actions and reward or punish appropriate or inappropriate behavior. The strength of social pressure to adhere to certain norms varies greatly and depends on the importance of the norms for society or its particular groups. For those norms called customs (or rules of behavior), society's reaction to their violation can be quite tolerant. For example, we condemn people who wear dirty clothes or who are late for meetings, but we do not consider them immoral or criminals. The main mechanisms by which customs are maintained (i.e., sanctions) are gossip and ridicule.

The stricter norms are the 'mores' (moral norms). These norms strictly condemn and prohibit murder, theft, violence, and betrayal. Mores are such norms that are necessary for the survival of society and its peaceful existence. Violators of such norms are considered immoral or criminal and may be fined, imprisoned, flogged, or executed. If, for example, a man walks down the street in summer without clothes on the upper half of his body, he is violating customs and passersby may turn around at him or say something to each other, but this will not have more serious consequences. If, however, he walks down the street without clothes on the lower half of his body, this is a violation of manners (morality), and he

24   Sociology in Jokes

will be taken by the police to the station and fined. The moral norms of society are the most important source of laws.

Laws are norms that are established by the state power and supported by its organs. The state has the right to use force when these norms are violated. The possibility of legal application of physical coercion is a specific difference of the norms of the law. Laws change more easily than customs and morals.

Values are ideas about what is good, right, just, or desirable that are shared by most members of a society or some social group. The difference between norms and values is that values are abstract, general concepts, while norms are concrete rules of action in specific situations. Values are the criteria for evaluation.

* * *

— *"Very well,"* said the ophthalmologist, *"you have One."*
— *"What does that mean?"*
— *"Your vision is perfectly normal."*
— *"Normal is like everyone else's?"*
— *"No, only 30% of the population has normal vision."*

There are two concepts of norm. The norm as an ideal, as proper, as something to be strived for. For example, laws or rules of behavior. Let's say, to cross the street only at intersections and only when the lights are green. These are formal norms. Moreover, some norms are adhered to by the majority of the population. In Ukraine when crossing the street, most people focus on the real situation, on the danger, not on formal rules. When coming to Germany for the first time, tourists are surprised to see Germans on an empty street at night, standing at the traffic light when it is red.

* * *

Peter noticed that his wife trims the ends of the sausages before cooking. *"Sonya, why do you do that?"*
— *"I don't know; my mom always does it."*
He went to his mother-in-law's room. *"Ida Solomonovna, why do you cut off the ends of the sausages before cooking?"*
— *"I don't know; that's how my mom always cooked them."*

– "*Can you call and ask?*"
– "*Okay, well, I was going to call her anyway. Mommy, my son-in-law, wants to know why we cut off the ends of the sausages before cooking them.*"
– "*Idochka, are you and Sonya still cooking sausages in my little pot?*"

This is an illustration of the question of cultural reproduction. We perform some actions without knowing how this or that tradition or custom originated. Often, its introduction was rational at first, but then it lost its original meaning and now such customs look meaningless, but they are still followed.

* * *

The norm is an idiocy that has been accepted.

This variant of norm formation is also quite possible. Why do we sit down for a moment before traveling? Or shake hands (which, incidentally, contributed to the spread of the coronavirus)? Why do we say, "Harping on the same string" or "Everything went to hell in a handbasket. " (this is all down the drain)? Does anyone have any idea what that means?

* * *

A guy walks into a flower store and asks the clerk to give him one rose.
– "*Who are you buying for, if it's no secret? Your wife?*"
– "*No, for my mother-in-law, it's her birthday.*"
– "*Why only one? Isn't that too little? Your mother-in-law won't be offended?*"
– "*Oh, you know, you're probably right. Let's have two roses!*"

In the former Soviet Union, the tradition is to bring an odd number of flowers to a funeral or the cemetery, you cannot give an even number of flowers on other occasions, only an odd number. Moreover, for example, in the United States, you give 12 flowers; in Germany, eight. This anecdote shows that many social norms are not universal; they are common more or less in societies. In our country, this norm dates back to paganism. However, universal norms and values are also formed (for example, the taboo on cannibalism).

26   SOCIOLOGY IN JOKES

* * *

— "Tell me, Rabbi, where did the custom forbidding an Orthodox Jew to walk with an uncovered head come from?"
The Rabbi answers: *"The Torah says: 'And Moses came down from the mountain to the people'".*
— "But where does it say anything about the head?
— "Where where? That Moses went out to the people without a kippah?"

Often, social norms, traditions, and customs have such an ancient origin that people may not remember where they came from and feel that they have always been there. The rabbi cannot even imagine that it was ever otherwise.

* * *

A grandson asks his grandfather, *"What is ethics?"*
— "I'll explain it to you with an example. Rabinovich and I have a store, as you know. And Rosa Solomonovna comes in to do some shopping. I wrap everything up for her, thank her for the purchase, walk her to the door, wish her a good day, return to the counter and see a purse with money in it. And that's where the ethical question comes in: should I share that money with my partner?"

Many ethical norms are not absolute; they may exist only within a certain social group. For example, thieves' norms. A thief strictly follows the norm to show an honest and respectful attitude to other equal members of the thief community ('honor among thieves'), which, however, does not apply to persons occupying a lower position or completely outsiders. They completely reject external social norms and rules, have no right to engage in socially useful labor, cooperate with the authorities, etc. In this case, the hero of the anecdote thinks about the observance of norms in relation to his business partner, while cheating the customer is the norm for him. Interactionism explains the existence and reproduction of crime by the fact that certain cultural norms and rules are passed on during socialization and upbringing. Hence, children in families of criminals are more likely to become criminals than in ordinary families.

* * *

— "Look, is there any other meaning to the word 'fight'?"
— "No, there isn't. Why the question?"
— "You see, all the time, time I hear: fight against corruption, fight against corruption. But in life I see something else, so I thought maybe I just don't know my native language very well."

And I had such a case. After the announcement of the policy of perestroika and glasnost in the Soviet Union, meetings with American sociologists began. During the meetings with Melvin Kohn, president of the American Sociological Association, it was planned to conduct the first international project in Ukraine "The Impact of Social Structure on Personality"[5]. I discussed with Melvin Kohn the methodology of surveying by interview and we could not understand each other for forty minutes, no less. It turned out that because of the isolation of Soviet sociologists, an interview in the Soviet Union was usually understood as what was called a handout questionnaire in the rest of the world (the questioner gives a questionnaire to the respondent, waits for them to fill it out, and answers questions if they arise, i.e., the respondent reads the questions and fills out the questionnaire). That is what I was referring to. Melvin meant what has now become our definition of an interview — a survey in which the interviewer asks the respondent questions and the interviewer records the answers (the respondent is not shown the questionnaire). This is, of course, a rare case. However, the fact that in different languages, even traditional translations of words do not cover all the nuances is a problem in international research projects.

* * *

An attempted rape was committed in the building of a large firm. An investigator interviews the victim in the director's office.
Director: *"There's no way our employee did this!"*
Investigator:*" We'll look into it. Victim, did you get a good look at your attacker? Do you remember any signs?"*
Woman: *"No, he attacked from behind. I just remember dirty shoes."*
Director: *"I told you! We're a solid firm. It's probably one of the visitors."*

---

5   The project was carried out for about 15 years; see the results. Social Structures and Individuality: Studies by Melvin Kohn and His Spivpratsivniki, Kyiv: Vidavnichy dim "Kyiv-Mohyla Academy", 2007. 558 c.

28 SOCIOLOGY IN JOKES

> Investigator: *"Victim, do you remember anything unusual about the behavior of the attacker?"*
> Woman: *"First he was very persistent, active, even aggressive. But as soon as there was a small obstacle, something there was not immediately unbuttoned, he immediately wilted and ran away."*
> Director sadly: *"Yes, it seems to be one of ours after all."*

In organizations that have existed for a long time, a so-called corporate culture is formed. These are norms, rules, and patterns of behavior that are shared by the majority of the organization's members. The management usually tries to influence its formation in such a way that it contributes to the efficiency of the company's work. For example, at KIIS, we are trying to make the motto "Reputation is more important than profit" an element of the corporate culture (I do not know how successful we have been).

* * *

> — *"Rebbe, we had a child before we were married — is that a big sin?"*
> — *"What, a sin! How could a child know when you were getting married?"*

Sin is a type of deviation from the norm; it is the name used for deviations from religious norms (such as the commandments). In different societies, the sanctions for violating these norms can vary greatly. In some societies, the violator may be burned (as was the case in the Middle Ages) or stoned, while in other societies, the sanctions are slanted glances from neighbors. Society strives to make external norms become internalized so that the rules of behavior are supported not by external sanctions but by conscience or other feelings of a person (for example, once sexual relations between parents and children were generally accepted, but now the norms prohibiting sexual relations between parents and children have become an internal norm, and it is so effective that people feel unpleasant just thinking about it; such norms, as mentioned above, are called taboos).

* * *

> — *"Rabbi, what should I do? I can't keep so many commandments. I try, I try, I try, but it doesn't work."*

CULTURE   29

> — *"The important thing is not to be discouraged. Keep trying. I have to confess that I can't fulfill one commandment either."*
> — *"Yes, Rebbe? Which one?"*
> — *"Well, that depends on the circumstances."*

People are always looking for ways to justify their behavior, to present it as socially approved, corresponding to norms. For this purpose, euphemisms and substitutions of negative characteristics with positive ones are used (for example, not greedy but frugal, not rude and boorish but truthful and frank, not boring but thorough).

* * *

> — *"Sofochka, is it true that your brother is in jail for theft?*
> — *"No. He was released early for good behavior!*
> — *"I can't imagine how proud you all are of him!"*

In addition to the common culture of a society, there are also cultures of different social groups within the society. They are called subcultures. A subculture can be distinguished by its system of values, habits, clothes, language, behavior, etc. If the values of a given subculture are very different and contradict the values of the whole society, this type of subculture is called a counterculture. The previously mentioned "thieves in law", who very strictly followed their norms and rules, followed their ideas of honor (perhaps much more strictly than ordinary citizens followed the rules of society as a whole)—this is a typical example of counterculture. For example, a thief-in-law was not supposed to accept any job, not to cooperate with law enforcement (even as a witness), not allowed to kill (unless the thief's honor was at stake), etc. It is not excluded that in some of the subcultures, it was possible to be proud of early release from prison.

Here is another counter-culture anecdote.

* * *

Thieves are sitting in a prison cell. One thief brings a bowl of bread, and suddenly, a huge rat runs out of somewhere, grabs a piece of bread and tries to run away. A young convict grabs a bowl and throws it at the rat with all his might. The bowl hits the rat, after which the

30 SOCIOLOGY IN JOKES

rat falls and lies without signs of life. There is silence; everyone is silent. One of the convicts asks him:

– *"We're all thieves sitting here. You're a thief too, aren't you?"*
– *"Yes"*, replied the one who killed the rat.
– *"A rat stole our bread ..."*
– *"Yeah, so what?"*
– *"Like what? If a rat stole our bread, he's a thief too. So you killed our comrade. If you, asshole, don't come up with an excuse by morning ... you're dead."*
The convict who killed the rat stayed up all night.
– *"What do you say?"* The old thief asked him.
– *"What can I say? The rat stole our bread. So he's a thief too, our comrade. Isn't he?"*
– *"Well, yes,"* replied the old convict.
– *"Why couldn't that damn rat just sit with us? What, does it think it's too good for us?"*

* * *

In an Odessa school, a teacher asks a question to the class: *"Children, who knows what happened in 1799? Who does? Shame on you for not knowing. In 1799, the great Russian poet Alexander Sergeyevich Pushkin was born! Children, who knows what happened in 1812?"*
Iziah stands up and answers: *"In 1812, the great Russian poet Alexander Sergeevich Pushkin had a bar mitzvah ..."*

There is no such tradition in Ukrainian culture; the overwhelming majority of the population has no idea what a bar mitzvah is. In Judaism, bar mitzvah means something like a rite of passage. When a boy reaches the age of 13, he reads the Torah in the synagogue, then they organize a celebration and give gifts. As far as I know, even non-religious Jews often organize such celebrations without a synagogue. Apparently, for Iziah's family and its immediate social circle, this was a common tradition. So he assumed that Pushkin, at the age of 13, also had such a celebration.

4. Macrosocial Structures

What is a society? A society is a social association of people that meets certain conditions: 1) is self-reproducing (reproduces its structure), 2) has a defined territory, 3) has common elements of culture, and 4) a system of political power that is not subordinate to other societies. Every society is structured. The concept of social structure is one of the central concepts of sociology; it is because of social structure that human life gives the impression of being organized and regular. Much of what sociologists call social structure consists of political understandings and agreements — a network of implicit rules and regulations — that guide people's behavior. Many problems never arise, and many institutional rules never provoke opposition because people regard these rules as self-explanatory and their implementation as routine.

Social structure is a certain set of relatively recurring and ordered relations between the components of a social system (the macrostructure of society). One way of structuring everyday life from a microsociologist's point of view is to combine certain cases and assign them names, i.e., labeling: "family", "church", "government", "Ukraine," or "United States". Vander Zanden believes that "strictly speaking, there are no such things, only a collection of certain actions of individuals which we take to be ordered and designate by a certain name." In the social structure, people are distributed according to social positions and stable attributes of the subjects who enter and leave the social system. The people who make up the university come, learn or teach, then leave, but the university remains. Kyiv-Mohyla Academy, where I teach, has the slogan, "Time flows, and the Academy is eternal." In 2015, it celebrated its 400th anniversary. A church may exist for millennia; there may be no houses left, no material objects that came to us from the founders of the church, and it continues to exist. So do families, orchestras, cat clubs, armies, and corporations. From a microsociological point of view, the two main components of social structure are statuses and roles.

Status is a position in a certain social structure of society with certain rights and responsibilities. For example — student, professor, dean, head of a department, head of the academic unit, department secretary — these are certain positions in the social structure of the university with certain statuses. Statuses are distinguished precisely by rights and duties that are determined by social norms. Every adult in modern society has several statuses (student, sibling, friend, public figure). In many cases, the different statuses of a person do not contradict each other. However there are situations of status incompatibility (inconsistency). Status determines when one enters society, so to speak, how one should behave around other people.

The most significant differences exist between the statuses that society establishes for a person independently of their actions: at birth, with age, due to changes in the statuses of relatives (the spouse of a student becomes the spouse of the president), and achieved statuses that a person can acquire (or lose) due to their activities.

In most societies, there are significant inequalities between different statuses. For example, a person with the status of a member of the US Supreme Court has more money, power, and prestige than a restaurant waiter. Alternatively, the head of a large Ukrainian corporation, who owns several television channels and leads a faction in the Verkhovna Rada (Ukrainian parliament), has a higher status in terms of income, power, and prestige than a schoolteacher. A set of members of societies that have approximately the same status (in terms of wealth, power and prestige) is called a social class by some sociologists (others, a social stratum). Members of a certain social stratum have greater access to public wealth and other resources of society than people with lower statuses, but less access than people with higher statuses. The fact that statuses are hierarchized has profound social consequences.

The second (besides status) basic element of social structure is role. Status is always associated with some expected behavior that is determined by the culture of the society. It is this expected behavior associated with status that sociologists like Linton, Merton, and Smelser call social roles.

The main difference between status and role is that a person occupies (or has) status while a person fulfills a role. A role is a set of expectations (expectations, norms) of people's behavior in relation to a certain social status (not the behavior itself, but a "project" of behavior, an expected "scheme" of behavior). Social roles are one of the main objects of sociological research. Roles have a normative nature. Therefore, they give us the opportunity to first "project" our behavior and then carry it out in an appropriate way.

With roles, we bring order to our social world by categorizing people. We assume that we can largely ignore personality when we go to the doctor, for example. We think that the doctor will listen to us carefully, look at the tests, diagnose us and prescribe treatment regardless of whether they are melancholic or sanguine, what party they vote for, what books and movies they like, or whether they are having an affair.

Role performance is the actual (actual) behavior of a person occupying a particular status. Each role is associated with at least one reciprocal role (doctor-patient). One of the factors that brings people together in groups is the network of reciprocal roles. Role relationships bind us to each other because rights on one side of the relationship are responsibilities on the other side.

* * *

> All the world's a stage,
> And all the men and women merely players;
> They have their exits and their entrances,
> And one man in his time plays many parts.
> —Shakespeare. *As You Like It.*

It is not an anecdote, but it captures the idea of role theory well. I even think that Shakespeare's play suggested the idea of statuses and roles to the authors of role theory. In Section 7 on social interactions, we will look at Erwin Hoffmann's dramaturgical approach, which develops this analogy.

* * *

34   SOCIOLOGY IN JOKES

Mark Twain wrote, *"A man is willing to do much to arouse love, but will dare anything to arouse envy."*

* * *

University entrance exams. The professor asks the applicant a lot of additional questions, and he answers them all. *"Okay"*, says the professor. *"Finally, the last question: Youngman, why did you choose our university for your admission?"*
– *"Dad, enough already; let's talk about it at home!"*

Each person has several statuses; sometimes there is a conflict of these statuses, and sometimes there are difficulties in the relationship between two people because it is not clear what norms should be used in the interaction, the norms of one status or another (for example, the norms of relations between a boss and a secretary or a lover and a mistress, a professor and a student or a father and a son). Here is an example of status conflict in relations with doctors, when the norms of behavior toward strangers in general and toward doctors differ significantly. If you take off your pants for the first time when visiting a strange woman, it will look strange, but if you do it in the office where this woman works as a doctor, it will be accepted behavior.

5. Social Differentiation and Stratification

All societies behave differently, with those who have certain characteristics and those who do not. Every society treats differently, for example, older and younger people and men and women. In addition, a society may treat its members differently, depending on their skin color, physical strength, religious beliefs, level of education, or any other characteristics that are considered important in that society. A common result of such differences is social inequality, the unequal sharing of social goods such as wealth, power, and respect.

Social differentiation and **social stratification** are concepts used to describe the structure of society, but they denote different aspects of social organization.

1. **Social differentiation** refers to the process or condition in which society is divided into different social groups or categories based on different criteria such as occupation, education, age or gender. The term is broader and describes the variety of social roles and functions that may overlap and interact with each other. Differentiation can be horizontal (division into groups of roughly equal status, such as different professions) and vertical (division by level of power or income).

2. **Social stratification is** a narrower and more specific term that refers to the hierarchical organization of social strata or classes within a society. Stratification always has a vertical structure and is based on inequality of access to resources such as wealth, power, and education. Social strata in a stratification system can be clearly demarcated, and there is often a barrier to social mobility between them.

Thus, the main difference between the two concepts is that social differentiation describes diversity and division in society based on different characteristics. In contrast, social stratification emphasizes hierarchical ordering and social inequality. The scientific view of stratification has changed and been refined over time. Karl Marx developed a view of stratification where society is divided into a class of capitalists (the bourgeoisie), who own the means of production, and the proletariat (the working class), who have only their labor power. The bourgeoisie was seen as the oppressing class, and the proletariat as the oppressed class.

Together with Melvin Kohn, in our research, we used a modification of Marx's concept proposed by Eric Wright and improved by Kohn (Kohn et al., 2007). We analyzed ownership of the means of production and the degree of control over them, defining classes based on their combination, such as employers, top managers, self-employed, etc.

The famous German sociologist Max Weber (1864–1920) proposed a three-dimensional concept of stratification, arguing that social ranking in society has not only an economic aspect but also aspects of status and power. Classes are defined by economic criteria, statuses by prestige, and parties by power. Some statuses can combine high ranking by wealth, prestige and power, such as doctors. At the same time, university professors in Ukraine may have high prestige but low economic status and power. However, these three dimensions of stratification are often interrelated and interact with each other.

Social inequality is a central issue in sociological debates. Historically, two different directions have emerged: conservative, which supports the existing social order, and radical, which criticizes the existing arrangements. Modern theories of inequality also fall into these two traditions: functionalist (which grew out of the conservative tradition) and conflict theories (which grew out of the radical tradition).

Functionalist theory

It holds that stratification exists because it is beneficial to society. The classic statements of this theory were formulated in 1945 by Kingsley Davis and Wilbert Moore[6], although it has been modified

---

6   Davis, Kingsley, and Wilbert E. Moore. "Some Principles of Stratification." *American Sociological Review*, vol. 10, no. 2, 1945, pp. 242-249.

and improved by other sociologists many times since then. Davis and Moore argued that social stratification is both universal and necessary and that no society will ever be completely classless. From their point of view, all societies need stratification if they are to fill all the statuses that exist in the social structure and motivate people to fulfill the duties associated with their positions. Different positions have different importance to society. Both presidents and servers are necessary for society. However, a server's mistake can lead to the consequence of a customer's spoiled clothes, but a president's mistake can lead to a war in which thousands of people will die. Therefore, more capable people should be chosen for the more important positions, and there should be competition for the roles. For this purpose, rewards are provided for the fulfillment of roles in these positions — higher economic status, prestige, power — they are built into the social system. Hence, the need for social inequality and social stratification; without them, there would be no motivation to fulfill more demanding social roles. Using a supply and demand model developed by economists, Davis and Moore concluded that positions that reward the most are those that 1) are engaged with the most talented and most qualified individuals (this is on the supply side), and 2) are functionally more important to society (this is on the demand side). For example, to guarantee a sufficient number of qualified, skillful physicians, society must offer them high wages and high prestige. Davis and Moore wrote that if we do not offer physicians such rewards, we cannot expect people to want to pursue the burdensome and expensive medical education. People at the top of the social hierarchy should be rewarded accordingly. Otherwise, these positions would remain unfilled, and society would disintegrate.

Conflictionist theory

The conflict theory of social stratification is based on Karl Marx's idea, which asserted that social stratification serves individuals and groups who hold power. Society is seen as an arena of struggle for privilege, prestige and power where social groups use coercion to maintain their advantages. In the feudal system, landowners

38   SOCIOLOGY IN JOKES

controlled the economy and dominated the serfs; in the capitalist system, capitalists replaced landowners and serfs replaced wage laborers.

Eric Olin Wright, a leading American conflict sociologist, emphasizes ownership of the means of governance as another source of power and believes that the structure of the Soviet Union and Eastern Europe illustrates this well.

The most constructive synthesis of the two approaches discussed above is the evolutionist approach proposed by Gerhard Lenski. According to Lenski, society is stratified, and individuals are distributed on the basis of their social status, such as income, education, occupation, and heredity. These social strata influence access to opportunities and privileges as well as the social mobility of individuals. Thus, Gerhard Lenski's stratification explains how social inequalities can arise and be maintained in society.

* * *

The crocodile ate the fisherman, put on his hat and started fishing. Another crocodile swam by; he peeked out of the water and asked, *"So, are they biting?"*
The crocodile in the hat, with a contemptuous glance, replied: *"Swim, swim, green shit!"*.

If a person changes their status or if they move from one social group to another, they will be suspected of loyalty to the old group in the new group must be "holier than papa" in proving loyalty to the new group. A reliable way to show that you already belong to the new group and that you cannot be suspected of loyalty to the old group is to demonstrate a negative attitude toward the group you came from, which far exceeds the statements and actions of other members of the new group.

* * *

A man is sitting, fishing with a rod. A young male frog comes out and says, *"Uncle, can I dive from the float?"*
— *"Well, dive."*
The frog, proud of the permission of the big uncle, dives in. In his

SOCIAL DIFFERENTIATION AND STRATIFICATION   39

> pleasure, he says: *"Uncle, can I sit with you and fish?"*
> — *"Well, sit down."*
> He sits down, enjoying himself, whistling. Then he asks: *"Uncle, what's your name?"*
> — *"Well, Uncle Kolya."*
> The frog is even happier, just delighted. Another young frog pops up and asks: *"Uncle, can I dive from the float?"*
> The first frog (threateningly): *"Get out of here, you asshole! All the fish will scare away!"* And ingratiatingly: *"Am I right, Uncle Kol?"*

Same as "swim, swim, swim..." but with some nuance. The first frog clearly has the necessary qualities for career advancement. He not only shows contempt for the group he came from but also ingratiates himself with those of higher status.

* * *

> Fima and Sema decided to be baptized into Orthodoxy. Fima was scheduled to be baptized on one day and Sema on another. So Sema stood in front of the church, waiting for Fima to come out. As soon as he came out, Sema rushed to him: *"Well, how was it? Tell me,"* to which Fima replied, *"Get out, you kike!"*

It is the same as the anecdote about the two crocodiles.

* * *

> Two classmates ran into each other on the street. One got out of a luxurious car, wearing high heels and elegant clothes, and the other one was unbrushed, wearing some kind of sweater with different buttons and a bag of empty bottles.
> — *"Masha, what's wrong with you? How are you dressed? What's that sweater?"*
> — *"You know, ever since Versace was killed, I've been wearing anything."*

While the women were studying, their status was practically the same. Now, apparently, one of them has raised it significantly, and the second one occupies a low position on the ladder of stratification. So, should I admit defeat in the race for status? No! The case is presented in such a way that her status was at the top of the social hierarchy, she was dressed by Versace himself! And now she

40   SOCIOLOGY IN JOKES

cannot get down to an average tailor, like a frog who says, "I'm sick, but I'm white and fluffy."

* * *

A frog is sitting on the shore, and a crocodile swims by and asks: *"Why are you, frog, so slippery, sticky, disgusting?"*
And the frog answers him: *"I'm just sick, and I'm actually white and fluffy."*

* * *

A new conductor has been appointed to the Philharmonic. He conducts a rehearsal with the orchestra. The rehearsal goes well, but the first violin keeps wrinkling its nose in frustration. The conductor announces a break and approaches the soloist: *"I noticed that you are upset and dissatisfied. Tell me honestly, you don't like my interpretation of Beethoven?"*
— *"No, not at all! I like it very much. I'm glad you've been appointed to our theater."*
— *"So what's the matter? You tell me, my dear fellow, what's going on. It's hard for me to go on."*
— *"Well, how can I explain it to you... to be honest, I've hated music ever since I was a kid."*

This anecdote supports Davis and Moore's functionalist theory. If it were about a janitor or a locksmith, it would not be funny. In a situation where the profession requires tremendous effort, years of continuous labor, and many benefits are usually available, it is hard to imagine a person not loving what they have spent so many years pursuing.

6. Socialization

From birth, the human infant is incomplete and helpless. The newborn knows almost nothing and cannot live more than a few hours without the help of other people. Unlike other living beings, the human infant must learn virtually all forms of its subsequent behavior. In one way or another, this initial biological being must be transformed into a fully human being, an individual who can participate effectively in social life. In other words, we are not born human; we become human only in the course of interaction with those who have already become human. This transformation, that is, our humanization, occurs through a process called **socialization.** As defined by Vander Zanden, socialization is the process through which a person acquires the knowledge, attitudes, values, and behaviors essential for effective participation in social life. Socialization is the link between the individual and society. It is so essential that neither the individual nor society can survive without it. An individual acquires social norms, values, languages, skills and other social aspects through socialization. Society uses socialization to transmit its culture from generation to generation.

Socialization occurs throughout the life course. There is also a theory about the influence of early upbringing, which allows the formation of certain parts of the brain. I once read a funny story (I cannot remember whose) about a lonely mathematical genius who advanced the development of humanity so much that he was persuaded to give his sperm so that his outstanding genes would not be lost. A talented and selfless woman was then chosen who agreed to artificial insemination. The child was surrounded by attention and taught by outstanding teachers and mathematicians. The result exceeded all expectations, and the child became a genius who surpassed their father. Many years later, a laboratory assistant at a research institute that carried out artificial insemination admitted that they had accidentally broken a test tube with the 'genius' sperm and in horror of what he had done, he persuaded the watchman, Vasya, to hand over his sperm for a small sum. As a result, the genius was brought up on the basis of the watchman's heredity, and it was the child's early upbringing that worked. Personality is formed from cognitive, thinking elements (thoughts, beliefs, perception, memory), emotional (love, hate, envy, sympathy, anger, pride and other feelings,) and behavioral components (skills, abilities, capabilities, aptitudes). A unique life pathway determines what skills and abilities a person will come to possess.

Since the middle of the last century, scientists have been debating whether personality is determined by heredity (nature) or upbringing (society). These two factors are closely related and cannot be separated from each other. In most cases, the relationship between heredity and socialization is not clear. Take, for example, honesty, sincerity, and legal consciousness. These qualities seem to be completely determined by upbringing. However, I once read an article about families of people with schizophrenia. It was about 60 years ago when I was still in school. My mother subscribed to the S.S. Korsakov Journal of Neurology and Psychiatry, and I read it regularly (maybe that is why I was interested first in psychiatry and psychology and then in sociology). So I cannot give a link. However, I still remember that the authors showed that there are many 'schizoids' (people who look like people with schizophrenia but are not outside the medical norm) in the families of people with schizophrenia. Schizoid – a personality characterized by traits such as introversion, detachment, and emotional restraint. At the same time, in the article I read, excessive truthfulness was mentioned as almost a primary criterion for classifying this type."

With regard to legal consciousness and law-abiding behavior, it turns out that there are 'crime genes' that contribute to violence. The presence of these genes does not mean that a person will become a criminal, but it is more likely, especially if they live in a dysfunctional family. It seems that heredity makes a person prone to certain behaviors and sets limits, and the environment shapes the influence of hereditary capabilities. For example, intelligence is partly determined by genes inherited from parents. However, the family in which an individual is brought up, where to some extent their intellectual activity is stimulated and supported, and the quantity and quality of school education—all these influence the development of human intelligence.

Social interaction always takes place according to the norms and values of each society's culture. For example, during World War II, Americans saw the Japanese as brutal and treacherous, but now Americans more often than not see the Japanese as resourceful and hardworking. Even more to the point, I think, is how Ukrainians, Russians, and Belarusians viewed the Germans during the war and how they view them now. Furthermore, what of the "Russian and Ukrainian brothers"? These dramatic changes are described in the second part of the book.

* * *

A postal worker rings the doorbell. A boy of about ten opens the door, a cigar in his teeth and a bottle of wine in his hand. The postal worker is confused: *"Are your parents home?"*
The boy looks with interest, takes a cigar out of his mouth and asks: *"What do you think with your own head?"*

Prohibition of smoking and alcohol for children is a universal norm, and it exists in most societies and almost all families. Therefore, the postal worker's question made the boy question their mental capacity.

* * *

A mother told her daughter a fairy tale about Kolobok and summed it up: *"See, Kolobok did not listen to his grandparents and was eaten by the fox!"*
— *"If I had listened"*, says my daughter, *"they would have eaten him at the very beginning of the story! And so, at least, he went for a walk ..."*

It is important to emphasize that fairy tales can have different interpretations, and therefore, different lessons can be learned from them. This anecdote, moreover, is similar to the previous one in that the process of upbringing is not one-sided and not always the educator is more reasonable than the pupil.

* * *

44 SOCIOLOGY IN JOKES

> — *"Petechka, my son, where did you get so dirty? Your pants are dirty, and your hands are dirty — just like a piglet.*
> — *"Mom, is a piglet the son of a pig?"*

This anecdote, like the previous one, shows the difficulties parents face in raising children from an early age. And about Kolobok, not to discuss or say a superfluous word. Or here is another one:

* * *

> A mother, having caught her five-year-old daughter examining the contents of her handbag, begins to explain to her: *"Masha, rummaging through someone else's bag is very bad! Bad!"*
> The daughter, with surprise and some suspicion: *"Mom, where did you get someone else's bag?"*

Finally, another anecdote that shows the dangers of an adult trying to raise a child.

* * *

> A little boy is riding in a taxi with his older brother and thinking out loud: *"Now, if my dad were an elephant and my mom a female elephant, then I would be a little elephant. Now, if my dad were a lion and my mom a lioness, then I would be a little lion cub."*
> This continues throughout the entire journey. The boy-brother is glued to his mobile phone and not paying attention to him; this irritates the taxi driver terribly. Finally, he can't stand it any longer and asks irritably: *"Tell me, boy, if your dad were a drug addict and your mom a prostitute, who would you be then?"*
> To which, after thinking, the boy replies: *"Probably a taxi driver."*

* * *

> What is the difference between a gentleman by upbringing and a gentleman by birth?
> It is the same situation.
> A gentleman rents a hotel room, enters the bathroom, and there is a naked woman washing. A gentleman of education: *"Madam, a thousand apologies, etc."*
> A gentleman by birth: *"Excuse me, sir. I think I left my glasses here somewhere."*

SOCIALIZATION   45

People believe that their character depends on their date of birth, zodiac sign, name and eye color, but completely forget about their upbringing.

* * *

A disobedient Jewish boy was given to the Rebbe for training and education. After a short time, the Rebbe came to his parents in horror and said that he could not cope with this bandit.

Then, the boy was given to the priest. After a while, the boy became like silk.

When asked what had influenced him, the boy said: *"When I saw a crucified Jew on the cross, I realized that it was better not to get involved with them."*

* * *

— *"Do you have anything on the psychology of raising children from 5 to 12 years old?"*

— *"A soldier's leather belt in good condition."*

* * *

— *"Mistakes in raising boys are more dangerous than mistakes in raising girls. Poorly-brought-up boys grow up to be murderers, and poorly-brought-up girls just grow up to be grumpy wives."*

— *"Well, I don't know; maybe it's better to kill once rather than to torture your husband, son-in-law, or grandson, who will eventually become a murderer."*

Statistics show that men indeed become killers much more often than women. From an evolutionary psychology perspective, this is due to the fact that most human societies are polygamous. In such a society, the more successful males monopolize reproductive access to a few females, while other males are denied the opportunity to reproduce at all. Meanwhile, almost all females have this opportunity. This means that the difference between winners and losers in the reproductive game is much greater among males than among females. Therefore, males are forced to compete fiercely in order not to be permanently from the reproductive game. This competition among men leads to high levels of violence among men (murder, assault, and hand-wringing). The high murder rate among men (compared to the murder rate among women or between the sexes) is a direct result of this male competition for mating. Of course, this does not appear to be direct male competition for women but occurs indirectly. Most murders are committed because of what are called 'superficial spats'. Conflicts start over issues of reputation, honor or status (e.g., one man insults another); men do not give in to each other; they want to defend their dignity and eventually turn to violence, which can end in murder. Compliant men are less likely to leave offspring. These theories support the following pattern:

> Men commit crimes more often than women, but most of those crimes are about women.

* * *

> A father sent his father to a home for older people.
> The son asked for the address.
> The father thought about it and sent his son to the orphanage.

An interesting question is what influences the formation of a child more: parents' instructions or their actions. Actually, the instructions are more related to the process of upbringing as a purposeful process. At the same time, the actions of parents are more related to the process of socialization (i.e., all factors, both directed and non-directed). The father apparently adhered to the theory that his actions have a greater influence on his son than his instructions.

* * *

> Her mother raised Sveta strictly and brought her up to be an economic girl so that she could boil borscht, clean the apartment, wash, and iron, but Sveta did not need all this; she grew up beautiful!

This is more about social exchange theory than nurture. Beauty increases your value in the marriage market, and if it is not certain that you will grow up to be beautiful, then your economic skills are useful. They also increase your value. Raising children in their own image, parents somehow hope that they will be better than them.

SOCIALIZATION   47

* * *

Young mother: "*My parents forbade me to read lying down when I was a child. I let my children read even standing on their heads, but they still don't read ...*"

The pace of change in society is constantly increasing; whereas a few centuries ago both the level of knowledge and values changed slowly, now it happens within one generation. Can you imagine that young noble children taught their parents or governesses anything? And now, in 90% of families, 10–15-year-old children are better versed in cell phones and computers than their parents, much less their grandparents[7]. Furthermore, it is the children who are called in for advice and help. However, they do not want to read long texts — "too many letters".

* * *

Many years after graduating from high school, my wife and I were once visiting my favorite high school teacher of Russian literature, Sofia Yakovlevna Freidina (alas, she is no longer alive). She told me this story: "*I come home and want to tell my daughter a story about our cleaning lady, and I can't remember the word. A simple Russian word. The whole family was involved – my daughter, son-in-law, grandson and granddaughter – all the words were wrong. I barely remembered 'padla'. And why did I need to remember this word? The thing is that our cleaning lady sent her daughter to study violin at the music school. And she herself went with her, sat at the lessons to help her daughter. So she put her daughter and her violin in the school lobby, mopping the floor, and from time to time she shouts at her: You're holding the violin the wrong way, asshole! You're picking the wrong note, asshole!*"

You have probably guessed by now why I brought up this story — playing the violin is an education, and "padla" is part of socialization.

In the story Mumu by Ivan Turgenev, written in 1852, the main character Gerasim, a kind and simple-minded servant,

---

7   This is not survey data, but my expert opinion. There are, of course, families where parents are engineers or programmers and are better at computers, but are unlikely to be as free to use cell phones as their children.

48   SOCIOLOGY IN JOKES

commits a tragic act, struggling with the contradiction between his feelings for Mumu and the order of his mistress. He drowns his only friend, a dog named Mumu (tragic consequences of observing cruel and unjust rules and norms at that time).

* * *

Gerasim threw Muma into the water, but she did not drown; she got into the nets and was fished out by two fishermen: *"Thank you, guys. You guys saved me from death. I won't forget!"*
Men (shocked): *"Oh my God, a talking dog!"*
Mumu (in even more shock): *"Oh my god, talking men!"*

I like the hypothesis of the authors of the anecdote that Mumu was saved. Her life experience was limited only to communicating with Gerasim, so how could she know about the existence of talking men! Upbringing and socialization set the ideas about the surrounding world, its norms and values. For example, children who grow up in unstable families do not always have stable marriages themselves.

* * *

British scientists have discovered that infertility is hereditary. If your parents did not have children, you will not have children.

* * *

The children of psychologists never get cranky in toy stores with "buy one, buy one!" cries. They start with a distracting topic, for example, was your childhood was hard and joyless too?

As I said, my mother was not a psychologist but a neuropathologist (and psychiatrist); she subscribed to the journal of neurology and psychiatry, named after Korsakov. S.S. Korsakov, which I read in high school with great interest. This probably contributed to my choice of profession (though I did not go into psychiatry, I did not want to cut up corpses).

* * *

SOCIALIZATION   49

> — *"Did you get a B on your Russian dictation while Lesha got an A?*
> Sometime later ... *"Why did you get another B?"*
> — *"Lesha got a C on this assignment!"*
> — *"What does Lesha have to do with this? We're concerned about you, not*
> *Lesha. Who cares what he got?"*

This, perhaps, belongs to pedagogy rather than sociology. How effective is this pedagogical method in setting an example to a child of some of their classmates or siblings ("and here I am when I studied at school..."). My cousin was born and went to school in Marganets, and I in Kyiv, so we met very rarely. Although she was an excellent student, her mother always put me as an example to her, and she hated me. Later, when we got to know each other better, it turned out that I was not so bad.

* * *

> A neatly dressed, well-groomed boy with glasses is walking home from school, and in the yard, some men are sitting around drinking beer.
> — *"Good afternoon!"*
> — *"Good afternoon, Timmy. You must be a straight-A student. We're having a debate about spelling. Do you know how to spell that bad word starting with 'F'?"*
> — *"Mr. Johnson, I'm polite and well-mannered. I don't know any bad words!"*
> — *"All right, but do you know how to spell the bad word starting with 'C'?"*
> — *"No, I really don't know. How could I? I'm polite and well-mannered; we don't learn such words in class."*
> — *"Okay then. But surely you know how to spell the bad word starting with 'A'?"*
> — *"Mr. Johnson, I'm telling you, I'm polite and well-mannered ... Wait, hold on, what kind of word starts with 'A'?"*

The use of 'mate' also shows the difference between upbringing and socialization, as well as between the official ideas about a well-bred person and the real requirements for a socialized member of society. Actually, mate consists of only four words and their derivatives and a person who does not know these words will face certain difficulties in communication with other people. It would be logical for people to learn mate at school (**Now, children, write down the words that you should never say out loud**).

7. Social Interaction

The most basic unit of human behavior is action. Anything you can do is an action: getting out of bed in the morning, getting dressed, eating breakfast, walking into a classroom, reading a sentence, etc. Some of our actions are not performed for anyone but ourselves, but most of our actions affect our relationships with others and thus constitute interaction with them. Such actions that affect our relationships with other people are called **social actions.** Social action is behavior that is either oriented toward or influenced by other people. Even if a person simply behaves so as not to disturb other people, i.e., not to affect their interests, this is a social action. For example, a person in the reading room of a library tries to work quietly, and this is also a social behavior.

When people take each other into account in their behavior, then their social actions consist of social interaction. Social interaction is the mutual and reciprocal influence of people on each other's behavior. Without social interaction, a person cannot acquire the knowledge or skills they need to become a functioning member. Without social interaction, any social institutions or groups would be impossible. Microsociology is concerned with the detailed study of social interaction: what people do, think and talk about in their daily lives—minute by minute. Macrosociology focuses on large-scale and long-term processes. It is often characterized as a branch of social psychology: the scientific study of the influence of social factors on human personality and behavior. Many prominent sociologists, such as Charles Horton Cooley, George Herbert Mead, Emile Durkheim, Max Weber, Georg Simmel, and Talcott Parsons, paid attention to social and psychological issues as an integral part of their sociological research.

In modern sociology, there are several approaches to social interaction, and the main ones are the following approaches at the microsocial level:

1. Interactionist
2. Dramaturgical

52   SOCIOLOGY IN JOKES

3. Ethnomethodological
4. Social exchange.

Interactionists point out that we live in two environments — physical and symbolic. We interpret and evaluate what we see around us. For example, Ukrainian embroidery is not just a visual and tactile experience; it is also endowed with a certain meaning related to clothing, social position, culture or patriotism. Interactionists believe that our definitions of situations are important for social interaction. Our actions are determined by the meanings we attach to events, people, and things, in general, to everything that happens around us. Facts (the ways people define a variety of situations) do not exist independently of the meanings people give to them. It is like the parable of the three bricklayers, each of whom sees his work differently: one says that he lays bricks, the second that he makes money, and the third that he builds the temple of God, which will stand for centuries.

When people come to a common understanding of the need to integrate their actions with those of others, they quickly reach the same definition of a common situation, which allows people to live together. American sociologist William Thomas' theory, states that "If people define situations as valid, those situations are valid in their consequences". If people imagine Black people or Jews as having certain traits, then whether these perceptions are true or false, such definitions affect the behavior of those people who have these perceptions. In human history, very negative perceptions have periodically caused genocide and war.

The **dramaturgical** approach is that of the American sociologist Erving Goffman, in which the social world is portrayed for the first time (except for Shakespeare) as a natural theater. We all play the roles of actors and spectators of everyday life. Moreover, our social roles are determined by our interactions with others. Goffman points out that we often try to control how other people perceive us in order to present ourselves in an attractive light. He calls this process impression management. We provide 'onlookers' with a definition of who and what we are in the hope that they will find us convincing. Furthermore, we try to hide behavior that is incompatible with the image we are trying to create. For example, when we decide what to wear for a party, job interview, a date, or university exams.

Harold Garfinkel and his colleagues in the 1960s raised the question of how we create an ordered and structured vision of social life in our thoughts and conversations. They began to analyze the ordinary everyday actions people take for granted through an approach they called **ethnomethodology.** This approach allowed them to study how we establish the factual nature of our interpretations and evaluations and how events are interconnected.

Ethnomethodology is a theoretical approach to the study of the procedures and rules we use in everyday life to understand social life and society. It is based on the ideas of the German social philosopher Alfred Schutz, who noted that we assume the existence of an objective world independent of our experience. Ethnomethodologists explore how we create representations of external social reality and convince each other of its existence and how, under different assumptions and logic, people create different representations of the world.

Ethnomethodological research has shown that social structures largely exist only because a sufficient number of people agree to act according to the rules that have developed. Even the state and its organs exist only when a sufficient number of people behave toward them as if they really exist. However, when a large number of people question the authority of the existing state, revolutionary changes can occur.

Social exchange theory, proposed by American social scientist George Homans in the early 1970s, states that interactions between people are based on their attempts to balance their costs and rewards. Rewards are defined as what a person is willing to expend and engage in certain interactions for. **Expenses** are all the things a person tries to avoid or minimize. **Profit** is defined as rewards minus expenses. Exchange theory argues that people follow a "minimax" strategy; that is, they try to minimize their expenditures and maximize their rewards. However, measuring rewards and costs in comparative units can be problematic. Social interaction, from the point of view of exchange theory, consists of an exchange of actions between at least two people. In this process, both parties make a profit, a reward for the actions provided, and at the same time incur costs. However, if the expected profit does not satisfy one of the parties, the relationship may end. If someone marries a person who is much older than they are, they are likely to be much richer. In general, marriage can be regarded as an act of social exchange, where all advantages (appearance, age, character, health, certain skills, apartment, wealth, status, prestige, etc.) are taken into account, and an approximate equivalence of the advantages of each is achieved. Of course, this pattern is statistical, and there may be exceptions (then we speak about unequal marriages).

* * *

At the buffet, everyone pounces on the food, but one of them doesn't eat. His neighbor asks him: *"Aren't you eating?"*
— *"Not hungry."*
— *"Do you only eat when you're hungry? Like an animal?"*

Very many human actions are not purely physiological but fulfill social functions. People often eat not only to satisfy hunger, but also use food as a certain social ritual. It can be a celebration of certain events, a business dinner to discuss business issues or a romantic dinner as a prelude to a closer relationship. People do not always enter into sexual relations just to conceive a child or to get pleasure. It may be due to a sense of duty and the need to maintain relations in the family, a way to move up the career ladder, a way to earn money, revenge on a spouse for cheating, etc.

* * *

There's a man on a train. At the stop, another man comes on and says: *"Hello! Let's get acquainted. Where are you from? I'm from Berdichev."*
— *"Oh, so you're Jewish?"*
— *"If a sparrow flies out of a stable, is it immediately a horse?"*

The formation of stereotypes is very useful for the perception of social reality; people cannot perceive surrounding people (except for close acquaintances) in the entirety of their characteristics. They are forced to save their efforts and memory to create typologies and stereotypes. Robin Dunbar, an English anthropologist, showed that the maintenance of social ties rests on the thinking abilities of animals and requires the expenditure of considerable intellectual resources. He introduced into scientific circulation the so-called **Dunbar number** — the number of acquaintances with whom a person can maintain permanent social ties. According to different estimations in human communities, it lies within the range from 100 to 230; conventionally, it is considered that, on average, it is equal to 150. Kyiv International Institute of Sociology has estimated that this number for Ukraine was equal to about 160. However, here the result strongly depends on who is considered to be an acquaintance with whom social ties are maintained. Because of stereotyping, prejudices and overgeneralized and unreliable stereotypes arise, as in this anecdote.

* * *

— *"Syoma, what do you think is the similarity between a sex worker and a decent woman?"*
— *"Well, both are trying to sell the same thing for more money. What's the difference?"*
— *"A sex worker sells retail, and a decent one sells wholesale."*

The interlocutors clearly think in terms of social exchange. The joke also reflects certain sexist stereotypes, labeling and judging women. This may also be related to the fact that men in our society tend to tell jokes more often than women

* * *

— *"Daddy, can I kiss you?"*
— *"Of course, you can, but there's no money. Your mom already kissed me."*

56   SOCIOLOGY IN JOKES

Social exchange theory in its truest and most straightforward form. This joke is also somewhat sexist, as it implies that the wife has no income of her own and is dependent on her husband.

* * *

Two friends meet.
— "*Andrei, what's wrong with you? You don't look well; you look exhausted.*"
— "*Health issues.*"
— "*And what exactly is that?*"
— "*Yeah, I don't even want to say it. It's embarrassing.*"
— "*Look, I'm your best friend; who better to talk to than me?*"
— "*In general, problems with women not working out .....*"
— "*I have a wonderful therapist who can help you. Write down the phone number.*"
After a while, they met again.
— "*Oh, I see you're in a different mood! Did the therapist help?*"
— "*Look, I'm so grateful to you. It's a wonderful doctor. I'm just a different person.*"
— "*That's good to hear! So you're doing well with women now.*"
— "*No, it's the same with women as it was, but now I'm proud of it!*"

This anecdote illustrates the thesis that the perception of a situation has more influence on a person's behavior than the situation itself.

8. Gender, Sexuality, Marriage and Family

Sexuality.

Humans spend much more time having sex than other primates. Sexuality is an important part of the human experience throughout life. Even in early childhood, children may show interest in their bodies and explore the genitalia of their peers and adults. However, over time, they realize social limitations and begin to hold back. It is the same in older people — erotic interest and activity do not necessarily stop with age, including in healthy men and women over 80. The peak of sensation may have passed, but this does not mean that sexual attraction and pleasure have ceased to exist for them.

The social nature of sexuality.

Most of us look at sexual desire and orgasm as purely physiological phenomena. While sexual behavior certainly has a biological component, it is determined by social symbols and meanings. Let us say sexual behavior, like kissing. Younger boys may think kissing is "girly nonsense," and girls do not think it is sexy. However, when teens start spending time together, it turns out that kissing is erotically exciting. The act itself remains the same; only the meaning attached to it changes.

Family and marriage are important social institutions in modern society. However, they are also subject to change and evolution in accordance with social, economic, and cultural changes in society.

Family — a social group whose members are united by blood, marriage, adoption or marriage, who live together, maintain a common household and raise children;

Marriage — a socially established sexual union between two or more persons (in the case of polygamous marriages) that is entered into, in a sense, for a long time. A classification of types of marriage can be made on different grounds. The first of these is with whom one can marry, whether it can be members of one's own family or not. Each society regulates the conventional range of candidates from which an individual must choose a spouse. Two types of regulation must determine the 'right' spouse: endogamy and exogamy. **Endogamy** requires that marriage take place within certain social groups. People must marry within their class, caste, race, ethnic group, or religious grouping. **Exogamy** requires marriage to take place outside the group, whatever it is: nuclear family, clan, or tribe. The regulation of relations under exogamy, of course, forbids ties with close-blood relatives. However, not everywhere the same persons are considered close blood relatives — it is a matter of social definition. Thus, society determines not only whether or not blood relatives can or cannot marry but also who the relatives are. Not only are consanguineous marriages banned by society, but they are also actively condemned by most people. Sociologists and anthropologists continue to research this controversial issue of how and why incest prohibitions — the rule that prohibits sexual relations with close blood relatives — arose.

There are many different forms of marriage and family in modern society, including traditional marriage between men and women, same-sex marriage, civil unions, unregistered marriages, polygamy and other forms of family relationships. The union between a man and a woman can be of four types: 1) monogamous: one wife + one husband (exists in all societies and not so long ago was considered by Western society a sign of civilization and all other marriages as barbaric.); 2) polygamous: one husband + two or more wives (also quite common and related to a man's economic position and status); 3) polyandry: one wife + two or more husbands (rare marriages, usually when a family cannot marry each of its sons, so the eldest and the younger brothers have equivalent status as husbands, e.g., among Todas, one of the peoples of India); and 4) group marriage: two or more husbands + two or more wives.

A common public perception is that the basis of marriage is love (an emotional state that includes affection, care, attraction and mutual respect between two people), or, due to the fact that the word has many meanings, we can talk about romantic love, which according to Vander Zanden it is a strong emotional and physical attraction between people. However, in some cultures and societies, marriage may be based more on social, economic or religious considerations than on love. Marriage can also take place without deep emotional feelings, and the relationship between the partners may be based on other aspects such as respect, trust, cooperation and commitment.

Engels, in *The Origin of the Family, Private Property and the State*, points out that romantic love, unlike sexual attraction, has two differences and two characteristic features. First, greater selectivity (this does not mean that in purely sexual attraction, without love, there is no selectivity; as studies show, selectivity is to some extent characteristic of animals, such as dogs), but love can be felt simultaneously, as a rule, to one person (less often to two people at the same time). In contrast, sexual attraction can have many more objects. Second is the greater importance of reciprocity (sexual attraction can be satisfied without even having to wonder if the partner feels the same way). Engels, by the way, believed that in the future (that is, somewhere in our time), the economic reasons that are the basis of marriage will fall away. Marriage will become stronger because only love will remain, and it is unique; one can love only one.

Factors in spouses' choices. It is sometimes said that "opposites attract." It is unknown how true this is in terms of character traits. Still, as far as social traits are concerned, all studies show conclusively that the opposite is true: similarity and homogamy dominate here. Homogamy (not to be confused with homosexuality) is the tendency to choose a partner similar to oneself in terms of age, race, religion, nationality, education, and other social characteristics. Physical attractiveness is one of the factors that influence the choice of a partner. People think that the more attractive ones find it easier to get married and be happy or to get a good job. Experiments in which women talked to men on the phone showed that they were more animated and friendly when they thought they were talking to handsome men. The matching hypothesis, which has empirical support, indicates that the greatest benefits are achieved when people are similar in terms of physical attractiveness and that people often choose partners who are comparable in appearance.

Regarding psychological traits, the situation is unclear. Some sociologists believe that the principle of complementary needs

60   SOCIOLOGY IN JOKES

works, i.e., we choose those who complement us, say, a dominant person marries someone passive. Social exchange theory combines all three of the above explanations. We seek rewards and avoid punishment, which can be varied, such as love, gratitude, respect, security, material goods, or contempt, disrespect, and poverty, among others. We exchange rewards and try to maintain balance in the exchange process. In choosing a partner, we run the risk that an attractive partner may neglect us, which is a strong punishment. So, we try to maximize the ratio of rewards to punishments.

Since in all societies, we see how the institution of the family plays a central role in human relationships, it is not surprising that each of the major schools of sociology (functionalism, conflict and interactionism) attempts to explore all aspects of marriage.

Functionalists view the family as a necessity for society as a whole, as a social institution that fulfills certain functions in society, such as raising children, transmitting cultural values, supporting emotional wellbeing and strengthening the social structure. The family is presented as a structure with certain roles and functions of each of its members aimed at maintaining stability and harmony in society.

In contrast to functionalists, **conflict theorists** see the family as a field of struggle and conflict between different social groups and individuals, including disagreements over roles, power, resources and privileges within the family structure. Family relations can be a site of conflict, struggle for resources and social positions, and manifestations of inequality and domination.

Symbolic interactionists note that human beings create, use, and communicate through symbols. Interactionists view the family in terms of interaction and communication among its members. Emphasis is placed on interaction, meaning-making, and the construction of reality during social interactions within the family. Attention is given to the micro-level of social relationships and communication between family members, their roles, interactions, and interpretation of situations.

Each of these theories offers a unique understanding of the family and its role in society, emphasizing different aspects of family relationships and dynamics within the family.

In modern Western society, in most cases, there is a tendency to establish a close and meaningful relationship with another person. Despite certain changes in the family model in recent years, Americans are rather conservative (conventional) in their family relationships. Although the divorce rate has increased, they are not giving up on their marital relationships. However, a growing number of Americans do not see marriage as a permanent institution but as something that can end and begin again. Although divorce is becoming a seemingly common event, it is hardly becoming a sustainable practice. Most divorcees remarry. Often these are single-parent families (stepfamilies). Despite the significant changes that have taken place in the family model over the last decade, adult children are the ones who take on the care and responsibility for their elderly parents.

The positive thing about the rapid proliferation of different ways of living is that Americans and Europeans see the opportunity to tailor relationships to their preferences.

Lifestyle: the generally accepted pattern goes along with biological, social, and economic needs. Among those preferred by Americans, for example, are single, unmarried cohabiting, childless marriages, single parents, gay and lesbian families and communes.

* * *

Autumn. Two passersby stop at a crosswalk at a red light, and suddenly, a car whizzes by and splatters them with mud. *"If this happened in the UK"*, said one of them thoughtfully, *"the driver would come back, apologize, invite you into the car and take you to his country house. There, he would give them something to change into, and the soiled clothes would be sent to the cleaners. Then he would invite to dinner in a beautiful hall with a fireplace, allocate a cozy bedroom, and in the morning, after a delicious breakfast, would return the cleaned clothes and take them to the same place where everything happened."*
— *"You talk about it as if it happened to you."*
— *"Well, not to me, my wife, but who cares?"*

62   SOCIOLOGY IN JOKES

In social sciences and feminism, "gender" is understood as "social sex", i.e., socially determined roles, identities and spheres of activity of men and women that depend not on biological sex differences but on the social organization of society. The struggle for women's equality is not about wanting to achieve equality in biological characteristics but in social characteristics and gender equality. If the above anecdote causes laughter, it means that there is no equality yet, that there is a double standard, some moral standards for men and others for women. The narrator's wife paid for the driver's concern by spending the night with him. If the narrator himself had spent the night with the female driver, the anecdote would not have been funny; this anecdote can serve as a 'litmus test' to determine whether there are still double standards for men and women. Freud tells a similar anecdote in his book *Jokes and Their Relation to the Unconscious*.

* * *

> A most luminous prince is touring his estates and notices a man in the crowd who resembles his high personage. He calls him over to ask, *"Did his mother ever serve in the castle?"*
> — *"No, your lordship,"* was the reply, *"my mother didn't, but my father did."*

From my point of view, in this anecdote, the humor is created by a double standard (a prince who spent the night with a maid is not condemned, but a lady who spent the night with a servant is quite another matter). However, Freud himself interprets this anecdote as an example of so-called "resourceful witticisms". "Resourcefulness consists in the transition from defense to aggressiveness, in turning the spearhead from oneself to the side of the opponent, in repayment in the same coin, hence in creating an unexpected unity between attack and counterattack."[8] This interpretation, however, does not contradict my interpretation but lies in another plane.

---

8   Freud, Sigmund. *Jokes and Their Relation to the Unconscious*. Complete Psychological Works of Sigmund Freud, Vol. 8. Translated by James Strachey, W.W. Norton & Company, 1990.

GENDER, SEXUALITY, MARRIAGE AND FAMILY   63

* * *

Husband to wife: *"Look, sociologists have found that women say twice as many words a day as men. I've long thought women are chatty."*
— *"It's not about being chatty; it's just that men don't get it very well; you have to explain everything to them twice."*
— *"What did you say? I didn't understand!"*

I like this anecdote because, first, it aims to break down gender stereotypes, and second, it mentions sociologists.

One of the mysteries of the functioning of society is the origin of anecdotes. Almost all people tell anecdotes, many people know many anecdotes, there are books of anecdotes, programs on television, and anecdotes are printed in many magazines and newspapers. New anecdotes are constantly appearing, promptly reacting to new events. Hundreds of thousands of anecdotes function in society. Nevertheless, no one ever sees the authors of the anecdotes! I have not seen any anecdote authors either, but I have seen a person who creates aphorisms (maybe aphorisms turn into anecdotes in the course of functioning in society?) This is Eugene Golovakha[9], who has long been delighting us not only with his scientific and journalistic but also with his meta-scientific activities. In particular, he is the author of a number of alternative dictionaries[10] (on psychology, sociology, politics, etc.). In 2011, Golovakha's gender dictionary was published. Here are a few definitions.

Mutual love — the agreement between two people that no one else wants them.

Gender revolution — the new position of women in relation to men in modern society, which even the authors of the Kama Sutra could not have imagined during the triumph of male chauvinism

The head of the family is an influential member in a patriarchal society, but in our society, it is increasingly the family pet

---

9   A famous Ukrainian sociologist, doctor of sociological sciences, director of the Institute of Sociology of the National Academy of Sciences of Ukraine, editor-in-chief of the journal *Sociology: Theory, Methods, Marketing*

10   Є.Головаха. Alternative Gender Dictionary. Kyiv: SPD Moskalenko O.M., 2011.

64   SOCIOLOGY IN JOKES

Domestic violence is a form of family relations, the prevalence of which indicates the strong foundations of the family institution, which cannot be dislodged by any beatings.

Feminine movements are the movements of women that men enjoy the least.

Love is a selfless feeling that does not favor those who deserve it more.

The "better half" is the one that the "worse half" always has.

Knights are noble cavaliers who, in the past, were always willing to lay down their lives for beautiful ladies and, in modern times, are always willing to drink to them.

Liberal feminism is a moderate current in feminism whose admirers do not insist on surgically removing male chauvinism in the hope that through reform, it will gradually fall away on its own.

Masculinity is a set of typical traits that distinguish a man from human being.

Sexual behavior is the only form of social behavior that allows pleasure to all participants in the reproduction of social relations.

The sexual revolution was a revolution that resulted in far more pleasure for the oppressed masses than all of the socio-economic revolutions together.

Shame is a moral feeling that one gains by entering the realm of sexual relations and loses by entering the realm of politics.

A bachelor is a person whose instinct for self-preservation trumps that of procreation.

Marriage squeeze — a shortage of men for unmarried women arising from the fact that many men are willing to die rather than marry

Now that the reader is enriched with knowledge of gender terminology, I can already provide an anecdote summarizing the difference between sex and gender.

* * *

GENDER, SEXUALITY, MARRIAGE AND FAMILY   65

Zoo. Gorilla cage. A woman standing in front of the cage addresses a man standing next to her:
— *"Do you know if that gorilla is a woman or a man?"*
— *"It's a male."*
— *"A man, then."*
— *"No, it's not a man, it's a male."*
— *"Well, what difference does it make?"*
— *"A big one. A man has money."*

* * *

At intermission, a wife and husband stroll through the theater. *"Why are you staring at that girl like that? It's indecent."*
— *"She's got weird hair."*
— *"Yeah, the hair! Cause I don't know what you were looking at. She's got cleavage down to her navel."*
— *"Yeah, I hadn't noticed."*
— *"Of course, that's why I believed you! All you men are like that, looking left, cheating on your wives."*
— *"Aren't women like that?"*
— *"Of course not! For women, family and children are important."*
— *"And women don't cheat on their husbands?"*
— *"Virtually no cheating. Those are the rare exceptions."*
— *"Do all men cheat on their wives?"*
— *"Well, almost all of them."*
— *"If all women are faithful to their husbands, and all men cheat on their wives, then pray tell, with whom are they cheating on them?"*

A very accurate question from a sociological and statistical point of view. Barring statistically insignificant cases of same-sex marriage, all men are married to women, so the number of married men should exactly match the number of married women. This could be used to control for errors in our surveys if it were not for one thing. The fact is that in statistical censuses and many surveys, marital status is determined by a person's self-esteem (are you married or not?) In full accordance with the anecdote, there are couples in which the woman considers herself married, and the man does not consider himself married. For example, in the Soviet Union, the number of married women was statistically about a million more than the number of married men. Unfortunately, Ukraine has not had a census for almost 20 years, so I looked at what is going on

66 SOCIOLOGY IN JOKES

with this ratio in Ukraine according to our September 2019 survey[11]. It turned out that among all persons in registered or unregistered marriages, men are about 46% and women 54%. That is, there is a significant number of couples in which men do not consider themselves married and women do.

* * *

A husband and wife watch hardcore porn on videocon. In the middle of the movie, the husband, yawning, goes to bed and wants to turn off the TV. Wife: *"No, don't turn it off, I want to finish watching! And I wonder: will he marry her after all this or not?"*

In Western culture, sex is quite strongly associated with marriage, and sexual relations outside of marriage have been discouraged for many years. "As an honest man, I am now obliged to marry her" remains in the minds of a part of the population as an approved social norm.

* * *

A couple has been married for several years, and lately, their intimate life has become boring and predictable. They decided to consult a sexologist to diversify their intimacy. The sexologist listened to them and said: *"I can recommend you to experiment in bed. For example, try having sex (make love) with your eyes closed or in a new place. Or even try different role-playing games!"*
The husband and wife nodded gratefully and went home. In the evening, they decided to experiment — they lit candles, turned off the lights and started having sex with their eyes closed. But in the middle of the process, the man could not resist and opened his eyes. Seeing this, the woman became angry and shouted: *"What are you doing? Close your eyes, we had a deal!"*
The man grudgingly replied: *"Imagine how I feel when I'm lying here and I don't know who I'm having sex with!"*

* * *

---

11   Omnibus, F2F survey of 2000 respondents.

A party. Everyone's drinking and having fun, but one man sits looking sad.
— *"What's wrong with you?"*
— *"My wife got AIDS. What's wrong with you? Why are you all so pale? I was just kidding."*

* * *

— *"Kitty, where are you?"*
— *"I'm in the kitchen, honey!"*
— *"Shut up, asshole! I'm looking for the cat!"*

* * *

An old joke from Soviet times.

* * *

The Kyiv-Kharkov train compartment for two people. A circus performer and a respectable passenger. The passenger looks attentively at his traveling companion and asks: *"Are you, by any chance, a circus performer? Could I have seen you in a show last week?"*
— *"Yes, I was on tour in Kyiv."*
— *"Tell me, do you really guess the thoughts of other people?"*
— *"Yes. Can you tell me what I'm thinking?"*
— *"See, I have a performance tomorrow; and I need to rest, rest, not work."*
— *"Pardon me, but how much do you get for one concert?"*
— *"Fifty rubles."*
— *"Look, if you guess and answer my two questions correctly, I'll pay you for a full concert."*
— *"All right, ask away."*
— *"So, my first question is: where am I going?"*
— *"To Kharkiv."*
— *"Amazingly Kharkov. Amazingly accurate. And my second question: why am I going?"*
— *"To get a divorce!"*
— *"Fantastic!"* Exclaimed a fellow traveler. He took a hundred rubles out of his wallet and gave them to the artist.
— *"But we agreed on fifty!"*
— *"It's not for guessing my thoughts. It's thoughts for the idea!"*

* * *

68 Sociology in Jokes

— "Rozochka, make me some tea, please."
— "Oh, Sema, I'm so tired. I've been running around all day. I've just laid down; make it yourself, please. Please."
— "Arent I tired? You're at home, and I'm at work!"
— "Well, let's not quarrel. We're both tired. Let's do it this way: I'll make tea for you, and you for me. Is that fair?"
— "Okay, here's the deal."
— "Well, you do it. I'll lie down for a minute, and then I'll go too."
— "Rosa, here's your tea!"
— "You know, Semochka, I don't feel like it. Drink it yourself, please."

Conflict resolution and behavior management apply to business and family issues as well.

* * *

A mother brings her 18-year-old daughter to the doctor: *"Doctor. My daughter vomits all the time."*
The doctor examined the daughter and said: *"Your daughter is pregnant; five months."*
— "You can't say that, doctor. How can you say that? My daughter has never been with a man!"
— "Really, my daughter?"
— "I never even kissed a man", says the daughter.
The doctor silently walks to the window and starts to stare into the distance. Five minutes pass.
— "Doctor, is something wrong? Mother asks.
— "No, no ... just that in such cases, a bright star rises in the east, and three wise men come down from the hill. Here I stand, waiting ..."

Different societies have different norms and ideas about decent (proper) behavior. They can be different in different social groups. They can be observed with different strictness in different families. Sometimes the stricter the rules in the family, the more surprises await the parents.

* * *

— "Do you renounce Satan, my son?"
— "I cannot, Father."
— "How come? How come?"
— "We've been married ten years, we have two kids, I can't leave them."

GENDER, SEXUALITY, MARRIAGE AND FAMILY   69

* * *

A son asks his father: *"Dad, what is marriage?"*
The father replies: *"Marriage, son, is an eight-letter word that means two things: no arguments and no money."*

* * *

The wife says to her husband: *"Honey, it's our wedding anniversary to-day. What will you get me this time?"*
The husband replies: *"I have two pieces of news: good news and bad news. The good news is I bought you a beautiful dress. The bad news is it's a lot more expensive than I planned to spend."*

* * *

— *"How was yesterday's April 1st? Did you prank anyone? Any luck?"*
— *"That's a good one. I get to work, and I call my wife. I told her I'd been screwed over, my business was ruined, everything was gone, we were in debt. I come home in the evening — no wife, no mother-in-law, no belongings."*

The motives of marriage. This prank is like a social experiment or a sociological survey.

* * *

The house is broken into by masked robbers with guns; a man and a woman are in the house. *"All right, hands up, face the wall. This is a rob-bery."*
— *"Look, please, I'll show you where the money and the jewelry are. You won't find it without me. Just let her go."*
— *"That's how much you love your wife!"*
— *"It's not my wife, it's my neighbor. And my wife will be home from work soon, so let's hurry up."*

Apparently, the husband still loves his wife and values his family — at least more than money and jewelry.

* * *

Statistics show that for every man over the age of 85, there are seven women. But, alas, it is already too late! ...

* * *

Two shouting aunts came to the wise King Solomon and brought a young man. *"He's going to marry my daughter!"* Screams one of them. — "*No, mine!*" Yells the other.

The king thought about it and said: *"Bring a saw. We'll cut him in half, and each half will get half. Agreed?"*

The first aunt: *"Agreed, O wisest of the wisest!"*

Second aunt (after thinking): *"Why should an innocent soul be ruined ...?"*

Then King Solomon said he would marry the daughter of the first woman.

Second aunt: *"But she just wanted to kill him, didn't she?"*

Solomon: *"There, there. She is the real mother-in-law!"*

* * *

A man comes to a priest: *"Father, help me. Twenty years ago, I was cursed. Since that time, I have lost my luck. I have insomnia, headaches, an empty wallet, and no health. I beg you to help me. Please get rid of this curse."*

The priest pondered for a while and said to the man: *"All right, I will try to remove the curse, but you must tell me exactly what words were spoken to cast the spell. Can you remember? I bet you do."*

— "*Those words ring in my head like it was yesterday: 'I pronounce you husband and wife!'*"

* * *

A little boy asks his mom: *"Mom, why is the bride wearing white at the wedding?"*

Mom replies: *"Because this is the happiest day of her life, baby."*

The boy hesitates and says: *"Then why is the groom dressed in black?"*

* * *

When the lights come on in the cinema after the movie is over, the wife suddenly sees her husband sitting in front of her. *"Ah,"* she cries out, "*so this is how you do the kids while I take care of my sick mom!*"

* * *

GENDER, SEXUALITY, MARRIAGE AND FAMILY   71

Two people meet: *"Married recently? I guess now you know what true happiness is!"*
— *"Yes. I do now. But it's too late."*

* * *

— *"My spouse and I were happy for 20 years."*
— *"And later?"*
— *"And later, we met."*

* * *

The wife says to her husband: *"Darling, how did you spend your time while I was away?"*
The husband replies: *"Very simple, dear. I found the photo album of our wedding and was reminiscing about what a happy bachelor I was."*

* * *

— *"Young lady, do you have a boyfriend?"*
— *"No."*
— *"How? Such a smart, sophisticated, sexy girl doesn't have a boyfriend?"*
— *"He freaking died of happiness."*

* * *

— *"Fedya, you were late for work again. Been out all night?"*
— *"No, not at all. Sometimes I wake up early, like 6:00 this morning."*
— *"Wow! We have a 10:00 a.m. start time, and you don't live too far away."*
— *"Well, I've got some things to do in the morning."*
— *"What's there to do at 6:00 in the morning? What's your problem?"*
— *"All right, I have sex with my wife in the morning."*
— *"In the morning, at 6:00 a.m.? Why not in the evening?"*
— *"Evening's more convenient. But this way, I'm sure I'll be first today."*

* * *

— *"Why are you so pensive? Did something happen?"*
— *"I was leaving for work this morning and my wife snuggled up to me, kissed me and said, 'You're the best.'"*
— *"Oh, great, she loves you."*
— *"You see if she's saying I'm the best, it means she held some kind of casting somewhere."*

72   SOCIOLOGY IN JOKES

* * *

Wife to husband: *"Sweetheart, did I tell you that you're the best?"*
— *"No!"*
— *"Damn, who did I say that to yesterday, then?"*

* * *

— *"You see, my daughter, there was some torn wallpaper."*
— *"Daddy glued it back on almost imperceptibly. And he fixed the closet door. The iron works fine. As soon as it breaks, Daddy fixes it immediately. And Dad fixed the TV. How well it works now! Yeah, I know Dad can fix anything.*
— *"Yes, daughter, if you find a husband like that, you'll never have anything new in your house."*

An unexpected ending, like in a detective story. It reminds us that all sociological laws, unlike, say, the laws of mathematics, are statistical. If Pythagoras' theorem is 100% correct, it is rare in sociology. But if, say, 99% of women would like to have a husband who can fix everything in the house and willingly does it, then, as we can see, some women will be dissatisfied.

* * *

One friend asks the other. *"Are you still seeing Kolya?"*
— *"Well, I guess so."*
— *"You say that with some doubt."*
— *"It's just that besides Kolya, I'm also dating Ivan, Borya and Petya."*
— *"So, what, you cheated on Kolya? Why is that?"*
— *"You can only cheat if you're legally married. And that's called casting."*

* * *

In a small town, they were celebrating the birthday of a well-known local figure. The local newspaper sent a reporter for an interview. After the usual questions about the secret of his longevity, work achievements, and so on, she asked: *"Why have you never married? Do you not like women?"*
— *"I often fell in love. I had many women, but for marriage, I was looking for the perfect woman."*
— *"And out of billions of women, you never found her?"*
— *"Once I did find her, she was beautiful — in face, figure, and soul. I*

dreamed of marrying her."
— *"And why didn't you marry her?"*
— *"Alas, the thing is, she was looking for the perfect man."*

9. Religion

Religion is a mode of social thinking, feeling, and ways of acting that relates to the supernatural or "otherworldly." For convenience in discussing the problems of religious behavior, we use sociologist Ronald L. Johnstone (1975) scheme, which divides religion into these types: simple supernaturalism, animism, theism, and a system of abstract ideals[12].

Simple supernaturalism prevailed in pre-industrial society. Believers attributed supernatural qualities called obsession (mana) to nature. People manipulated these forces to achieve practical goals, such as luck in battle or success in love. Rituals and amulets were used to protect against the "evil eye" and envy. Belief in spirits or otherworldly beings is animism. Spirits are believed to live in animals, in nature, and sometimes even in people and are guided by the same emotions and motivations as humans. People use love, punishment, respect, gifts, and even deception when communicating with spirits. Rituals can be used to 'force' supernatural forces to act in a desired way — this is called a spell.

Theism is a religion centered on the belief in gods who are seen as powerful, interested in the affairs of people, and should be worshipped. Judaism, Christianity, and Islam are forms of **monotheism** or belief in one god. Proponents of theism create religious organizations, religious leaders, or priests, traditional rituals, and holy scriptures. Furthermore, the religion of the ancient Greeks and Hinduism (prevalent mainly in India) are forms of **polytheism** or belief in many gods of equal or relatively equal power. The gods of the Hindus are often local, tribal, or caste deities whose power is limited to a particular place — a house, a field, a mountain — or a particular object such as an animal or a tree. Finally, some religions focus on a **system of abstract ideals**. In this case, more than the worship of the gods, the focus is on the attainment of moral and spiritual perfection. Such are most of the religions of Asia, including Taoism

---

12   Johnstone, Ronald L. *Religion in Society: A Sociology of Religion.* Englewood Cliffs, NJ: Prentice Hall, 1975.

76   SOCIOLOGY IN JOKES

and Buddhism. Buddhism is aimed at achieving an elevated state of consciousness, liberation (by purification) from suffering, ignorance, egoism, and belief in the cycle of new births (reincarnation).

In the Western world, humanism is, in fact, a religion based on ethical principles. Proponents of this religion reject all theological beliefs in God, heaven, hell, and immortality. They try to live well in the here and now. They see heaven as an ideal society on Earth and hell as a world in which war, suffering, and ignorance flourish.

The soul is a person's unique personality, and immortality is our deeds that will remain as beautiful or bitter memories in the lives of future generations. Figure 1 shows the major religions of the world and the number of their adherents in 2010[13].

Figure 1. Number of adherents of religions of the world 2010

№	Religion	Numbers	%
1	Christians	2 292 454 000	33,2
2	Muslims	1 549 444 000	22,4
3	Hindus	948 507 000	13,7
4	Agnostics	639 852 000	9,3
5	Buddhists	468 736 000	6,8
6	Chinese religion	458 316 000	6,6
7	Folk religion	261 429 000	3,8
8	Atheists	138 532 000	2
9	New religions	64 443 000	0,9
10	Sikhs	24 591 000	0,4
11	Jews	14 641 000	0,2
12	Other religions	45 615 000	0,7
	Total	**6 906 560 000**	100

---

13   Wikipedia, citing J. Melton's encyclopedia *Religions of the world*.

Religious organizations

Norms, beliefs and rituals create the cultural basis of religion. However, it is still more a religious institution than a cultural heritage. Just as in other institutions, it has its structure and network of people involved, with certain, relatively stable ties between them. It is interesting to learn not only about people's religious practices but also about why they structure their religious life in this way and not in other ways.

Sociologists have agreed on these conventional-ideal types of religious organizations: churches, sects, denominations, and cults. Churches and denominations adapt to the larger society. Sects and cults do not. They are against established social organizations and practices. Still, cults are different from sects. The supporters of a cult see in it a path — one of many — to truth and salvation. In this respect, cults are like denominations. In contrast, the sect, like the church, believes that it is solely the only one that leads to truth and salvation. This model is depicted in Figure 2.

Figure 2. Types of religious organizations

	Attitude toward society	
	Positive	Negative
They only consider themselves legitimate	Church	Sect
Allow for the legitimacy of others	Denomination	Cult

This construct helps to understand the confusing aspects of religious organizations. In practice, however, some religious organizations have mixed characteristics. In the Church of Scientology, Rajnushism can be a denomination, a sect, or a cult, depending on which of their characteristics is emphasized.

The church.

A church is a religious organization that demands legitimacy and seeks to attract more members. If parents belong to the church, their children automatically belong to the church. The purpose of the church is clearly worldwide and universal and ignores competing 'firms'. The church agrees with the secular side of social life and chooses the dominant values of society but resists social reform. The church controls all aspects of social life by teaching and rewarding members.

Sects.

A sect is a religious organization that asserts its right to exclusivity, denies the values of the dominant society, and considers itself the chosen religious elite.

The denomination.

A denomination is a form of religious organization more adapted to a secular society that treats other religions with respect. In many cases, it is a sect in an advanced state of development and adapted to a secular way of life. The denomination (to the secular world) is comprised of middle-class parishioners. The denomination's moral rigor and religious fervor are weakened. The denomination has an established clergy and cares for a program of development and education for the children of the congregation. The denomination does not claim exclusivity and believes that all religions are worthy in the eyes of God. Examples of denominations are most religious groups in the United States: Presbyterians, Baptists, Congregationalists, Methodists, Unitarians, Lutherans, and the like.

The cult.

The cult recognizes the right to exist of other religious communities but often conflicts with the state. It does not claim exclusivity of its path to truth but criticizes society. Cults do not follow traditional religious practices but seek truth in the tenets of faith and secular views of the sacred. Cult membership does not require passing tests or submitting to one another. Cults may focus on solving their members' problems or have a specific purpose, such as spiritual healing or self-discovery.

Theory of religion (perspectives on religion)

What role does religion play in social life? Why is it such an important part of social experience? Why do people believe that the world around them is full of invisible forces, spirits, and gods? From functionalist doctrine, we learn about the social rituals that create social solidarity. From conflict theorists, we learn that ideas are weapons and that they serve the interests of privileged circles. There are not many sections of sociology where the positions of functionalists and conflictionalists are clearly stated.

Functionalist theory

The theorists of functionalism pay attention to the contribution of religion to social life and the survival of society. They believe that if any known society has something like religion, then the emergence of religion cannot be socially accidental. So, what functions does religion fulfill in social life?

The function of religion

1. Religion as a societal glue.

Émile Durkheim analyzed the functions of religion and concluded that its primary function is to create, reinforce, and support social solidarity and social control. Through religious rituals, people move from individual awareness to a collective mindset, creating shared consciousness that strengthens social bonds and moral authority. Religion acts as a symbol of society, allowing people to worship a representation of themselves and reinforcing a sense of unity. When society rejects religion without finding a suitable alternative, it risks losing cohesion, as individuals may start pursuing their own interests without considering the needs of the larger community. In general, according to functionalists, society has achieved its unity primarily because of its members' shared ownership of core values and goals (ends).

2. Social control

Durkheim sees religion as a "societal glue" but also notes that it reinforces social control through priests, idealism, and supernatural factors. Heaven and hell become realities for certain groups, with heaven symbolizing security and a decent place in society and hell symbolizing punishment for breaking laws. By identifying the morality of this world and that world, members of society internalize social standards: social control becomes the individual's control.

3. Dealing with life's "breaking points"

Religion always helps people at the turning points of life when they face crises and problems such as epidemics, diseases, wars, social disorders and the mysteries of life and death. It provides 'answers' and hope and helps people in their erratic and treacherous lives. Most religions explain and celebrate the major milestones of people's lives — birth, reaching maturity, marriage and death — through rituals of transition.

4. An impetus to social change

Religion can also drive social change. For example, Black religion has historically contributed significantly to the mobilization of protest that found expression in the public rights movement of the 1950s and 1960s. The Southern Christian Leadership Conference, led by Rev. M. Luther King and other Black ministers, was at the forefront of the Black protest movement in the 1960s.

Functional equivalents

Behavior that looks religious may be associated with other areas of life, such as communism, nationalism, science, and sports. These areas may have religious qualities but are not religions in the classical sense, like Christianity or Judaism.

Conflict theory (The Conflict Perspective)

With the help of functionalist theorists, we have seen religion as a life-giving source of social integration and solidarity. Conflict theorists look at it from a very different perspective. Some of them portray religion as a weapon in the hands of the ruling elite, which is necessary to keep under control the explosive tensions arising from social inequality and injustice. Others see religion as a source of social conflict and point to the religious wars of the Middle Ages and contemporary religious strife in the Middle East, India, and Ireland. In addition, religion is seen as a source of social change. Marx believed that religion was an opium for the people that diverted the attention of the oppressed class from seeking social change. Religion, in his view, creates false consciousness and prevents the working class from acquiring real class consciousness. It also creates alienation of people and oppresses them. Marx was not alone in his opinion: many sociologists agree that religion can be used to maintain the established order and legitimize change in favor of powerful and wealthy groups. However, Leon Trotsky (a revolutionary and one of the leaders of the October Revolution in Russia in 1917) believed in the similarities between revolutionary Marxism and religious sectarianism, so much so that in late 1890, he successfully recruited the first working-class members of the South Russian Workers' Union from among the supporters of religious sects.

An engine of social change.

Some conflict theorists have recently changed their view of the relationship between religion and social change. They see religion not as a passive imprint of social relationships but as an active force shaping social life. It can play a crucial role in the birth and consolidation of new social structures and new formations. Assuming that some aspects of religion prohibit change, they emphasize that other aspects of religion challenge existing social structures and inspire change. In some contexts, religion can be a powerful revolutionary force that shows people exactly how things should be. Thus, religion is not an invariable functional or conservative factor in society

82   SOCIOLOGY IN JOKES

but is often one of the main (sometimes the only) drivers of social revolutions.

Science requires axioms and proofs. Religion requires neither. Philosophy stands in the middle.

* * *

One buddy to another. *"You're a philosophy major. Can you explain something to me?"*
— *"I don't know, what are you interested in?"*
— *"For centuries, science has struggled with religious prejudice, and religion has persecuted science. Scientists have even been burned. And now, here in the 21st century, unprecedented development of science and religion also continues to exist, and the overwhelming majority of the population on Earth are believers. How is this possible?"*
— *"Science and religion can very well coexist. For example, you need science to make a bomb, but you need a religious person to detonate it."*

* * *

The Russian Orthodox Church (ROC) is conducting an internal investigation into a priest who conducted the rite of consecration of a spacecraft before the launch. According to the investigation, diluted holy water and counterfeit items of church utensils were used.

This anecdote lays out another variant of combining science and religion. The consecration of cars, buildings, etc. is familiar and not funny, but the consecration of a spaceship is the basis of humor in this anecdote. This means that science and religion are usually seen as opposites of each other.

Absolute faith (Christian parable).

* * *

It was a dry summer, and the farmers in the small village were concerned about what would happen to their crops. One Sunday afternoon after Mass, they went to their pastor for advice. *"Father, we must do something, or we'll lose the crop!"*
— *"All you have to do is pray with absolute faith. Prayer without faith is not prayer. It must come from the heart,"* answered the priest.
At the next week, the farmers met twice a day and prayed that God would send them rain. On Sunday, they went to the priest. *"It's not*

RELIGION   83

working, Father! We get together every day and pray, but it still doesn't rain."
— *"Do you really pray in faith?"* The priest asked them. They began to assure him that it was so. But the priest objected: *"I know you pray without faith because not one of you brought an umbrella with you when you came here!"*

Sometimes, experiments like this are conducted. Volunteers have it explained to them that in order to develop means to combat burns, a hot object (for example, a coin) will be applied to their shoulder, and then they will be treated. And a cold object is applied. But many develop a burn. If the subjects have doubts that the object is red-hot, there will definitely be no burn. The same is true for the requirement of faith, which is a specificity of many religions. If people begin to wonder, religion will not be able to fulfill its functions effectively (especially since sacred books are usually archaic and contain many contradictions). Atheistic literature tries to shake faith based on these contradictions. For example, Mark Twain comments on the thesis that man is a perfect being that god created in his own image. "What do men's nipples serve? From a practical point of view, they are useless, and as an ornament, they do not stand up to any criticism."

Other considerations that come to mind in connection with this anecdote are how cleverly the pastor was able to justify the apparent ineffectiveness of religion in dealing with a particular problem. It brings to mind Churchill's statement, "A politician should be able to predict what will happen tomorrow, a week from now, a month from now, and a year from now. And then explain why it didn't happen." As a social institution, the church has its functionaries who are interested in expanding the flock and strengthening the church's influence. Top church hierarchs can receive perks for supporting the authorities in doing business (which is consistent with the conflict theory of religion) and living in luxury (driving expensive cars, wearing $30,000 watches, etc.). For example, according to Wikipedia, Patriarch Kirill has a private jet, a yacht, an armored train, a villa in Switzerland, a house in Peredelkino, a palace in Gelendzhik, and a fleet of cars: a Victory, a Cadillac Escalade, a Toyota Land Cruiser, a limousine, and a super-luxe S-series

84   SOCIOLOGY IN JOKES

Mercedes. I once saw on TV a comment by our Ukrainian patriarch Filaret on the fact that Pope Francis refused to give up the papal car: "This is an ostentatious gesture. In any case, I am not going to give up my Mercedes, I need it to drive around the flock". However, the church has used the ability to impress the flock since ancient times. For example, in the 1st century CE, Heron of Alexandria, commissioned by the priests of an ancient temple, created a machine for selling holy water, which made a strong impression on the faithful (this invention was forgotten and revived only in the 19th century). A singing mechanical bird was also created for the Delphic Oracle (the priest pressed a secret button, and the bird sang, which meant "yes" in response to the believer's question).

On a side note to the ROC, *"it turns out that Jesus did not have an SUV, an expensive watch, or a country residence and did not dress in gold-embroidered robes."* The authors of this anecdote point to the contradiction between the propagated values and the actual behavior of many church representatives.

* * *

– *"Izya, it's Christmas, let's have a drink!"*
– *"Fima, what a strange suggestion! It's not our party!"*
– *"Listen, Izya, do you think two Jews can't have a drink at a third Jew's birthday party?"*

Why is that funny? Because it's not immediately obvious what it is about. The worldwide Christian religion arose on the basis of the Jewish religion, and the fact that in the sacred books of Christianity, almost all the actors, including Jesus Christ, his mother, and the apostles, are Jews is forgotten or deliberately glossed over. A new religion that replaces an old one tries to incorporate some elements of the old one to ease the transition from the old religion to the new one. For example, Roman gods and festivals copy Greek festivals. Christian holidays were celebrated at the same time as pagan or Jewish holidays. Christmas was probably celebrated in place of Saturnalia, and New Year's Day was the day Jesus Christ was circumcised. Catholics celebrate the "Circumcision of the Lord" on January

RELIGION   85

1, and although we say the year is from the birth of Christ, we are actually counting from his circumcision.

* * *

Once, a Catholic pastor and a rabbi were in the same compartment of a train. They got to talking. *"What surprises me,"* said the pastor, *"is that you don't have any promotion in your church."*
— *"Is that interesting?"*
— *"You are a rabbi and you will die a rabbi. What's the point of trying?*
— *"What kind of promotion can you have?"* Asked the rabbi.
— *"I may eventually become a bishop."*
— *"Let's say. What's next?"*
— *"A bishop can become a metropolitan."*
— *"Let's say. What's next?"*
— *"A metropolitan can become a cardinal."*
— *"Let's say. What's next?"*
— *"Well...a cardinal could become pope."*
— *"And then?"*
— *"Well, you know! A man can't become Lord God!"*
— *"I don't know. A Jewish boy did it."*

This is an anecdote on the same theme as the previous one.

* * *

In kindergarten, a girl draws something with rapture.
Teacher: *"What are you drawing?"*
— *"God."*
— *"But no one knows what He looks like!"*
— *"They're about to find out!"*

It seems that this anecdote came from a real story, but someone wrote it down. The girl is good, and her self-confidence causes respect. However, the attitude to the image of god could influence the development of a culture of different peoples. For example, according to one hypothesis, the fact that Judaism for centuries forbade any image of God influenced the fact that among the Jews until the 19th century, there were outstanding philosophers, scientists, and musicians, but there were no outstanding artists.

* * *

An older Jew came down with coronavirus in an infectious disease ward. He asks to call a priest. The priest came and said: "*My son, I absolve you of your sins ... etc*".

Then this Jew says to the priest: "*Here, father, is the key to the safe deposit box for safekeeping and my will. If I die, please take the money and give it together with my will to the rabbi of our synagogue*".

– "*All right, my son. But why didn't you call the rabbi about this?*"

– "*Where to? To the infectious disease ward?*"

A contradictory attitude to an Orthodox priest—complete trust but no love. The attitude to other people's priests is more or less clear. It is interesting how different religions treat their priests. For example, do Jews treat rabbis better than Orthodox Christians treat popes? If so, is the reason for this the lack of such a developed hierarchy, which was discussed in another anecdote, and the more modest life of rabbis compared to many Orthodox priests (at least in public opinion). Unfortunately, I do not know if there are any such studies.

* * *

– "*Are you a believer?*"

– "*God forbid! Thank God my parents were non-believers, and no one was able to instill these delusions in me. God had mercy!*"

* * *

On confessions: "*Father, I am a sinner: I indulged in gluttony, drank, fornicated ...*"

– "*I know, my daughter.*"

– "*How?*"

– "*I am subscribed to your Instagram.*"

It is not even funny; ROC priests regularly consecrate cars, SU-34 bombers, space rockets, submarines and weapons of mass destruction (В РПЦ предложили больше не освящать оружие массового поражения—BBC News Русская служба[14]). Therefore, the fact that they use social media is far less surprising. And here is another anecdote about the modern church.

---

14   https://www.bbc.com/russian/news-48702605

RELIGION   87

* * *

A man is sitting in a bar, drinking. A nun walks by and says reproachfully: *"How can you live your life in this shelter of fornication and debauchery?"*
— *"There is no debauchery here, Sister Anna,"* replies the man angrily. *"I'm just drinking."*
— *"And it disgusts God,"* says the nun.
— *"Have you ever tried it yourself, Sister Anna?"* Asks the man.
— *"No!"* Exclaimed the nun indignantly. *"How can you say so?"*
— *"Here, I'll buy you a drink now, and you'll try it."*
— *"Never! For people to see a nun drinking liquor?"*
— *"I'll ask to have it poured into a cup for you",* says the man. The nun agrees.
A man comes to the counter and says: *"Listen, give me two glasses of vodka; only pour one into a tea cup."*
The bartender turns around: *"What, Sister Anne's here again?"*

* * *

There was a terrible car accident, and three women died. They went to paradise. There's music, fireworks, cheerful voices. But the Apostle Peter is guarding the gate. He looks at them and sighs. *"I see that there is no evil in you; you have lived in the world as birds. However, you still need to know some basic things about Christianity. I'll ask you one simple question. If you answer correctly, I'll let you in, but if you don't, I'm sorry. Turning to the first one: What is Easter?"*
— *"It's when the tree is decorated, and presents are given, champagne is drunk."*
— *"Get out of here!"* The apostle turns to the next one: *"You tell me."*
— *"Easter is when everyone dresses up as ghosts, puts candles in a pumpkin and scares each other. It's a great holiday, I love it!"*
Peter chased away the second one. He asks the third. She says cautiously: *"Easter happens in the spring ... uh. Every year a different number of ..."*
— *"That's good."*
— *"Next, everyone dresses up and goes to the Holy Mountain, where Jesus Christ is buried. In a cave, behind a big rock."*
— *"Well, let's say. What's next?"*
— *"They push back the stone. Jesus comes out. And if he doesn't see his shadow, it means that spring will be early."*

88 SOCIOLOGY IN JOKES

The first person remembered the Christmas tree, a New Year's Eve celebration that is associated with paganism, the Julian calendar and Saturnalia. True, Christians later celebrated the day as the day of Christ's circumcision. However, the Christmas tree is associated with the green branches used during the Saturnalia. The second person speaks of Halloween, which is also associated with paganism with ancient Celtic customs. The third talks about Groundhog Day, which also goes back to Celtic and Germanic traditions. In Germany and other parts of Europe, people observed the behavior of animals such as badgers and hedgehogs to predict the weather. Hedgehogs were also revered in ancient Egypt, but it is not known whether they were used to predict the weather. The religions mentioned are polytheism (paganism, Groundhog Day) and monotheism (Christianity).

10. Economic System, Work, Free Time

The economic system is a social institution that is responsible for the production and distribution of goods and services. It provides solutions to the three main problems facing every society: 1. What goods and services should be produced, and in what quantity? 2. How do we apply limited resources — land, water, minerals, fuel, and labor to produce desired goods and services? and 3. For whom should society produce goods and services? How a society answers these questions has very serious consequences for culture and social structure. If a society decides to produce weapons in large quantities, the standard of living of its citizens will be much lower than if the society emphasizes the production of consumer goods. Deciding whom to produce for affects the distribution of wealth, income, prestige, etc., i.e., the system of stratification. In the course of history, there have been different economic systems: the hunter-gatherer society, agricultural and industrial society. Changes in what and how people produce, distribute and consume are accompanied by changes in family, religion, and political institutions.

Modern economic systems.

There are two types of modern economic systems: the capitalist market economy and the socialist command economy. They differ primarily in two ways. First, they give different answers to the question, "How is the economy organized — as a market economy or as a planned economy?" Second, different answers to the question "Who owns the means of production — the individual or the state?" Of course, the answers to these questions are not exclusive. Every modern society is somewhere between the two extremes. The Soviet Union had a planned economy; the owner of almost all means of production was the state, and the United States had a market economy. The owner of most means of production is a private individual (although they have some state ownership); these two countries are opposites. Therefore, if you give a definition, they say that a capitalist economy is an economic system based, for the most part, on the free market and private ownership, and a socialist economy is an economic system based, for the most part, on state planning and public ownership of the means of production. However, Nazi Germany had a planned economy that was controlled by the state but, for the most part, had private ownership. Yugoslavia (as it was before the collapse), on the contrary, had a market economy and state and collective ownership.

In sociological terms, property is a social reality consisting of a set of rights that show what one party can do and the other cannot do. It is a force-backed right to some scarce object. The concept of property is culturally universal — all societies have rules governing the ownership and disposition of property, focusing on private ownership as the right of individuals, on public ownership as the ownership of the state, and on communal or community ownership as the ownership by a family, clan or group.as the right of the state.

Ownership by a family, clan or group.

Comparison between market and command economies. Recall that to compare economic systems it makes sense to see how they answer three questions.

1. What goods and services should be produced, and in what quantities? In a market economy, this is decided by the consumer, voting with currency. If more people buy a good or service, the producer can expand production, and thus, the system keeps track of demand. This mechanism is called consumer sovereignty. There is an underlying assumption that if each economic unit has free choice in pursuing its interests, then it is better for all. Critics say that everyone is not necessarily better off under this assumption. For example, if children eat whatever they want, it will be a lot of chocolate or candy, which may not be good for them. In a command economy, the government decides what and how much to produce. This is why, writes Vander Zanden, the Soviet Union has fewer cars and more volumes of Lenin than the consumer wants.

2. How do we apply limited resources — land, water, minerals, fuel, and labor — to produce desired goods and services? In a market economy, competition forces the use of resources efficiently because to do otherwise increases costs and decreases profits. The command economy is based on the assumption that only a rational decision, free from the random operations of the market economy, can give society what is more useful to it.

For whom should society produce goods and services? In a market economy, this is determined by money, with capitalists — the owners of capital — receiving the most. Critics say that this leads to inequality and is unfair. However, under state ownership, the state receives the profits and distributes them according to what is good for society. What is not good for the society is decided by the management.

Capitalist economy.

The elements of a capitalist market economy emerged in the Middle Ages, between 1500 and 1750, when private property rights, banks, insurance and the like appeared. Sociologist Peter Berger (1986) explored the relationship between capitalism and the type of society. Max Weber, in his work The Protestant Ethic and the Spirit of Capitalism (1904), showed the influence of Protestantism on the development of capitalism. The economic boom in Singapore, Hong Kong, Japan, South Korea, and Taiwan showed that capitalism is possible not only in societies with an emphasis on individual autonomy but also in Asian societies with respect for tradition and group solidarity. Berger concluded that capitalism is necessary but not sufficient for democracy because there is no society with democracy without capitalism. However, it is possible to have capitalism without full democratic development, as in the case of Taiwan.

92 SOCIOLOGY IN JOKES

Socialist economics.

The capitalist economy has its flaws. Karl Marx gave the most influential criticism of capitalism. These are, for example, instability, recession or depression. The socialist system established in the Soviet Union has been effective in mobilizing resources, for example to build a military arsenal or space programs. Social programs (free education, health care) provide social protection. For a certain period (the period of extensive economy), there were quite high rates of economic development. However, then the rates began to fall steadily, and constant shortages, corruption, low discipline, lack of interest in the results of work, etc, characterized the last years of the Soviet Union. Other socialist countries (including the developing world) also had great difficulty in achieving economic growth, individual freedoms, and social equality.

The academician Victor Glushkov, director of the Kyiv Institute of Cybernetics of the Academy of Sciences of the Ukrainian SSR, proposed a certain modification of socialism. Since the planned economy does not have such an automatic regulator of supply and demand as the market, production did not keep up with changes in demand, and because this information was too slow to reach the planning authorities and there was too much of it, the planning authorities did not have time to process it in time. Glushkov believed that it was necessary to put automated control systems (ACS) everywhere, which would automatically collect information and transmit it to the center. There, large computers would quickly process it, and then the socialist system would not have such critical shortcomings and would be more efficient than capitalism.

The leadership of the Soviet Union decided to conduct an experiment in Ukraine and build in the early 1980s what Glushkov had proposed — the Republican Automated Control System (RACS). Valery Khmelko and I once took part in evaluating the effectiveness of one of the subsystems of the RASU, the health management system. The experiment showed that the problem is not only with the speed of information exchange but also in the lack of private property and the lack of interest from the workers in providing the ACS with the necessary information. For example, in one of the articles I read, it was described how a transportation company introduced an ACS system that optimized operations. Trucks were carrying cargo one way and empty on the way back, so the system planned the return trip so that they would also carry cargo on the way back. However, realistically, on the return trip, the drivers were carrying 'left cargo' and earning most of their wages[15]. Hence, the implementation of the system caused them to quit, and the system could not be implemented. Thus, the experiment with RASU showed that the shortcomings of socialism are more serious than the insufficient speed of information exchange. Nevertheless, as previously stated, each of the societies has a mixed economy to some extent.

Corporations.

After World War II, multinational corporations (these are firms that have a central office in one country and branches in other countries) have become increasingly important. Often, these corporations have profits greater than the gross national product of these countries. More than half of the world's largest economic units are no longer countries but multinational corporations.

For example, according to the State Statistics Committee, Ukraine's gross national income for 2019 amounted to approximately UAH 4.1 trillion, i.e., $146 billion, and Apple's turnover in 2019 amounted to $260 billion (and Apple's market value is more than $2 trillion, i.e., more than $2,000 billion). Furthermore, the market value of the Saudi Arabian Oil Company is about 2,500 billion dollars, i.e., 17 times more than the national income of Ukraine (to buy such a company, Ukrainians must not eat, drink, or buy anything and could accumulate enough money in 17 years). Even individual owners of corporations can have a fortune comparable to

---

15 'Left cargo' is an expression that refers to illegal or unaccounted goods that drivers transported without the company's official permission. In simpler terms, these were goods that were transported unofficially, bypassing the accounting system and without paying taxes, and drivers earned more from this than from their official work.

the national income of the state. For example, Elon Musk had 188 billion dollars at the beginning of 2021.

However, corporations not only compete with nations (countries) on the level of profit but also form a supranational economy, which lies beyond public regulation or ordinary international rules. In their quest for profit, they pursue their global interests, which may not coincide with those of nations. In some cases, they may be a threat to the sovereignty of the countries in which they are located. For example, in the early 1970s, ITT (International Telephone and Telegraph) contributed to the organization of a military putsch, the overthrow of the legitimate government of Salvador Allende and the establishment of a military dictatorship in Chile.

Labor.

Labor is one of the most important aspects of our lives. It ensures an income and affects our position in society, and our social status. Therefore, when people get acquainted, they ask about each other's profession. Let us consider in more detail the social meaning of labor.

The social significance of labor.

Why do people labor? The most obvious answer is because of economic necessity. This may be one of the main reasons, but it is far from the only one. During sociological surveys, the vast majority of Americans surveyed note that they would not quit their jobs even if they had enough money to live comfortably. However, maybe this is only during the survey, and the actual behavior is different. Another study analyzed the behavior of people who won millions of dollars from a lottery that is regularly held in the United States. The vast majority did not leave their jobs. Thus, economic necessity is not the only reason. It turns out that people work out of interest in the content of the work, out of a sense of duty, to gain the approval of others, to avoid boredom, to socialize, to avoid loneliness and the like.

Melvin Kohn (1983) and his colleagues have pointed out several ways in which work affects our lives. More complex work requires education and longer periods of study. Therefore, this work holds a higher status within the stratification system (refer to the functionalist theory by Davis & Moore, which we discussed in Section 5 on social stratification). More meaningful and interesting work has a positive impact on intellectual development. Kohn showed that higher status in the hierarchy provides more opportunity for self-actualization of the worker through two intervening variables: the ability to self-regulate (self-directedness) and the degree of control over the worker (closeness of supervision). People who have more intellectual jobs choose more intellectual activities in their free time. In general, those who have more freedom at work and a higher level of self-regulation feel the value of freedom and self-regulation is higher; they are more open to new ideas and less authoritarian in their relations with other people[16]. Moreover, they bring up their children, instilling these values in their children. The general conclusion is that work affects our identity, who we are, and what we are as individuals; that is, it affects both our social status and our personal qualities.

This is not an anecdote but a real story. My car is parked in a multi-story garage, and a security guard sits downstairs, checking passes. Once, he saw me on TV, and from then on, he liked to ask questions and share his opinion about the situation in the country and the world. Furthermore, it was in those years when Leonid Kuchma was the president of Ukraine. The first time he saw me, he asked me: How's Kuchma doing? This reflects a great respect for television: if a person is shown there, it means that they are at the top. Of course, he used to tell me all his complaints about the actions of the president and the government.

One day, he asked me a really serious question: "Tell me, what are we building, capitalism or socialism? It does not look like socialism, so it's capitalism? Moreover, if it is capitalism, why doesn't anyone talk about it? Why haven't I and other people been asked whether we want to build capitalism? They asked about Ukraine's independence — we supported it. There was also a referendum on

---

16 Social Structures and Personality: A Study by Melvin Kohn and his collaborators, Kyiv: Publishing House Kyiv-Mohyla Academy, 2007.

reducing the number of deputies. Nevertheless, they did not ask about what to build."

This is a very important question! What can we say here—he is absolutely right. No one really wants to call our system capitalism (probably fearing the negative connotation that was formed over decades in the Soviet Union).

* * *

> Soviet anecdote (when there was a food shortage in the country and many goods rarely appeared in stores, long queues built up, and goods were quickly bought). An engineer catches his wife in bed with her lover. *"You're doing something stupid here. Across the street from the bread store, they are giving away bananas!"*

That goes for socialism, too. Scarcity. A commodity that is not available to everyone (but at the same or almost the same price!). To get it, you need either connections, goodwill in stores, privileges (distributors), the expenditure of considerable time (half a day running around stores...), luck, or chance, as in this anecdote. There is another aspect to this anecdote: "doing stupid things". From some perspective, this fussing in bed (especially for those not involved) seems silly, like some writer recalling that as a child, she was surprised by the discovery that people connect with their lower abdomens. There was also an anecdote about spaceships meeting.

* * *

> Earthlings show aliens a movie about the system of life reproduction.
> — *"It's a man, it's a woman, they copulate, and nine months later, a baby is born."*
> — *"In nine months? Why were they in such a hurry at the end?"*

There is some disconnection between the significance of the events and their perception, and maybe some rituals are missing, such as weddings.

* * *

It is possible that acquaintances can also get a position under capitalism. However, it exists only under socialism on such a systematic and large scale, a phenomenon specific to socialism, which has been called *blat*. *Blat* refers to informal connections or acquaintances that help a person gain advantages, bypass official rules, and solve personal or business issues. In the USSR and post-Soviet countries, *blat* was often used to obtain scarce goods, secure employment through connections, or access other benefits that were difficult to acquire within a planned economy. This phenomenon also involves mutual favors and informal obligations between people. In the absence of a market economy, connections are often more important than money, and there is a natural exchange of services. Under capitalism, when the demand for a commodity increases, its price rises until the rate of sales equals the rate of production. Under socialism, prices for goods are stable; neither producers nor trading organizations have the right to raise them without the approval of higher departments or ministries. There is a shortage, and sellers keep goods for themselves and sell them to acquaintances at higher prices or in exchange for services. Blat or protection in universities is also a characteristic feature of socialism. There are no private universities, higher education is free of charge, and there is competition in the more prestigious universities. Admission to a university is an important, momentous event; the leadership of universities and faculties, as well as party organs supervising universities, use their influence as a very important favor; blat is the currency of socialism.

> Entrance to the institute. The first applicant enters by a big blat, the second just by a blat, and the third without a blat. The first person is asked a question: *"Over which country was the first atomic bomb detonated?"*
> — *"Over Japan."*
> — *"That's right, top score — five points."*
> The second is asked two questions: *"Over which country was the first atomic bomb exploded?"* and *"In what year?"*
> — *"Japan, 1945."*
> — *"That's right, five points".* A third is asked the same question, and then another: *"How many people were killed in the explosions?"*
> — *"Two hundred forty-four thousand. Please list their names."*

98   SOCIOLOGY IN JOKES

* * *

A husband and wife live in Moscow, but the mother-in-law lives in the provinces. So she comes to visit and tells her son-in-law. *"Well, son-in-law, I want to see if you're worthy of my daughter. If you can provide for your family. I'll give you three tasks. If you do them, I'll respect you. The first one is to get red caviar and sausage servilat."*
The son-in-law fussed, ran somewhere and on the second day, he bought caviar and servilat.
— *"Good for you"*, says the mother-in-law. *"I've saved some money; get me a sheepskin coat."* This task is more difficult. The son-in-law started calling his friends and running around the city but got the sheepskin coat.
— *"Well done, says the mother-in-law. Here's the last task. I want, at least after my death, to make a name for myself. I want to be buried in Moscow, in the Novodevichy Cemetery. And it will be easier for you and my daughter to remember me. So, do whatever you want, but get me a place there."* The son-in-law spent a week making phone calls, writing all sorts of statements, taking a vacation at work and disappearing somewhere all day long. Finally, he came running in happy. *"It worked! I got you a spot in the cemetery! But the funeral's tomorrow at noon!"*

Typical of socialism, the shortages concerned everything: food, clothing and services. Of course, and cemetery places. Money was not the most important thing here (especially since the prices for everything were fixed and low). What mattered were connections and a system of mutual services and goodwill. Novodevichy Cemetery was the most prestigious cemetery in Moscow during the Soviet era (maybe now too), where the leaders of the country, Nikita Khrushchev, Boris Yeltsin, famous writers, composers such as Anton Chekhov, Nikolai Gogol, Sergei Prokofiev, Dmitry Shostakovich and many others were buried.

* * *

This is the early 1990s, Ukraine's transition from socialism to market relations. Madame Hershkovych trades at Privoz in Odessa (a famous bazaar in the port city). She decided to expand her business and take a loan to buy goods but the banks do not give her anything without collateral. Finally, someone advised her *"Vova Bank"*, they said, *"go to see the bank director, Vova; he is an unconventional man, so he introduces*

ECONOMIC SYSTEM, WORK, FREE TIME   99

himself to everyone as Vova." She managed to get to the principal's office surprisingly easily. He invited her to sit down, and she started to speak, but Vova interrupted her. *"How much do you need and for how long?"*

— *"Can you give me sixty thousand?"*

— *"Uh, sure."*

— *"And a hundred thousand? For a month, until September 10."*

Vova stood up, went to the safe, pulled out a ten pack and put it in front of her.

— *"Here you go! All the best to you, good luck."*

— *"Wait, I haven't told you yet, I don't have a deposit."*

— *"I don't need security."*

— *"Do I have to sign somewhere? Do I need a passport?"*

— *"There's nothing to it!"*

Madame Hershkovich is puzzled: *"I don't get it. No collateral, no receipt, no passport? And if I don't give the money back, don't return it?"*

— *"How can you not give it back? You'll be ashamed of yourself!"*

— *"What? Am I going to be ashamed? When, in front of whom?"*

— *"Before the Lord God! When you stand before him, you will be ashamed!*

— *"When will that be?"*

— *"What do you mean, when? If you don't hand it over on September 10, you'll appear on September 11!"*

This is an example of business ethics and informality. They say that the initial accumulation of capital in other countries was also not always done exclusively by law-abiding people. And it is hard to say how many bandits became big businessmen and came to power in Ukraine.

Two classic Soviet anecdotes.

* * *

A brother from America writes letters to Rabinovich, but he does not reply. Here comes the so-called détente of international tension. Relations between the USSR and the USA improved. The year 1972 came, President Nixon's visit to the USSR was being prepared. Rabinovich's brother asked his senator, and the senator included this question in his request to the Soviet authorities — what about Rabinovich? And so Rabinovich is summoned to the KGB and told: *"Why don't you write to your brother? Do you want to undermine the policy of détente between the Party and the government? Sit down and immediately write a letter to your brother."* And Rabinovich sits down and writes: *"Dear brother, I finally found the time and place to write you a letter."*

* * *

USSR. Two Soviet violinists are traveling on a train, returning from the Paganini Competition in Genoa. And it should be said that the winner of the contest is given the right to play Paganini's violin. One took the second place, the other last. The one who took the last place is cheerful, satisfied, drinking cognac, while the one who took the second place is very upset. *"Why are you so sad? Second place is also very good."*
– *"Yeah, but whoever gets first place gets to play Paganini's violin."*
– *"Fuck that violin! Well, you didn't play it, and to hell with it. You'll play another one."*
– *"How can I explain it to you so you'll understand? You see, for me to play Paganini's violin is like for you ... to shoot Dzerzhinsky's Mauser."*

Those who do not live in the Soviet Union will not understand this anecdote. In Soviet times, it was very difficult to travel abroad. For example, as a non-partisan, I was not allowed to go even to socialist Bulgaria, which was very close to the Soviet Union. If someone was allowed to go abroad, they were accompanied by a KGB officer, who made sure that they did not stay there. This officer pretended to be an ordinary member of the delegation.

* * *

Grandma made a bet with Sema that if he couldn't eat her 25 dumplings, he would have to clean the apartment. So Sema finishes the 24th dumpling and realizes that the 25th is not on the plate. That's all you need to know about making contracts.

* * *

– *"Doctor, tell me, what should I do with the two teeth that hurt?"*
– *"Just extract them!"*
– *"And how much will that cost me?"*
– *"150 dollars."*
– *"Wow! 150 dollars for two minutes of work?"*
– *"Okay ... I'll pull your teeth slowly."*

ECONOMIC SYSTEM, WORK, FREE TIME   101

This is to the question of pay by results or hourly work.

* * *

— "*Why are you so nervous? Did something happen?*"
— "*Well, my cottage was burgled. That was two weeks ago. Over the week-end, we dropped off new furniture and got two dogs, a sheepdog and a Rott-weiler, for security.*"
— "*Well, that's right, well done. So, what are you nervous about?*"
— "*You know, what if one dog relies on the other?*"

This is from the field of sociology of organizational business. Func-tional responsibilities should be divided in such a way that the sphere of responsibility of each employee is clearly defined.

* * *

On the streetcar. Conductor: "*Can I see your ticket, please?*"
— "*You ask everybody, but do you have a ticket yourself?*"
— "*I don't have one, but I don't need one.*"
— "*What do you mean you don't need one? He doesn't have a ticket himself, but he asks others!*"
— "*Look, I'm the conductor, and I don't have to pay for the ticket.*"
— "*Why is that? I'm an electrician, so what, I shouldn't pay for electricity?*"

This anecdote is also related to business organization. Here is why, really, the conductor should not be paid. What can he say to the electrician? If it is at the conductor's expense, will they demand a wage increase, or will they save money and need conductor after conductor? Moreover, this will increase the cost of the streetcar company for control. It turns out that, in reality the streetcar com-pany transports more people and does not pay tax to the state for some of them. In general, there are a lot of questions here and it will not be so easy to convince the electrician. By the way, the question of how environmentally friendly streetcars were displaced by air-polluting buses is interesting. Look up the Great American Street-car Scandal on the Internet. Another aspect of the control problem is how big the losses are if there is no control and whether the in-troduction of control pays off in increased profits.

* * *

102 SOCIOLOGY IN JOKES

An anecdote from twenty years ago, when there were virtually no cell phones.

> An older Jewish person is sitting outside a large bank selling seeds. A passerby approaches him and says: *"I see you have a lot of change. Could you change three dollars into quarters (25 cents) for me? I have a lot of calls to make."*
> — *"Unfortunately, I can't."*
> — *"But why? It's more convenient for you to have paper money than change."*
> — *"You see, I have a contract with the bank: I don't do financial transactions, and the bank doesn't sell seeds."*

* * *

> Business School. Startup and investment seminar. Business coach: *"There is a common misconception that you need a large amount of money to start a business. Sure, there are businesses with a high financial threshold to enter the market, but a huge number of businesses can be started with minimal funds available to almost anyone. Think about this for a moment. Have you? Now, let's talk about it. You, young man, what could you open with the money you have?"*
> — *"Me? Just the window."*

11. Sociology of Crime and Law

What is deviation? In a stable society, most people adhere to most social norms most of the time. That is why, in a stable society or, more precisely, in a stable phase of social development, social life has quite regular and predictable forms. However, this picture of social life, even in stable societies, is not complete. If we look at it more closely, we can see that people not only adhere to social norms but also violate them. People steal from and rape other people. People wear extravagant clothes, use drugs, adopt religions atypical for Ukraine, utter absurd slogans or preach pretentious ideas. All this means that a complete picture of society should include both compliance with social norms and deviations from them. What is deviance? Strictly speaking, this concept should cover any behavior that does not conform to social norms. However, in practice, in life, many norms are not considered very important. Non-conformity of behavior to such norms can be perceived quite tolerantly or even ignored. The social reaction to a person being late for a date, crossing the street in the wrong place, or accidentally wearing unmatched socks will be very different from the reaction to someone slapping an older woman on the street, participating in an orgy, or claiming to be Napoleon.

Small deviations from the norm, or deviations from norms that no one particularly cares about, have, if anything, very few social consequences and are, therefore, of little interest to sociologists. The sociology of deviance is concerned primarily with those disorders that a significant number of people perceive as offensive, repugnant or very bad. From this perspective, deviance or deviation is behavior that violates significant social norms and is condemned, as a result, by a significant number of people. The definition of specific actions as deviant varies greatly from time to time, place to place, and social group to social group. For example, what was considered heretical in some times may be considered holy in others; a 'freedom fighter' from one group's perspective may be a 'terrorist' to another group; conservative views in one society may be considered dangerous radical for the other. The act of a person who kills another person may or may not be considered an aberration. Sometimes the conditions under which such an act is committed may incline some people to consider it heroic and others to consider the same act criminal.

In 1776, George Washington was branded by the British authorities as a traitor. However, 20 years later, he became the first president of the United States and went down in history as the 'father of the nation.' However, if the Americans had not won their war of independence, Washington might have become a prisoner or been shot.

Because deviance is defined according to social circumstances and power relations, the definition of some forms of behavior as deviance is subject to change. For example, in recent decades in the United States, some groups, including gays and lesbians, have entered the political arena and achieved official recognition. However, the majority of the population still stigmatizes them. Still, universal human values are gradually being formed. If killing and eating an enemy was once the norm in many groups of primitive people, nowadays, killing under certain circumstances is still the norm. In contrast, eating a human is an aberration in all modern societies.

Social control. In order for society, most people, to fulfill their needs, they must follow certain rules. Without social order, it would be difficult for us to interact because we would not know what to expect. To ensure that members of a society adhere to its basic norms, societies develop special forms of social control. Social control is a set of methods and strategies that regulate the behavior of people and society. Sociologists distinguish between the three main processes of social control. The first is the *process of socialization*. During childhood, behavior conforms to social norms through external control. Later, there is an internalization of these norms when they become part of the personality. Group norms also play a role in shaping behavior and self-identity. Social control thus becomes self-control. The second process of social control is culture, which limits our social experience and we often fail to consider alternative standards of behavior. The third process of social control is the process of punishment for violating the norms of society (discontent, hostility, or even imprisonment and death) and reward for conforming to those norms (approval, popularity, prestige, etc.).

However, the question arises — why do people break social rules, why does crime occur? Why are some actions defined as deviant, deviant, or criminal, while others are not? Moreover, why do forms of deviance, in particular crime, differ from group to group and from society to society? This kind of question has long been of interest to sociologists. Other disciplines, especially biology and psychology, also study processes of deviance. However, they study slightly different aspects of the phenomenon. Biologists and psychologists study those people whose behavior is defined as deviant and seek answers to the question of how the biological or, respectively, psychological properties of these people differ. Sociologists focus on the study of social factors that generate deviations.

In modern sociology, there are four main approaches to explaining deviance (and crime): 1) anomie theory, 2) cultural transmission theory, 3) conflict theory, 4) and labeling theory.

1. The theory of anomie or structural tension.

The first sociological explanation of deviance was given by Emile Durkheim, who proposed the theory of anomie. "Anomie" means an "absence of norms" and occurs in times of crisis and radical change, when social norms become opposing, unclear or disappear. Durkheim analyzed suicide statistics and found that suicide rates are higher than usual in times of economic downturns. He attributed this to the disruption of the collective order and the disorientation of people. Durkheim's theory remains important in explaining deviant behavior. Durkheim's theory was further developed in the works of the famous American sociologist Robert Merton. Merton believes that the cause of deviations is the gap between the goals of society and socially accepted means of achieving them. Some people resort to illegal means to achieve a desired goal, for example, through criminal activity. This theory draws attention to the processes that produce deviance in society. It proposes reforming society according to the ideals of democracy and equality to solve the problem of crime. Programs such as the "War on Poverty"

106   SOCIOLOGY IN JOKES

were proclaimed in the 1960s but failed to achieve their goals and were subsequently canceled.

2. The theory of cultural transmission.

The concept of structural tension enables us to understand how society can contribute to deviance (particularly crime) because of divergences in its structural goals and structural capabilities. At the same time, quite a few sociologists emphasize the similarities between the ways in which criminal behavior and ordinary behavior are shaped. During the 1920s and 1930s, sociologists at the University of Chicago were struck by the concentration of high rates of juvenile delinquency in certain Chicago neighborhoods. Through a series of studies, sociologists concluded that deviant and delinquent behavior is passed from one generation to the next through culture. Youth who live in neighborhoods with high crime rates acquire delinquent lifestyles. Moreover, when new ethnic groups move into an area, their children learn delinquent behaviors from those who already live there.

Building on these findings, sociologist Edwin Sutherland developed the concept of differential association in the late 1930s. According to this concept, people become deviant if they are surrounded by an environment where deviant ideas and behaviors are considered normal or desirable. For example, they may learn illegal behaviors such as drug use or stealing.

The concept of differentiated communication gives a scientifically developed version of the old expression "you are the company you keep " (or "good campaigns make good guys, bad campaigns make bad guys"). When parents change where they live to, as Americans say, "take Mike away from bad friends altogether," they are applying the principle of differentiated communication. Incidentally, it follows from this concept that incarceration can be socially harmful to youth when they serve time with experienced criminals. The disadvantages of this approach are that it does not explain all forms of crime, and not all people who grow up with patterns of criminal behavior become criminals. Different subcultures have different values and norms, but the question is which group can turn their values into the rules of society and enforce them.

3. Conflictionist conceptions of deviance (crime).

Conflictionists cite examples where, during the war fought by the United States in Vietnam, anti-war groups argued that the real criminals were those who waged the war. Alternatively, take, for example, those in the former Soviet Union who denounced as criminal the war in Afghanistan (e.g., academician Andrei Sakharov) or the use of psychiatry to punish people (human rights activist Semyon Gluzman). These very people were seen as deviant criminals, and there was even a special term, "dissident". Semyon Gluzman received seven years of camps and three years of settlements. The authorities decide what is a norm and what is a crime.

Conflictionists point out that the interests of major social groups — classes, genders, racial and ethnic groups, business organizations, and trade unions — are often at odds with one another. Thus, conflictionists say we should ask, "Who gets the lion's share of the profits from the existing social order?" Another way of phrasing this question is to say that some people benefit and gain from it, while others suffer harm and loss and are even stigmatized as deviants or criminals. In recent decades, the conflictionist approach has given rise to many new directions, but its roots, as we have already mentioned, can be traced back to the Marxist tradition. According to Orthodox Marxism, the capitalist ruling class exploits and steals from the masses but avoids punishment for its crimes. The victims of capitalist oppression (from a Marxist perspective), in their struggle for survival, commit acts that the ruling class regards as criminal. Other forms of deviance — alcoholism, drug addiction, family violence, sexual immorality, and prostitution — are seen as consequences of a social structure based on the unscrupulous pursuit of profit and the oppression of the poor, women, people of color and other minorities.

The modern Western Marxist approach to deviance was developed mainly in the 1970s by the American sociologist Richard Quinney. "Law," he says, is the instrument of the ruling class. The capitalist ruling system makes illegal behavior that is offensive to those in power and threatens their privileges and property. Not even crime, but ordinary vulgar behavior — gambling, unauthorized sex, drunkenness, idleness, loafing, truancy — threatens the interests of the powerful by its challenge to basic capitalist values such as poise, personal responsibility, delayed rewards, diligence, and hard work.

The conflictionist approach has led sociologists to investigate how those in power control the creation and implementation of laws. Many sociologists have noticed that crimes are defined primarily in terms of guilt against property (theft, robbery, vandalism, and so on). In contrast, corporate crimes (crimes committed by firms and other business organizations) are treated more leniently by law and jurisprudence. This was emphasized in the mid-1980s by the famous sociologist James Kuhlman, president of the American Sociological Association in 1991–1992. He also emphasized that while the punishment for property crimes is imprisonment, the most common form of punishment for corporate crimes is monetary fines.

Sociologist Amitai Yetzioni found that between 1975 and 1984, 62% of the 500 largest US corporations were involved in at least one form of illegal activity, 42% in at least two forms of illegal activity, and 15% of corporations in at least five forms of illegal practices. These crimes include overcharging, paying bribes at home and abroad, fraud, misrepresentation, patent infringement, and so on. However, unlike robbers, corporations and their employees got off easy enough (although they took much more money from people illegally than the thieves). American sociologists also draw attention to the fact that the United States Federal Bureau of Investigation keeps records of every murder, robbery, car theft, and similar crimes, but no government agency keeps records of crimes committed by corporations.

4. The concept of labeling

Some people acquire power and, with it, the ability to turn their value advantages into rules regulating institutionalized life. Now, they get the opportunity to determine who exactly are the violators of these rules and, so to speak, "label" them negatively. A number of sociologists have taken these ideas into account and investigated them. They have considered the process by which some people are defined as "deviants" and "transgressors" and begin to think of themselves as transgressors and to adhere to norms of deviant behavior, to make, so to speak, a "career of transgression" (e.g., criminal). This approach is seen as a kind of sign (or symbolic) interactionism. It was formed precisely due to the fact that it put in the center of its attention, first, who exactly evaluates people's behavior from the point of view of deviation, and second, how the environment behaves with a person after they are labeled a deviant.

In the early 1960s, American sociologist Howard Becker proposed a concept that was in many ways opposite to the explanations of deviation that prevailed at that time, and that was based on the so-called 'medical model'. According to this concept, a person defined as a violator or deviant was considered to be 'sick' in a certain sense. That is, it was believed that the cause of deviant behavior lies with the person. The formation of those criteria by which a person was defined as deviant remained unattended by researchers. Such approaches, as Howard Becker noted, did not take into account, in particular, political aspects of deviation. Becker concluded that, in fact, deviation is largely due to the power of influential groups in society (he meant legislators, judges, doctors, etc.) to impose certain standards of behavior on others. "Social groups," he wrote in his book The Outsiders, "create deviance because they make up the rules whose violation is considered deviant. In addition, they impose these rules on certain people, who are "labeled" as outsiders. From this point of view, a deviation is determined not by the quality of the act a person performs but rather by the consequences of other people's application of rules and sanctions against the 'violator'. Becker's concept and similar approaches by Edwin Lemert and Kai Erikson are called labeling theory because they explain deviant behavior in terms of the power of powerful groups to label members of less powerful social groups as deviants.

They noticed that a person could be treated as if they had broken a rule (even if it was not true) just because other people claimed that the rule had been broken. This is how Black people in America are often treated. They were persecuted and were even lynched based on false accusations of raping white women. Some people believe that the same situation is now happening in the US with the Me Too movement, which fights sexual harassment. They claim that there are cases where people have been fired from their jobs, had their movies banned, etc., because of allegedly baseless accusations and attacks in the press. For example, the French actress Fanny Ardan writes, "I don't respect a movement based on denunciations. I prefer to trust justice. I hate it when the press engages in lynchings without evidence in hand. The press cannot play the role of a court of law; it is very dangerous. This is where freedom ends and obscurantism begins"[17].

Most people break some rules of social life. Teenagers sometimes smoke marijuana. Administrators of business organizations sometimes overbill. A fairly large percentage of married people have sexual relations outside of marriage. The people around them often look at these behaviors with a blank stare, and the person who violates certain norms in these behaviors, in such a situation, as a rule, does not consider themself a violator or a deviant". Edwin Lemert called this type of behavior **primary deviation.** It is defined as behavior that violates certain social norms but goes unnoticed by the agents of social control. However, the situation changes when someone close to that person, or a manager or employee, discovers these behaviors and publicizes them. Quite often, this leads to **secondary deviance**. This is what Lemert called deviant behavior that adapts to the reaction of the environment and adapts to that reaction.

The fact is that when a person is labeled as a deviant, at first, the people around them begin to treat them as a deviant, and over time, the person often begins to behave in accordance with this role. Moreover, a person often begins to explain their deviant behaviors to others and then to themselves by the fact that they are "such"

---

17   https://meduza.io/feature/2019/11/20/ya-ne-uvazhayu-dvizhenie-osnovan noe-na-donosah)

(with sayings such as "I am an alcoholic," "I am a drug addict", "I am lecherous, etc.).

Becker asked the question: who are the people who can make others obey their rules? He argues that this depends on the distribution of political and economic power in society. For example, in American society, psychiatrists set the rules by which people are recognized as mentally defective. In the former Soviet Union, however, these rules were set not by psychiatrists but by the organs of the KGB, i.e., the secret police. The framework, so to speak, of the 'standard-setting" activity of these bodies was set by the leading functionaries of the Communist Party of the Soviet Union.

The greatest harm was probably caused by the 'crusade' in the name of creating new values, which led to the formation of the so-called communist ideology and the establishment of Bolshevik power in the former Russian Empire. Here was established such a system of new rules, according to which tens of millions of people — those who were recognized as "enemies of the people", "saboteurs", "agents of imperialism", and then "anti-Soviet", "dissidents", "servants of imperialism", "bourgeois nationalists", etc. became deviants. Such 'rules prevailed for more than 70 years. Unfortunately, this is not the first example of the domination of a brutalized system of rules. Mass exterminations of people, as is known, were committed in the Middle Ages by the Inquisition, which had the right to interpret people's deeds on behalf of the Christian Church. The Inquisition became widespread in the 13th century, and in some countries of Western Europe, especially in Spain, destroyed 'heretics', i.e., deviants from the point of view of the then church, and in the second half of the 16th century, i.e., for more than 300 years. Many aspects of such events are explained precisely by labeling theory, that is, a concept that describes the process of forming new attitudes toward people who are considered deviants. In general, it should be noted that none of the sociological concepts we have considered provides a complete explanation of deviant behavior. However, each of them highlights important sources of deviation. Deviant behavior has many forms, and we must approach each form with the specific factors involved. This is most relevant to the study

112 SOCIOLOGY IN JOKES

of criminal behavior, which is especially prevalent in modern industrial societies.

* * *

"I did what the Internet advised me to do to learn English: I went to England, made a mess, and went to jail. I spent a whole year in state custody among native speakers. Now I know Arabic perfectly, not bad Chinese and some African dialects. English: still with a dictionary ..."

There may be two problems here. First, crime may actually be higher among migrants, which is explained by the above theories of cultural transmission and labeling. Second, it may be a problem of selective justice, where the court treats the same crime committed by a migrant and a native differently. The selectivity of justice is especially pronounced in relation to people of different social statuses. The famous Swedish-Danish TV series *The Bridge* begins with the discovery of a corpse on Europe's largest bridge, the Eresund Bridge, which connects Denmark and Sweden, which turns out to be made up of parts of two murdered women — a homeless Swedish woman and a member of the Danish Parliament. The perpetrator did this to show that the justice system works differently — the homeless woman's murder case is quickly closed, while the MP's case is worked on by the best professionals in the two countries. Since 2011, the remake of this movie has been filmed in the United States, France and Russia.

Furthermore, if even in such developed countries as Sweden, Denmark, France and the USA, selective justice is a problem, what can we say about Ukraine? As for Russia, with its blatant lawlessness and crackdowns on dissenters, justice is out of the question. It is increasingly becoming a dictatorial country led by a criminal wanted internationally. On March 17, 2023, the International Criminal Court in The Hague issued an arrest warrant for Russian President Vladimir Putin. Criminology is the science that studies criminals who get caught, the unlucky criminals. The science that studies successful criminals is otherwise known as political science.

This anecdote illustrates conflict and labeling theories well. Those who come to power determine what is a crime and who to

SOCIOLOGY OF CRIME AND LAW   113

call a criminal. "Rebellion cannot end in fortune; otherwise, it is called otherwise".[18]

* * *

Scientists have discovered that your fingerprints can indicate whether you are Black or white. More specifically, if your fingerprints were found at a crime scene, you are probably Black.

This and the following anecdotes also speak to both selective justice and the theories of criminality described above.

* * *

In the hall of a large bank, a man sits at a separate table with a bank officer and is about to sign a mortgage contract. He hands the man a pen. *"So, you understand that you will have to pay the bank money every month for 40 years?"*
– *"Yes, of course, I understand."*
– *"And you know that the interest rate will be 23% per annum?"*
– *"Yes, of course, I know that"*, the man replies, pushing the documents toward him.
– *"And you realize that the total cost of the apartment, taken in the mortgage, together with all the interest for all 40 years will be four times its original price?"*
– *"Oh yeah, I get it. Let me just sign these stupid documents!"* The man sighs and puts his pen over the paper. Suddenly, a masked man bursts into the bank hall, points a machine gun at the guards and shouts: *"Nobody move! This is a robbery."*
– *"Eh, buddy"*, the man replies, not even turning in his direction and not taking his eyes off the mortgage agreement. *"Yes, I realize that this is a robbery. But, damn, I need the apartment urgently ..."*

Under the conflictionist approach, large corporations, including banks, often do far more damage than thieves but are not held accountable. Below is another anecdote on the same topic.

* * *

---

18   This is a verse by the English poet John Harrington, who lived in the 16th and early 17th centuries, translated by S. Marshak. "Treason doth never prosper, what's the reason? For if it prosper, none dare call it Treason."

114   SOCIOLOGY IN JOKES

> — *"Dad, I've decided to pursue a career in organized crime."*
> — *"Civil service or private sector?"*

* * *

> Interviews with passersby: *"Tell me, please, how do you think crime should be dealt with?"*
> — *"Well, people should be brought up honest from childhood. And now, we need to strengthen law enforcement. All criminals should be punished more severely: murderers to the wall, thieves to the dungeons. Bribe-takers should be tried regardless of their position! It's time to end selective justice! TAKE AWAY THE CAMERA! TAKE THE CAMERA AWAY! What is it? I'm a wanted man!"*

This speech is very similar to the speeches of some MPs. However, the origin of large capital is a complex topic and, as we know from our history, you can be a wanted person or steal hats, but this does not prevent you from becoming an MP or even president (Yanukovych, who was president of Ukraine from 2010 to 2014, was convicted of stealing hats in his youth).

* * *

> A rape case is being heard. A plaintiff in an ultra-short skirt appears in the courtroom. The judge asks her: *"Are you suggesting we start by examining the crime scene?"*

One section of criminology is called victimology, and it studies victims of crime.

For example, someone is several times less likely to be killed by a stranger than an acquaintance. One concept (although debatable) is that some people are more prone to crime than others. For example, some clothing could increase the likelihood of being a victim of rape. Here is an anecdote about the likelihood of being killed by a loved one.

> "After a murder, the first thing the police do is find out if the victim's spouse was involved. And that's pretty much all you need to know about marriage."

* * *

SOCIOLOGY OF CRIME AND LAW 115

– *"Tell me, Holmes, how do you solve a crime?"*
– *"We need to determine who benefits from it!"*
– *"What if everyone benefits?"*
– *"Then it's kind of not even a crime anymore ..."*

* * *

Article in the newspaper: *"Comrades! We hasten to share the joyful news! In our city, once and for all, finished with crime. Yesterday, the last bandit was killed by some maniacs ..."*

* * *

A student is taking an exam in sociology. The teacher asks: "Is *crime rising or falling?"*
The student faltered and then exclaimed: *"It is falling! After all, in the time of Cain and Abel, it was 50 percent."*

* * *

The brilliant criminals of the past needed ingenuity, artistry and strategic intelligence to commit the perfect crime. Nowadays, it's much easier: you don't post a video of your crime on YouTube, and you're elusive.

* * *

The following are anecdotes about lawyers. Some of them characterize the judicial system, and some of them characterize the attitude of the population to lawyers.

* * *

After a successful trial, the attorney and client relaxed and talked. *"You know"*, said the lawyer, *"I used to dream of being a pirate when I was a kid."*
– *"I congratulate you"*, the client replied, writing the check; *"not everyone gets to realize their childhood dream."*

It is said that in the United States, everyone hates lawyers but dreams of becoming one. If this is true, then the attitude toward lawyers is born of envy. In fact, hatred of lawyers is one of the

116 SOCIOLOGY IN JOKES

defense mechanisms described by Freud and his followers.[19] The works of Adler, Sullivan, Mead and others have shown that there are limits to what a person is able to discuss with themself and what they can give themselves an account of. In the process of socialization, each person forms a self-concept, a person's ideas about themselves and how others see them. Usually, one strives to preserve and maintain one's self-concept (especially if it is positive). If there is a threat to this self-concept, the person tries to eliminate it, and if it fails, defense mechanisms are triggered, and everything that is associated with a threat to the self-concept is pushed into the subconscious. One such mechanism is rationalization; in my opinion, this notion has ceased to be scientific and has long since become everyday. The fox in Krylov's fable, who could not reach the grapes and therefore called them green, was engaged in rationalization.

* * *

Judge to the defendant: *"Why didn't you get your own quarterback?"*
— *"All the lawyers refuse to prosecute my case once they find out that I really didn't take that five million."*

* * *

At the law firm.
"Fifty marks for two questions!" The customer is indignant. *"Isn't that too much?"*
Counsel dryly: *"Plus twenty-five marks for the third question."*

* * *

The lawyer's son, himself also a lawyer, calls his father: *"Father, congratulate me! Luck! I won the case you couldn't win for ten years!"*
— *"Oh, son, you're not going to be a lawyer anytime soon! What have you done? This case has fed us for ten years."*

* * *

A father teaches his son: *"That's it, you can't suck the blood all the way out."*

---

19   Shibutani T., Social Psychology, per. from Engl., M., 1969, pp.73-75.

SOCIOLOGY OF CRIME AND LAW   117

– *"Why?"*
– *"Because we're vampires, not lawyers!"*

Judge: *"Witness, you must tell the truth, the whole truth, the only truth and nothing but the truth."*
– *"Yes, Mr. Judge."*
– *"In such a case, what then do you have to say about the case under discussion?"*
– *"And what can be said with such limitations?"*

* * *

The famous Russian lawyer Fyodor Nikiforovich Plevako (1842–1908) had a habit of starting his speech in court with the phrase: *"Gentlemen, but it could be worse"*.
No matter what case did not fall to the lawyer, he did not change his phrase. Once Plevako undertook to defend a man who raped his own daughter. The hall was packed to the brim, and all waited, how will the lawyer begin his defense speech. Is it with his favorite phrase? Unbelievable. But stood up Plevako and coldly said: *"Gentlemen, it could be worse."* And then the judge himself could not stand it. *"What,"* he shouted, *"Tell me, what could be worse than this abomination?"*
– *"Your Honor,"* asked Plevako, *"What if he had raped your daughter?"*

* * *

On Trial. *"Citizen Drozdova, we are considering your suit against Citizen Berezkin. Tell the court the whole truth, just the truth,"* the judge warns.
– *"Your Honor, I swear."*
– *"When did this incident of rape happen?"*
– *"This one? It happened all summer!"*

* * *

– *"Do you continue to say that the defendant called you a fool?"*
– *"Yes, citizen judge. But he didn't say it directly; he said it allegorically. He said: As far as intelligence goes, you and I are on the same level."*

* * *

"Your Honor", said the lawyer, *"can my client's actions be called robbery?"* As the investigation has established, he said the following: *"Please, sir, take pity on me; help this poor unfortunate man who is very hungry and cannot find work. All I have in this world is this gun."*

118   SOCIOLOGY IN JOKES

* * *

Wife to husband.
— *"You know, our niece Anechka went to the doctor today, and it turns out she's having a baby. It's about time."*
— *"When's it coming?"*
— *"The doctor said sometime in September or early October."*
— *"Some accuracy, huh? My grandfather was told when he was going to die, and he died the same day!"*
— *"Wow! Was it some kind of eminent doctor?"*
— *"What doctor! A judge!"*

* * *

"Witness!" says the judge. *"I ask you to forget for a moment that you work for the State Statistics Committee and tell the court only the truth."*

Statisticians, like social scientists, suffer from distrust of their data. I think this is a manifestation of a more general pattern — people consider reliable data that they like.

A man is on trial for calling a madam a cow. The court awarded him punishment for the insult in the form of a fine. The defendant asked: *"Judge, would it be an insult to call a cow 'madam'?"*
— *"Of course not; you can call the cow whatever you want."*
— *"Then, as he was leaving, he bowed to the lady who had won this trial and said: Goodbye, madam."*

* * *

A lady walks into a gun store. *"I'd like a small gun to carry in this purse, please."*
— *"Do you want protection?"*
— *"No, I'm hiring a lawyer for my protection."*

* * *

— *"Look, with that hammer of yours, you've killed dozens of people and ruined the lives of hundreds. What do you have to say for yourself?"* —
— *"Defendant, sit down and stop clowning around!"*

12. Survey Methodology

Books are written on sociological survey methods and separate courses are undertaken. The methodological arsenal of sociologists is changing rapidly. Methods of sociological surveys have been computerized, and telephone interviews are conducted only with the help of a computer, apartment interviews are conducted with the help of tablets, and big data analysis is used, in particular social networks. However, we will speak here only of the survey as the method that most people primarily associate with sociology. So, one of the main classifications of methods is the division into quantitative and qualitative methods. This classification is based on the purpose of the method.

Quantitative methods of sociological data collection are usually used to obtain accurate quantitative information — they are based on representative samples and use statistical methods of data analysis. Conventional opinion polling methods tell us how many percent of people surveyed trust the church, how many percent feel happy, how many percent of men wash dishes; electoral surveys with ratings of parties and presidential candidates, or marketing surveys that tell us what percentage of the population prefers Colgate toothpaste are all quantitative methods of gathering sociological information. Content analysis (quantitative analysis of content) of texts, which shows what percentage of comments on articles in a given online publication contain hate speech, is also quantitative research.

Qualitative methods are methods that do not aim to achieve representativeness of the obtained data. They are used not to obtain the distribution of the population (or other objects of analysis) by certain characteristics but most often to get a general idea of this or that phenomenon. It can be an observation, a focus group (a discussion of 10–12 people, which is videotaped and analyzed), an in-depth interview, or a case study. The typical result, in this case, is not percentages but a set of expressed judgments, opinions, explanations of reasons and motives.

Another classification is based on the source of information. From this perspective, there are three main methods: observation, document analysis and interviews.

A questionnaire is a set of carefully designed questions that are asked in the same way to a group of people to gather information about what the researcher is interested in. Two types of surveys can be distinguished — interviews and questionnaires. On an interview form or from a tablet screen, the interviewer reads out the question and records the respondent's answers in it. When conducting a questionnaire, the questionnaire is handed out to the respondents to answer the questions printed there.

The structure of the questionnaire is an address to the respondent, followed by a series of questionnaire blocks combining questions related to one topic, then a socio-demographic block and service questions.

A list of pre-prepared response *options is* called a *scale or a set of alternatives.* Unlike sampling or data analysis, questionnaire design is still more of an art than a science; it is easier to say what should not be done than what should be done. Therefore, very often all recommendations take the form of describing possible errors in question design.

Here is a list of the most common mistakes.

1. *Tendency of the question or scale.* The neutrality of question-wording and response options is one of the main requirements for questionnaires. The preamble of the question sometimes specifically explains to the respondent the possibility of different points of view: "There is no right or wrong answer to the question, it is your opinion that interests us..." or "Some believe that..., others hold the opposite opinion..." (for example, "Some people believe that horoscopes can predict people's fate, others disagree, what is your point of view? — "can — 1", "cannot — 2", "hard to say — 3").

2. *The problem of average position.* Most researchers use scales with an odd number of answers and an average position ("as satisfied as dissatisfied") or use "hard to say" as an average position. This allows the respondent to 'walk away' from the answer and not make 'noise' in answering the other questions. Other researchers believe

that the presence of this position leads to the fact that "hard to say" is chosen by an unreasonable number of respondents who have an opinion but prefer not to think and minimize their efforts. Hence, such researchers exclude the "hard to say" option from the list of answers. Meanwhile, the inclusion or non-inclusion of this position can make a significant difference. Let me demonstrate this with the example of research on the scandal with Bill Clinton and Monica Lewinsky, which resonated all over the world (in Ukraine, it was instantly used in the pre-election struggle — the slogan "Better sex with Monica than with the whole country." appeared).

At the height of the Bill Clinton-Monica Lewinsky scandal, but before Clinton's confession, the Yankelovich Polling Center asked a representative sample of Americans, "Did Clinton have an intimate relationship with Monica Lewinsky?" with response options of "yes," "no," "hard to say." The CBS channel conducted the same poll, but only with two answer options — "yes" and "no" (no evasion option). The following results were obtained[20]:

Did Clinton have an intimate relationship with Monica Lewinsky? (% of responses received)

Research organizations	Yes	It's hard to say	No
Yankelovich	27	42	31
CBS	58	-	42

It turns out that according to Yankelovich's data, only 27% of respondents thought that Clinton had such a relationship, while according to CBS data, the majority, 58%, thought so. The results are qualitatively different, with a 31% difference in the data! According to Yankelovich, a majority believe Clinton. According to CBS, they do not. Where is the truth?

Rather, the situation was such that 27% of those polled strongly believed that Clinton had had an intimate relationship, 31% strongly believed that he had not, and 42% had difficulty and did not know what to say (of those, 31% thought it was more likely

---

20 These data are given in the network ("chat") of the American Association of Public Opinion Researchers AAPOR (American Association of Public Opinion Research).

yes, 11% thought it was more likely no). When people who are still undecided are not given the opportunity to avoid answering, those who leaned toward a "more likely yes" answer added to those who were strongly confident to form 58%, while 11% added to the 31% who were determined "no" to form 42%.

It turns out everyone is right, but Yankelovich's 27% are those who strongly believe, and CBS's 58% are both those who strongly believe and those who are wavering.

Thus, the presence or absence of a middle position can qualitatively change the result. Although both research centers are right, we think that 'nudging' a respondent who hesitates is not very good, and we usually get complete and reliable information using the middle position. Therefore, the use of scales without mean positions makes sense only in special cases (for example, to predict the outcome of a referendum in which there are only 'yes' and 'no' answers, and this question should be preceded by a filter question that screens out those who will not come to vote).

3. ambiguity of wording. When formulating a question, the researcher should think about how different respondents can understand it and whether there is no possibility of understanding it in a way different from what the researcher had in mind (one can imagine a university professor and a rural grandparent in the process of formulating questions). Our long-term experience shows that when there is such a possibility, it is sure to be realized for a part of respondents (not even Murphy's law[21], but ordinary statistical regularities work here — if the probability of misunderstanding is 0.05, then 5% of respondents will understand the question incorrectly).

Example (unfortunately very common): Your income? _____.

It is not clear: a) for what period, b) income of only the respondent or average for all family members, c) how to calculate it, d) in what it should be expressed — in hryvnias or dollars? This is

---

21 It is a joke statement: if there is even one chance that some unpleasantness can happen, it will happen (a scientific variant of the proverb "the sandwich always falls butter-side down").

an example of a question from Kohn's questionnaire which is formulated more correctly:

1. How many people now live together with you in the same household?

2. What is the total monthly income of everyone who lives together with you in the same household, including your income and all types of income of your household (their stipends, pensions, allowances, etc.)?

3. *Order of alternatives.* Our research shows that when assessing a number of objects on one scale, respondents can use their assessment of the first object in the list as a benchmark, comparing the rest with it[22]. Our research has also shown that the place of a party in the list has a certain influence on the rating of parties for the first part of the list. Therefore, in political research, which starts long before the elections and before determining the real place of parties on the ballot, it makes sense to use object rotation, which allows to eliminate the influence of the place in the list on the rating. The simplest kind of rotation is having two lists or two cards for a given question with different ordering of parties. According to the survey instructions, the interviewer shows card A when interviewing an odd-numbered respondent and card B when interviewing an even-numbered respondent. The same can be done in surveys on other topics. In a tablet survey, the program can change the list randomly for each respondent. These are only examples, there are many more such common mistakes.

The so-called sensitive issues pose a special problem. As mentioned above, there are a number of sensitive topics that we all do not like to discuss. Questions about these topics are called sensitive or embarrassing. These include issues that are too intimate (e.g., sex, relationships with loved ones), issues related to income, violation of some social norms, etc. There are several approaches to ensuring sincerity in such surveys — some of them are related to the organization of the survey itself (ensuring complete anonymity, use of voting boxes, etc.), and some of them are related to the specifics of question-wording.

---

22   See: Chernovolenko, Ossovsky, Paniotto, 1979.

124 Sociology in Jokes

Here are a few recommended approaches:

1. Violation of the principle of question neutrality. In some sensitive questions, we know for a fact that it is difficult for the respondent to admit to having done a certain action. Then, violating the rule of question neutrality, we do not ask them whether the action has occurred but ask how often it occurs or when was the last time it occurred. For example, in Kinsey's study, Sexual Behavior in Human Males,[23] respondents were not asked if they had masturbated; they were asked, "At what age did you have your first experience with masturbation?" The researchers made it clear that all people do it; it goes without saying, and it is common, normal behavior.

2. Everyone does it. Another approach is to make a direct statement about the prevalence of something difficult for the respondent to admit or to provide some motivation in the question that gives reasons to justify such behavior. For example, in questions about the shadow economy, the involvement of people in jobs that provide earnings from which taxes are not paid. "These days, the poverty rate has increased a lot, and the tax system is not being reformed; the state is trying to take money from the poor instead of the rich. Because of this, many people have to work part-time unofficially without paying taxes. Do you have any occupation of this kind from the list below that gives you additional income?"

3. The questions are given to the respondent to fill in for themself. Sometimes, the interviewer will drop the completed questionnaire or part of it into a special box, ballot box (a secret ballot) or place it in an envelope and seal it (the sealed ballot technique). As a last resort, if the ballot or sealed envelope technique is not used, the interviewer hands a card with question and answer options and asks for the answer number without reading it out.

All these approaches have their limitations, and there are other methods. The discussion on this topic often cites the ironic description of the application of such methods in the article by Allen Barton[24],

---

23   Kinsey, Pomeroy, Martin, 1948.

24   "Asking the Embarrassing Question" (*Public Opinion Quarterly*, Volume 22, Issue 1, SPRING 1958, Pages 67–68, https://doi.org/10.1086/266761

1. The Casual Approach: "Do you happen to have murdered your wife?
2. Numbered Card approach: Would you please read off the number on this card which corresponds to what became of your wife?" (HAND CARD TO RESPONDENT): Natural death/I killed her/Other (What?) (GET CARD BACK FROM RESPONDENT BEFORE PROCEEDING!)
3. The Everybody Approach: "As you know, many people have been killing their wives these days. Do you happen to have killed yours?"
4. The "Other people" Approach:(a) "Do you know any people who have murdered their wives?"(b) "How about yourself?"
5. The Sealed Ballot Technique: In this version, you explain that the survey respects people's right to anonymity with respect to their marital relations and that they are to fill out the answer to the question, seal it in an envelope, and drop it in a box conspicuously labeled "Sealed Ballot Box" carried by the interviewer.

* * *

A remote village. A guy with a folder of papers approaches an older man on the stoop. *"Did you bring your pension?"*
— *"No, I'm a census taker, Grandpa. We're trying to find out how many people live in Ukraine."*
— *"Well, you're wasting your time with me. I have no idea."*

The reaction of older people to sociological surveys is often "Ask your daughter; she knows better" or "My husband will come home from work". Therefore, at the beginning of the interview there is an address to the respondent, where it is explained who is conducting the survey, the purpose of the survey, and the confidentiality of answers. It is explained how they were selected ("we selected 2000 people randomly, like in a lottery") and that "there are no right or wrong answers in the questionnaire, any answer is correct, it is important for us that you are the one who answered".

* * *

126   Sociology in Jokes

We publish the first results of the All-Russian census: 2345 enumerators were beaten, 92 were robbed, one was missing, and 12456 were sent to the same address.

I cannot say anything about how the census is conducted in Ukraine; it has not happened for 20 years, but I have to say that during exit polls, our first reports look like this — "two polling stations did not open, the police detained an interviewer in one of the polling stations, a dog bit one interviewer, some strange people forbade the interviewers to work in two polling stations, etc.

* * *

News: Only 5% of Belarusians correctly answered the question of sociologists: "Do you like our president?"

* * *

The question "Do you use the Internet?" was answered in the affirmative by 100% of Ukrainians. This is the result of an online survey conducted recently on the Internet.

* * *

The latest sociological survey conducted in Russia by the Pravada Center showed that the president's rating exceeded 100%. Researchers explain this by the fact that some Russians like the president twice each.

* * *

What a freedom-loving people we are! Two hundred people were interviewed and not one of them wants to go to prison!

There is no point in wasting time on questions that are close to rhetorical. Sometimes, it happens that a question has several answer options, but most of them "don't work"; all the answers "pile up" into one point. To prevent this from happening, before the main survey, a so-called pretest — a small survey of 20-40 people — is conducted.

SURVEY METHODOLOGY   127

* * *

– *"Vovochka, why are you late for class?"*
– *"I argued with my dad. I wanted to go fishing and he wouldn't let me."*
– *"I'm glad Daddy explained to you that you can't skip school."*
– *"He didn't explain to me about school, he said there weren't enough worms for two."*

This is a typical situation for sociological research. Question-answer and the interviewer has the impression that they understand what the respondent wanted to say. If the dialogue had not been continued, the teacher (as sociologists usually do) would have had an erroneous view of the situation.

* * *

A journalist interviews a longtime resident: *"How did you manage to live such a long life and be so perfectly preserved in your 120 years?"*
– *"When the Great October Socialist Revolution was ..."*
The journalist interrupts: *"Revolution is irrelevant now. Tell me more about Pushkin or people who knew him."*
– *"When the Great October Socialist Revolution was ..."*
– *"God forbid the revolution. If you don't want to talk about Pushkin, tell us about the Russo-Japanese War ...."*
– *"Now, relations with Japan are very relevant. When the Great October Socialist Revolution was ..."*
– *"Again? All right, God be with you; what about the revolution?"*
– *"When there was the Great October Socialist Revolution, there was such a mess that when I was issued a birth certificate, I was assigned an extra thirty years."*

This is a question about the ability of interviewers to listen to respondents and the reliability of the data we get from them. The software that we now use for tablet-based surveys, Computer Assisted Personal Interview (CATI), can record parts of the interview. Using this method of control has shown that the situation described in this anecdote is far from an exception.

* * *

Ivan Petrovich, the boss, asks one of his employees: *"Please excuse me for asking you this question; I've been wanting to ask you for a long time and*

128 Sociology in Jokes

haven't dared to. You always dress so impeccably, and suddenly, you started wearing an earring in your ear. I thought that only young people nowadays decorate themselves like that."
— "You see, we are too uptight, too closed, conformist, always acting within traditions without thinking about how rational they are, wanting sometimes to step outside our rut to do something like this."
— "How long have you been having this urge?"
— "Well... since my wife found this earring in our bed."

This is an anecdote about the difference between the real reason and motivation. What Ivan Petrovich told the boss is the motivation; while the real reason came to the surface quite by accident, in most cases, it remains unknown and, worst of all, it is the motivation that is mistaken for the real reason. The most typical case is when the respondent does not realize or does not want to admit this reason and reports what "looks good" as a reason.

* * *

If you were offered a choice between your spouse and a movie star, which movie star would you choose?

This is an example of a so-called push question that imposes a certain answer on the respondent. Of course, this is a somewhat exaggerated example. Usually, such 'pushing' is less noticeable, but the difference is not very big. An example from a real questionnaire: "Which method of privatization of large enterprises do you think is more correct — sale at auctions or issue of shares?" For those who are against the privatization of large enterprises, there are no options.

* * *

A literature professor asks a student: *"If you could meet and talk to any writer, now living or already dead, which one would you choose?"*
— "The living one, of course!"

This is the problem of open-ended questions. The researcher is immersed in the problem and formulates the question without giving much thought as to what other interpretations of the question are possible. Some respondents may understand the question in a completely different way. In closed questions, this happens less often because the respondent receives a card with answer options and understands from the context what the authors of the survey meant.

* * *

"You are accused", says the judge, *"of hitting your husband on the head with a dish from the service. Don't you feel sorry for him?"*
— "It's pathetic! It's an antique set I got from my grandmother."

This is a very typical situation in sociology: when sociologists ask a question, they think one thing, but respondents think something else. They understand the question in a way different from what sociologists would like. A judge can clarify the question, and an interviewer can sometimes do it too, but in handout questionnaires or online surveys, this is no longer possible. Another anecdote is when the person asking the question means one thing, and the person answering means another.

* * *

— "Andrei, have you seen our new neighbors? He's such a suave and handsome man, and she's just lovely. And he's not afraid to show his feelings, and he's always hugging her, taking her hand, stroking her, pinching her butt. Why don't you do that?"
— "Liusya, what are you doing? I haven't even met them yet!"

* * *

There's a trial going on, and the lawyer goes to the plaintiff: *"According to your complaint, the defendant I'm defending said you were a fool. Is that true?"*
— "Yeah, that's the truth."
— "Then what are you complaining about?"

This is another example of a question that the author of the question and the respondent understand differently. The only difference is that here the author of the question deliberately asked it in such a way that the respondent misunderstands it.

130   SOCIOLOGY IN JOKES

* * *

A candidate for a position fills out a questionnaire. One of the questions is: *Have you been on trial or under investigation?*
The candidate answers honestly: *I have not.*
The next item, *For what reason?*
This was obviously intended for those who answered "*yes*" to the first question.
However, the candidate filled it in as well: *Not caught yet.*

A typical mistake in the formulation of questionnaire questions is the absence of so-called skip patterns. The first question should have been followed by "only those who answered 'yes' to the first question will answer the next question, and the rest will proceed to question 3".

* * *

Call on the phone: *"Vaska, hi, I haven't heard from you for a long time! How do you like your life after the wedding?"*
— *"I've never been so happy to live!"*
— *"Is she there or something?"*
— *"Every day is like a holiday for me now!"*
— *"All right, hang in there, bro."*

A typical situation during a telephone survey. The interviewer should conduct the survey in such a way that no one is present during the survey. This may influence the respondent's answers.

* * *

Mrs. Parker was invited to participate in the trial as one of the jurors. She declined because, according to her, she is fundamentally opposed to the death penalty.
"But, madam, this is not a murder charge!" The judge told her. *"This is about a woman's claim against her ex-husband: he promised to spend $25,000 to renovate her kitchen for her birthday, but instead, he lost it in a casino."*
— *"Well then, I'll take part"*, Mrs. Parker said firmly, *"And I may have been wrong about the death penalty."*

Mrs. Parker was convinced that she was fundamentally opposed to the death penalty, and if sociologists asked her if she thought it was possible, she would have chosen the most categorical denial. However, in a real situation, she is ready to act quite differently from her principles. The situation in which the respondent himself is not aware of his values and motives for his behavior is the most difficult for sociologists. Several defense mechanisms prevent people from realizing their values and reasons for their behavior. For example, **rationalization** is where people use their intellectual abilities to justify actions they have committed for reasons they had no idea about. The fox in Krylov's fable, who could not reach the grapes and therefore called them green, was rationalizing. A person who has failed reassures themself by reducing the value of what they are striving for. Typical behavior of a rejected suitor: "They are not my type," etc. Alternatively, another judgment: "I am not really interested in money; the main thing for me is spiritual development". Most often, it is said by people who, for one reason or another, have not been able to solve their material problems. However, in many cases, if they are given a choice between a more interesting and better-paid job, they choose the better-paid one.

* * *

- *"Mikola, if you had two yachts, would you give me one?"*
- *"Of course, Vanya, we're friends."*
- *"If you had two Mercedes, would you give me one?"*
- *"Of course, I would."*
- *"And if you had two chickens, would you give me?"*
- *"That's not fair; you know very well I have two chickens."*

If we ask an abstract question about an imaginary, only theoretically possible situation, we get a socially desirable answer. When the question is brought closer to reality, the answer can change significantly.

Another similar pattern is the degree of specificity of the question and the terminology that is used. For example, at the end of 2019, KIIS posed the question on the permissibility of selling land in the wording used most often in TV debates (referendum on the

132 SOCIOLOGY IN JOKES

sale of agricultural land); 55% were against the sale, and only 21% were in favor. Politicians have opposed the sale of land for decades and the result seemed predictable. However, at the same time, we asked whether a landowner should have the right to sell it, and 66% said they should.

* * *

— *"Well, buddy, imagine the situation: two friends are squirrels. One squirrel found a nut and hid it, but badly. And the other squirrel found the nut. It's not his fault that he found the nut of his friend Squirrelka!"*
— *"What are you talking about? What nut! What squirrel ... you slept with my wife!"*

People always build such a system of coordinates in which they feel decent. These are euphemisms (not killed, but neutralized), the choice of a positive word from the scale of qualities (not greedy, but thrifty, not stubborn, but principled, not lecherous, but uninhibited, etc.), it is also the so-called **fundamental attribution error** (explaining one's actions by the situation and the actions of others by their orientations), attributing negative traits to enemies and positive traits to friends for the same actions — hero or fanatic. These kinds of substitutions can be used in the study of sensitive questions when, in the question itself or the preamble to the question, it is necessary to present situations in such a way that it is easier for the respondent to "confess" to socially disapproved actions.

* * *

Mom comes back from a business trip, and her son tells her: *"Yesterday, my dad brought some aunt, and they drank wine, and then he brought the aunt to bed."*
— *"Wait, wait. When Dad comes home from work, you'll tell him about it in front of him! I'm going to pack; we're probably going to go to Grandma's."*
Dad came home from work, his wife brought him into the room and asked his son to tell him what happened yesterday.
— *"Yesterday, Daddy brought some auntie over. They drank wine, and then he brought the auntie over to the bed and they did the same thing there that Mommy does with Uncle Kolya when Daddy isn't home."*

I have two comments on this anecdote. First, the mother, like the interviewer sometimes does, assumes she knows everything the respondent is going to say without listening to the respondent. She was in for a surprise. In the same way, the interviewer can mark the answer option without even asking (e.g., not asking young people a question about pensions, recording that they do not receive them, although some of them may receive survivor pensions or retire early from ballet).

Second, people forgive themselves when they do not forgive others. The wife was full of indignation, although she did not behave perfectly, and probably, as in the previous anecdote with the squirrel, she was going to appear before her husband as a faithful wife, indignant at the despicable treason.

> — *"Tell me, Rebbe, who is more satisfied: Rabinovich, who has six children, or Abramovich, who has six billion dollars?"*
> — *"The one with six kids!"*
> — *"Why?"*
> — *"The one with six billion wants more. "*

The notion of satisfaction, it turns out, is not as obvious as it seems to us at first. Below is a purely sociological example.

> Sociologist: *"Please tell me, are you satisfied with your job?"*
> — *"Well, what can I tell you? When I drag myself home from work, crawl into the apartment and fall into the chair, I want absolutely nothing."*
> — *"That means it satisfies!"*

And what should the interviewer note?

> — *"Tanechka, hi! Long time no see. How are you doing? You haven't gotten married yet?"*
> — *"Aunt Sonia, what are you saying? Why would I need that!? Right now, I need to establish myself at work and build a career! And what is marriage — cooking and laundry? There are so many interesting things in the world now, I want to see something, read something, go somewhere ..."*
> — *"What, nobody wants to marry you?"*
> — *"They don't," —* and Tanya started crying.

One of the problems with sociological surveys is that people are often unaware of their motives and values. This is because there are psychological mechanisms that protect the mind from trauma. One such mechanism, as we have already mentioned, is rationalization. If you want something very much but cannot achieve it, you convince yourself that you do not need it. This situation is reflected in Aesop's fable about a fox who could not reach the grapes and said that they were unripe, and she did not need them, "the grapes are green." (Since childhood, I wondered why, in the fable, the fox craves grapes, she does not eat them. We should talk not about grapes but about the eggs of some bird whose nest the fox cannot reach and says that they are small). Because of rationalization, answers about values and motives may not correspond to reality.

Two anecdotes about how defense mechanisms work successfully:

* * *

Found a wallet today. As a good Christian, I thought, *"What would Jesus do?"* Anyway, I turned it into wine.

* * *

An Orthodox priest and a rabbi argued about whom God loves more. — *"I was flying in an airplane"*, says the priest, *"and suddenly I felt the airplane going down. I started praying, and the plane righted itself and landed safely. I was driving on the highway"*, says the priest, *"and suddenly I was skidding straight toward a wall. I only had time to turn to God before the car straightened out, and I arrived safely."*
— *"Once on the Sabbath"*, says the rabbi, *"I was walking down the street and saw a big wad of dollars lying on the ground. What should I do, Sabbath? I started praying to God. And what do you think? The goodness and power of God are truly boundless: God turned the Sabbath into Thursday for five minutes."*

* * *

At the Institute of Foreign Languages, a literary translation exam is taking place. The instructor gives a student a phrase to translate into Ukrainian. The phrase is as follows:

"Roses are red,
Violets are blue,

Sugar is sweet,
And so are you."

The student translates it into Ukrainian as best as he can. The instructor reads it and then gives the Ukrainian phrase to the next student to translate back into English. The student translates it as follows:

The crimson hue of roses mirrors your lips so divine,
The azure of violets reflects the depths of your eyes,
Your voice, a sugar melody, melts me like sweet wine,
In your radiant presence, my enchanted heart sighs."

The problem of translation adequacy is especially relevant for international comparative research (this is one of the main specializations of my institute, the Kyiv International Institute of Sociology; we named it so because we have had many such projects). The first time we encountered this problem was while participating in Melvin Kohn's project on the influence of social structure on personality; the project was carried out in the USA, Poland, Ukraine, Japan, and China[25]. The same understanding of the same issue in different countries is key. Otherwise, we will get differences and will not know what they are related to. Either they are due to the fact that social structure in one country affects it differently than in another or that the translation is unsuccessful and does not provide the same understanding of the issue. The standard way of ensuring adequacy is back-translation, just as in this anecdote. A question is translated, for example, from English to Ukrainian by one translator and then from Ukrainian to English by another translator. If the back-translation into English matches the original question, the translation is considered adequate. To our disappointment, we (our research group) found that this method does not always work. Sometimes, a blunt, straightforward translation of a question that we understood differently than in the US produced a better back-translation than an adequate translation that took into account the nuances of the situation but deviated from the direct translation.

---

25 See "Social Structures and Personality": A Study by Melvin L. Kohn and his collaborators / Translated from English, ed. by V.E. Khmelko. — K.: Vid. dym "Kyiv-Mohyla Academy, 2007. — 559 c.

136   SOCIOLOGY IN JOKES

I cannot remember now the specific questions on which we discovered this, so I will give another example. I spent almost a year at Johns Hopkins University, where Melvin Kohn, Valery Khmelko, and I analyzed the results of two surveys in Ukraine. On one of my first visits to a supermarket, as I was paying at the cash register, I put my groceries on the counter and held out my money. The clerk asked, "Paper?" I proudly replied, "It is not paper; it's real money! The clerk looked at me like I was crazy, shrugged, took the money, put the groceries in a plastic bag and handed it to me. The next day, I told Melvin Kohn about the strange behavior of the supermarket clerk, and he laughed a lot. It turns out that the supermarket was switching from plastic bags to special paper bags that were not harmful to the environment (by the way, this was back in the early 1990s) in order to support the environmental program. In order to make the transition soft and not to make customers nervous, paper bags were offered to everyone, but those who did not want one could take a plastic one. The clerk, of course, did not ask, "Do you prefer a paper or plastic bag?" but just "paper?"

In order to understand this phrase, as well as many other things in the language, you need to understand the context and know a lot about life in this country. That is why automatic translation has not been perfect so far and the situation started to change only in the last one to two years thanks to artificial intelligence that understands the context. If here the question was translated directly as "paper?", the back translation would be the same as the original, unlike the translation "Which bag do you prefer—environmentally friendly paper or plastic?"

We encountered another problem. Our researcher, Roman Lenchovsky, had to translate a questionnaire for schoolchildren. In English, there is no distinction between "you" and "you are"; it is all translated as "you". Understandably, high school students can be addressed as "you", but for junior high school students, such an address looks strange and can interfere with communication. At what age should one switch from you to you? It was especially difficult for Roman to decide how to address children aged 13. Here, too, no back translation helps; you need to understand the situation in the country well. The method we arrived at was as follows. After translating the questionnaire from one language into another, for example, from the original English into Ukrainian, we look for a person who emigrated from Ukraine to the USA, lived there for two to three decades but did not lose contact with Ukraine and knows both languages at the level of their mother tongue, as well as the situation in both countries. This person checks the adequacy of the translation. It turned out that this was not a problem and it was not so difficult to find such a person.

13. Statistical Data Analysis, Modeling of Social Processes

Paradoxically, as long as I was reviewing other people's work, the problem of compactly presenting some sociological concepts did not arise. The presentation of methods for collecting sociological information, to which I have devoted several books, has already caused complications. Moreover, my favorite topic, mathematics in sociology, had me stumped. I could not figure out how to present it in four to five pages and decided only to use anecdotes with comments.

Rutherford said that all sciences can be divided into two groups — physics and stamp collecting. Auguste Comte, who coined the term sociology in 1839, understood sociology as social physics; the more sophisticated methods we use to measure complex social concepts (social structure, patriotism, xenophobia, etc.) and the more we use mathematical methods to analyze empirical data and computer modeling of social processes, the more sociology moves away from stamp collecting to physics.

* * *

Two marketers are out hunting. A deer is running. The first shoots a whole meter to the left. The second is a meter to the right. First to the second puzzled: *"Listen, according to the statistics, we've already killed him."*

* * *

Statistics state that if you have a pot of boiling water and your neighbor has chicken, you have chicken soup on average.

These are two very cheesy anecdotes, which I cited only to demonstrate the nature of anecdotes about statistics. In my opinion, they are generated by an inferiority complex, lack of understanding of elementary statistical concepts and envy of those who understand them. The same applies to the famous expression that "there are lies, brazen lies and statistics". Another thing is the following story from

140 SOCIOLOGY IN JOKES

the book Physicists *Keep Joking*. It is a classic of the genre.[26] He sneers at the conclusions drawn by insufficiently competent researchers.

> Pickles will ruin you! Every cucumber you eat brings you closer to death. It's amazing how thinking people still haven't recognized the deadliness of this plant product and even use its name to compare it in a positive sense ("like a cucumber!"). And in spite of everything, the production of canned cucumbers is growing. Cucumbers are associated with all the main ailments and all generally human misfortunes. Almost all people suffering from chronic diseases have eaten cucumbers. The effect is clearly cumulative. 99.9% of all people who died of cancer ate pickles in their lifetime. 100% of all soldiers and 99.7% of all victims of automobile and airplane accidents ate cucumbers in the two weeks preceding the fatal accident. 93.1% of all juvenile offenders come from families where cucumbers are consumed on a regular basis. There is also evidence that the harmful effects of cucumbers last for a very long time: among people born in 1839 who subsequently ate cucumbers, the mortality rate is 100%. All persons born 1869–1879 have flabby, wrinkled skin, have lost almost all their teeth, and are practically blind (if the diseases caused by cucumber consumption have not reduced them to the grave long ago). Even more convincing is the result obtained by a famous team of medical scientists: guinea pigs, which were force-fed 20 pounds of cucumbers a day for months, lost all appetite! The only way to avoid the harmful effects of cucumbers is to change your diet. Eat swamp orchid soup, for example. As far as we know, no one has ever died from it.

About the placebo effect

> *"Doctor, why did you change my treatment? You started giving me different pills. Why do you think so? Are they any different? They look the same, but the pills you used to give me used to sink in the toilet, and these float."*

In experiments, the experimental group may be influenced by the very fact that the experiment is being conducted. For example, people feel better because of the very belief that the treatment is beneficial. In order to understand what is really affected, a control group

---

26 Physicists Keep Joking. A collection of translations. http://n-t.ru/ri/fz/ / Compiled by: Y. Konobeev, V. Pavlinchuk, N. Rabotnov, V. Turchin. — Moscow: Mir Publishing House, 1968.

is given a neutral substance under the guise of medication and the results are compared with the experimental group. This neutral substance is called a placebo, and the control group that is given the placebo is called the placebo group. The anecdote shows that there may be other uncontrolled influences on the outcome of the experiment besides what the authors of the experiment plan.

To evaluate the effect of a factor (e.g., medication on cure, teaching method on success, improved working conditions on job satisfaction), it is necessary to have a main group and a control group. The absence of a control group can lead to false conclusions. Nassim Taleb describes a similar situation.[27]

The Story of the Pious Drowned Men:

More than two thousand years ago, the Roman orator, fiction writer, thinker, stoic, manipulative politician, and (almost always) noble gentleman Marcus Tullius Cicero told the following story in his treatise On the Nature of the Gods. The Greek philosopher Diagoras, nicknamed the Godless, was shown images of people who had prayed to the gods and were saved in a shipwreck. The implication was that prayer saves from destruction. Diagoras asked: "Where are the images of those who prayed but still drowned?"

It is not easy for pious drowned people to speak their minds from the bottom of the sea for the reason that they are dead. As a consequence, the superficial observer can easily believe in miracles. Let us call it the problem of hidden evidence. The idea is simple but significant and universal. While most thinkers tried to trash their predecessors, Cicero gave a hundred points to almost all empiricist philosophers who lived after him.

Later, the essayist Michel de Montaigne and the empiricist Francis Bacon (two of my idols), speaking of the origin of false beliefs, referred in their works to this very example. "Such is the foundation of almost all superstition — in astrology, in dreams, in beliefs, in predictions, and the like," Bacon wrote in *The New Organon.*

---

27   *Nassim Nicholas Taleb.* Chornyi lebid: Kyiv: Nash Format, 2017–392 c.). Taleb, *The Black Swan*, p. 178 The Story of the Pious Drowned Marcus Tullius Cicero.

142 SOCIOLOGY IN JOKES

Unfortunately, such brilliant thoughts are soon forgotten if they are not pounded into our heads day by day."

Indeed, Taleb is quite right. My wife once dreamed that a kiosk had been built under the windows of our house. Indeed, when we got up, washed up, and came into the kitchen to have breakfast, I happened to look out of the window — there was a kiosk. It stood for only one day, and then they took it down for some reason. But I have remembered this story for years. During that time, I had thousands of dreams that did not come true, but they were not memorized. That is how superstitions are formed. What is not confirmed is not remembered.

Fraudsters on the New York Stock Exchange used a similar method to sell non-performing stocks. Rich people playing on the exchange began to receive predictions; they guessed which stocks would go up or down once, twice, three times, four times, or five times, and then they invested all their money in what the unknown well-wisher advised them. They managed to get a few thousand addresses of people playing on the stock exchange. Let us say four thousand. To half of them, they wrote that the stock price of, say, General Motors would go up and to the other half that it would go down. They waited. In the end, they had a group of 2000 people, they guessed. Half were told that, say, Google would go up, half that it would go down. They got 1000 who guessed two times, 500 who guessed three times, 250 who guessed four times, and 125 who guessed five times, and they were advised stocks to buy.

Similarly, the anecdote about parachutes.

In the store: *"Tell me, are your parachutes reliable? Do they always open?"* — *"You know, I've been working here for 20 years, and I've never had a customer come in complaining that a parachute they bought from us didn't deploy"*

A sociologist gave birth to twins. Her husband was thrilled and immediately called the priest to arrange a baptism. — *"Congratulations,"* said the priest, *"bring them to church on Sunday, and we will baptize them."* — *"No,"* replied the sociologist, *"we'll baptize one. We'll keep the other as a control group."*

STATISTICAL DATA ANALYSIS, MODELING OF SOCIAL PROCESSES   143

Indeed, this experiment will determine whether baptism affects the future life of the baptized. The Pulitzer Prize-winning novel by American novelist Thornton Wilder, *King Louis St.'s Bridge* (1927), tells the story of the collapse of a suspension bridge linking a village to the outside world, resulting in the deaths of five people. A Franciscan friar tries to understand if there was a divine purpose in the deaths of the five people and why God chose these particular people. Having learned the details of the life stories of the five unfortunates, he tries to measure the goodness and piety of the people and compare them with a control group of other villagers. By the way, a very good movie with the same title (with Robert De Niro) was made based on the novel in 2004.

> No, just think about it: 22 players, two coaches, ten substitutes, one referee, two side referees, six camera operators, 12 TV workers, 50 sports journalists and about 80,000 spectators, and this pigeon pooped on me!

The same question arises among respondents during sociological surveys: why was I selected? Indeed, the probability was negligible. Almost unbelievable events happen to us all the time. Often, a meeting with a future spouse hangs in the balance and may not take place. Our life itself is a big accident. Litvak's book The Principle of Spermatazoi[28] begins with an address to the readers: "First of all, I want to congratulate you on your big victory in a crazy race in which there were 50 million competitors". It goes on to explain that in the race to conceive, there are between 50 and 150 million spermatozoa. One won — that is you — and the rest died, the fiercest battle of your life. Thus, the probability of you being born was one in fifty million, a totally improbable event.

* * *

— "Why are you so upset, Seryoga?"
— "I went out for lunch, came back, and saw that someone had been messing with my computer while I was gone. I don't know who. We have a lot of people in there. I don't understand how they could crack the password. It's

---

28   M.Litvak. Principle of Spermatazoid. M.: Phoenix, 2013.

144 SOCIOLOGY IN JOKES

*four digits, that's 10,000 variants. Even if it takes five seconds per variant,
it would take ten days."*
— "What was your password?"
*— "It's very complicated. I made it up so no one would guess it. It's not like
a year of birth. It's the year of St. Dominic's canonization by Pope Gregory
IX! Can you believe it?"*
— "What year is that?"
— "1234."

Something happened that everyone foresaw but no one expected. This is about the question of prediction and the perception of predictions. The god Apollo gave Cassandra the gift of foresight, but then she refused to reciprocate and he made it so that no one believed her predictions. For example, pandemics were talked about a lot, novels were written, and movies were made, but when it happened, it took everyone by surprise. I watched the 2011 movie *Infection*, directed by Steven Soderbergh and was struck by the similarities to the situation in 2020. In this movie, Patient Zero is infected in China by a bat, and the virus begins to spread rapidly. The method of spread—airborne and through fomites (surfaces)—is completely the same. The recommendations of doctors (social distancing and hand washing) and reactions of people and authorities—worldwide quarantine, public panic, mass purchase of products, mass misinformation, conspiracy theories, problems of vaccine development, etc. are described very accurately. The movie starred such well-known actors (Matt Damon, Jude Law, Gwyneth Paltrow, Kate Winslet, Laurence Fishburne and Marion Cotillard) that it was hard to ignore. So what? The world was unprepared for the unfolding of the scenario described.

* * *

After all, how complex a person is, how everything in the body is interconnected. The condition of your feet is reflected in your head. I have noticed that when I wake up in my shoes, my head always hurts.

Analyzing cause-effect relationships is always a challenge. Attribute A causes attribute B (e.g., education increases wages) if three conditions are met: 1) A occurred before B, 2) A and B are statistically correlated (i.e., changes in A are accompanied by changes in B), and 3) there is no plausible alternative explanation for B other than A. Fulfilling condition 3 is always problematic: it is difficult to be sure that there is no other factor that could affect B. In this anecdote, such a factor is easy to find, but there are much more complicated situations. Here is another anecdote on the same topic.

* * *

— *"Doctor, help me. Something strange is happening to me. Which is to say, you know, sometimes I get drunk, and in the morning, I find blue spots on my body."*
— *"I sympathize with you. My wife has a temper, too."*

These two anecdotes illustrate the concept of "false correlation."

Here is more from the humor of physicists. At the physics department of the University of Milan, one of the Soviet physicists saw a 'statistical' document on the wall. I have reproduced it, extrapolating Ukrainian realities based on the population calculated for 2019.

UKRAINIAN POPULATION	37 000 000
Including those over 65 years old	8 900 000
Stays for work activities:	28 100 000
Under 18	6650000
Stays for work activities:	21 450 000
Non-working women	10 900 000
Stays for work activities:	10 550 000
University students	275000
Stays for work activities:	10 275 000
Employees of various institutions	3830000
Stays for work activities:	6 445 000
Unemployed, political party and trade union officials	2 560 000
Stays for labor	3 330 000
Military	780 000
Stays for work activities:	2 550 000

The sick, the crazy, the vagabonds, the regulars at race-tracks and casinos.	1 310 000
Stays for work activities:	1 240 000
Illiterates, artists, judges, etc.	880 000
Stays for work activities:	360 000
Hermits, philosophers, fatalists, rogues, etc.	240000
Stays for work activities:	120000
Ministers, MPs, prisoners	119 998
Remains for labor activity	2

It's you and me. Unfortunately, I am already weary under the weight of the burden that has fallen on me, and you are the only one left.

14. Marketing and Advertising

Quite a few anecdotes are either directly about marketing and advertising or may describe situations faced by researchers and marketers. Below are some anecdotes with my comments or with titles only, showing the relation of the anecdote to marketing and advertising, and in obvious cases, without comments and titles.

* * *

If you show an ass on TV every day, in six months, it will be interviewed (Vladimir Pozner).

I have to disappoint the politicians. Daily broadcasts on TV increase popularity, and interviews and autographs will indeed be taken. However, that does not mean they will vote. Popularity and ratings are correlated, but the relationship is ambiguous. Popularity is rather a necessary but not sufficient condition for rating. For example, former presidents are popular; everyone knows them, but they have very little chance of being elected again. The same is true for products: the number of impressions (number of hits) increases brand awareness but does not automatically increase sales.

* * *

The advertising department gets a call from the newspaper:
— *"Sorry, we are typing your ad for lighters and wanted to make sure there were no errors. Are you offering a set of 50 disposable wooden lighters for only three hryvnias?"*
— *"I also think we should charge more, but the marketing department claims that they won't buy matches for a higher price."*

I wonder if it is a fresh, uncluttered take on the product, a new take on an old one, or a non-trivial deception of the customer?

* * *

A young writer, Gosha Kavrigin, has written a book. He published 10,000 copies. He sees that no one is buying it. He decided to put an

148   SOCIOLOGY IN JOKES

ad in the newspaper. "*A young, handsome millionaire would like to meet a woman who looks like the heroine of G. Kavrigin's book.*" The next day, the whole edition was sold out.

* * *

The exodus of the people of Israel from Egypt. The people of Israel came to the Dead Sea. The Egyptian cavalry was already catching up behind them. Moses thought: *"How can I save the people of Israel?"*
Out of nowhere comes a PR man. He says: *"Let the Jews kneel down and pray. Then get up and go straight into the sea."*
Moses hesitated: *"Won't we drown?"*
— "*I don't know. But I guarantee publication in the Bible.*"

* * *

A copywriter, an art director and an account manager find a bottle from which, to everyone's surprise, a genie has escaped. The rescued man tells them: *"Each of you can make any wish you want. Just one."*
The copywriter wishes: *"I'd like to win a Pulitzer Prize."*
— "*No problem*", replies the genie. The copywriter instantly disappears.
The art director says: *"And I'd like to write about sunsets on the shores of the French Riviera, where I'll have a small but nice chalet."* As soon as he says this, he immediately disappears.
— "*Well, what about you?*" The genie asks the account manager, *"what do you want?"*.
The man replies: *"Make sure these two are back here in 15 minutes. I've got a project on fire."*

Well, the man has no creativity. He did not realize he could ask the genie to fulfill the project at once! But sometimes you want to hire a person who, even if they do not have the stars from the sky, does their job very responsibly, purposefully, without being distracted by all sorts of temptations and the flickering of genies.

* * *

Yesterday I felt what active marketing is all about. I go to my car in the morning, and I see that the wipers have been stolen. And an advertisement was on the glass: Rent concrete garages from us.

MARKETING AND ADVERTISING   149

It was in the Charlie Chaplin movie — the creative tandem of the Kid and the Glass Tramp. The Kid breaks the glass, and the glazier puts it back in. This kind of marketing simply has no strategic perspective.

* * *

A blind man sits with a sign "HELP THE BLIND", but almost no one gives money. One of the passersby says: *"You have the wrong sign. Write a different text, and people will give."*
— *"No, that won't work. I can't lie."*
— *"You don't have to lie. Listen to me, an experienced advertiser. Let me write you a text."* He wrote the text.
After that, things started to move. They started to give. The blind man was surprised, rejoiced and asked a passerby to read what it says. The man read to him: *"SPRING IS COMING. BUT I WON'T SEE IT."*

We also once tried to increase the response rate in a mail survey by writing a letter of complaint ("Our team has been working on this project for a year; if you don't respond, the labor of many people will be lost"), but it did not help much. I have the impression that this anecdote was invented in a civilized country with a high level of sympathy and trust. I am not sure it would work here.

* * *

Judging by the commercials, TV is watched by people who are miserable, tortured by dandruff, diarrhea, dirty dishes and stinky toilets.

* * *

London. In the center of the British capital, there was a celebration of the Coca-Cola company. During the festivities in the air, a hundred airplanes circled with the inscription "Coca-Cola", and 200 thousand charges of festive fireworks were released. On an improvised stage, Placido Domingo, Luciano Pavarotti and Jose Carreras sang. A 'cheap publicity stunt' was the evaluation of this event by specialists of the Kyiv beverage plant "Obolon".

* * *

150   SOCIOLOGY IN JOKES

Evaluating the effectiveness of advertising: *"Are you sure that advertising in your newspaper is effective?"*
— *"Yes, I am! Just yesterday afternoon, the Cascade company advertised that they needed a watchman, and already tonight the company was robbed."*

Advertising and political correctness

The Schmukler family has been making nails all their lives. Great-grandpa was a nail maker, grandpa, then dad. When they privatized this nail factory, Dad said to his son: *"Fima, I've been in production for 30 years and have never been on vacation. You stay as the director, at least for a month, I'll go away with your mother. I'll rest."*
— *"Dad, I am not a specialist. I'm a marketer, I'm in advertising!"*
— *"Sonny, we have a warehouse full of nails! You just manage, sell these nails, and I'll be back in a month and everything will be fine!"*
The son stayed, and the father left. Two weeks later, the father receives a telegram: *"Daddy, urgently come, we are out of nails."*
Dad returned and said: *"What do you mean out?"*
— *"Dad, I advertised."*
— *"Show me!"*
The son shows him a billboard advertisement. It shows Jesus Christ nailed to a cross and caption: *"Schmuckler Nails — held up for 2000 years."*
Dad says: *"Fima! You're obviously the perfect marketer, but you're an idiot! How could you depict Jesus Christ in an advertisement? Haven't we Jews been beaten and pogromized enough? Take it down immediately!"*
Dad gave the command, production ramped up, Fima shot a commercial, and Dad went on vacation. Two weeks later, again comes an urgent telegram: *"Daddy urgently fly out, these nails have run out."*
Dad flew in. *"What again?"*
— *"Yes, just calm down — no Jesus Christ, just like you asked."*
Dad looks at the billboard layout. There's a picture of an empty cross without Jesus and the caption: *"Now, if you had had Schmuckler nails..."*

Unfortunately, the issues of ethics and advertising effectiveness are often at odds. The important thing is not to cross the line. Here is a balanced version:

* * *

An advertisement for an American firm: *We'd rather deal with a thousand Arab terrorists than one Jew.* The ad looks anti-Semitic, but I think readers have already begun to guess what kind of firm this is: Goldberg Funeral Home.

* * *

— *"You advised me last time to give some interesting names to the barbershops in my chain, remember?"*
— *"Well, yes, we advised to give the names of writers, composers, and artists, so that there would be associations with creativity."*
— *"Well, in general, it worked; nine out of ten hairdressing salons became better, but in this tenth, people almost stopped going."*
— *"What did you name it?"*
— *"Van Gogh."*

It is an anecdote about the importance of names. I also think it is an anecdote from some cultured European country like France or Germany. To stop going to the barbershop you have to know something about Van Gogh's life.

* * *

Mashenka went for mushrooms and berries. She came back with nothing because you have to set specific goals for yourself!

Sometimes, people ask me: why is marketing necessary? Well, why is a blade of grass swaying in the wind or the croak of a frog in the pre-dawn mist necessary? It might seem they aren't. But without them, the world would be a little bit duller...

Strategic Marketing.

Below are three useful strategies for selling merchandise.

1. Calling a computer repair company:
— *"My printer has started to print badly!"*
— *"It probably just needs to be cleaned. It costs $50. But honestly, you can read the instructions and do the job yourself."*
Customer, surprised by this candor, asks,
— *"Does your boss know that you're hindering business this way?"*
— *"Actually, it was his idea. We make a lot more profit when we let our customers try to repair something themselves first."*

152 SOCIOLOGY IN JOKES

2. An older man is selling watermelons at the market under the sign "One watermelon — 30 rubles. Three watermelon — 100 rubles". A man comes up and buys first one watermelon for 30 rubles, then two more watermelons for 60 rubles and in farewell, happily says, *"look, I bought three watermelons and paid only 90 rubles! You don't know how to trade!"* The older man look at him: *"you took three watermelons instead of one. Don't teach me commerce ..."*

3. The Union of Pediatricians recommends Pampers. "Pampers is the only diaper recommended by the Pediatricians' Union." The Pediatricians' Union is the only union created specifically to recommend Pampers diapers.

4. A customer once went into an antique store. After hurriedly examining the goods on the counters and about to leave, they noticed a cute cat sipping milk from a beautiful, expensive porcelain saucer. Having estimated the cost of that saucer, he turned to the seller: *"Hello, sir. In your shop, such a nice kitty lives, but I am a lonely person. I have no children, no grandchildren, no pets. Maybe you can give it to me?"*
— *"I cannot. This cat is very fond of my young visitors, who often come to feed and play with her."*
— *"Oh, but I have such a soft spot for her. I'm sure we'll make friends, and she'll be fine at my house too. I can pay 20 shekels."*
— *"It is not for sale."*
They agreed on 20 shekels. The buyer takes the cat in his arms and says: *"I saw the kitty likes to drink from that saucer over there. She must have become used to it by now. Maybe you can give it to me, too. Can I have it for 20 shekels?"*
— *"No, no, no. This saucer is made of very expensive Chinese porcelain from the 12th century with gold painting and precious stones. It's my talisman. It brings me happiness. With its help, I sell dozens of cats a week for 20 shekels! I already have contracts with all the cat shelters in the city!"*

Here is a subtle marketing strategy to promote the product. True, it helps to develop not the business that was planned from the beginning; sales of antiques did not grow. However, the business person must be able to switch in time from an unprofitable business to a profitable one and not miss out on their luck.

Product characteristics

> One business person to another: *"You know, I bought a batch of Christmas toys in England the other day. They turned out to be defective."*
> — *"Maybe they are fake?"*
> — *"No, in nice boxes with holograms, and everything is as it should be."*
> — *"Not shiny?"*
> — *"Yes, they are!"*
> — *"What's wrong with them?"*
> — *"See, I got myself a box, brought it home, unpacked it — not happy!"*

This is what happens when a business person focuses on their own tastes rather than researching the reaction of the target audience when evaluating products. It doesn't matter what it is, but if it beeps, flashes, and requires at least six batteries, most men will want to buy it.

> — *"I need shoes that are inexpensive but comfortable and good-looking."*
> — *"Me too"*, the salesman sighed.

Promotions in marketing.

> When you buy the right shoe, you get the left shoe for free!

> An unprecedented promotion by Coca-Cola. Under every seventh cork, there is vodka.

> Promotion at the gas station: Fill up a full tank, and we'll top up five liters for free!"

> Recently the company Procter & Gamble celebrated the 10th anniversary of the shampoo Rantepe ProV 2 in 1. At the gala banquet the topic was raised whether to stop writing "New" on the label or to wait.

* * *

> *You'd have to be so disappointed in people to use the word "Friendship" to name a chainsaw.*[29]

---

29 The Druzhba chainsaw is the most famous chainsaw in the former Soviet Union. The saw has been produced since 1955 and is still in production.

154 SOCIOLOGY IN JOKES

By the way, I have long been surprised by the name of the airplane. The Antonov Design Bureau created a heavy military transport airplane in 1965 and named it Antaeus (after an ancient Greek mythological hero). Antaeus, the son of the earth goddess Gaea, lost his strength as soon as he lifted off the ground. Heracles was able to cope with him only by tearing him off the ground. What a name for an airplane!

> He bought "Parliament" cigarettes, but he didn't get into parliament; he ate "President" butter, but he didn't become president. And only "Kozel" beer really worked![30]

I hasten to state that this is an abstract anecdote, and any similarity with real people is coincidental.

Brand loyalty

> The president of Samsung always hides when he eats apples.

Stereotypes in brand perception:

> A new Russian complains to his buddy: *"You know, bro, it's all lies, you can't trust anyone! I bought a Ming dynasty vase for the office from Christie's auction for 50,000 bucks, but it's a decent place, a famous auction! I brought it back, checked it in the museum, and it turned out to be Chinese!"*

> * * *

> The Lord God decided to improve things in medicine and got a job as a district doctor in a polyclinic. He came to the clinic, and the first patient came to him, a person with paralysis in a wheelchair. God puts his hands on his head and says: *"Get up and walk."* He got up and walked. He goes out into the corridor, there is a line to the street, they ask him: *"Well, how is the new one?"*
> — *"Like all of them — he didn't even take my blood pressure."*

It's about measuring client satisfaction.

---

30 Kozel (the name translates as "goat") is one of the most famous brands of Czech beer. The history of the brand goes back about 150 years.

Customer loyalty

* * *

An Englishman decided to rest in a country hotel, but because he always took his favorite dog with him, he wrote a letter to the hotel administration asking whether he was allowed to keep a dog in the room. A reply from the hotel was like this: *"Dear Sir! In our practice, there has never been a single case when a dog burned the bed linen with a cigarette, took away towels from the room, poured wine on the carpet or left without paying. That is why we'd love to have your dog! If he vouches for you, we are ready to accommodate you together with him."*

The final stage of sampling: selection in the household

A woman, buying a coat, pays at the cashier's desk, taking out crumpled and wet money from their purse and responds to the perplexed look of the cashier: *"My husband was crying so hard, so hard ...."*

In marketing research, unlike social surveys, often the respondent is not selected randomly in the household, but the decision maker is selected. It seems that all sorts of biases are possible; in the case described in the questionnaire, the husband would probably report that he is the one who makes the shopping decisions. In my opinion, it is worth considering whether stochastic selection is better because it reduces the effective sample size but gives real representativeness. Typical marketing research (unlike most social research) has restrictions on the age of interviewees (for example, up to 60 or 70 years old). It is believed that these people do not buy much themselves; others buy things for them. In general, people of retirement age are considered unpromising buyers and are not of interest to businesses. This seems wrong because a significant part of consumers are ready to invest a much larger sum in buying for their elderly relatives than for their purchases (for example, a few years ago, when my 98-year-old mother was still alive, desperate to find a comfortable cell phone for her, I was ready to pay three times more for it than for my own). It would be wise to create an association that would test products for older people and put their own label (like they do now with "GMO-free"). I think the production of such

156   SOCIOLOGY IN JOKES

products is very promising (especially since the population is aging)

Posing questions in marketing research:

> A customer walks into a grocery store. The assistant, smiling, asks: *"What would the lady like?"*
> — *"The lady would like some Martini, but she came for bread..."*

The situation is not as trivial as it first appears. Real consumer behavior differs from verbal behavior not only because people correlate their desires with available resources but also for other reasons. Someone may have enough money, but they think that it is indecent to drink right from the morning, or they are driving, or they should drink only in good company, etc. A useful type of survey is one at the entrance to the store about what the respondent is going to buy and a survey at the exit about what was bought and why something was bought that the customer did not intend to buy.

* * *

> On a street in Cairo, not far from a mosque, two beggars are sitting. In front of each of them is a coin cup and a sign. One says: *"Give to a poor Jew"*, and the other: *"In the name of Allah the Merciful, give to AraBu, wounded in the war with Israel."* People coming out of the mosque defiantly walk past the Jew to throw a few coins at the Arab. Some of them chuckle and twirl their fingers at their heads when they see the Jew. Finally, one of the passersby says: *"Listen, do you realize anything? Why did you write in front of the mosque that you are a Jew, take it down or go to your synagogue?"* When the passerby has left, the Jew turns to his neighbor and says: *"Have you heard, Izya? That jerk is going to teach us about commerce!"*

I cite this anecdote not because I want to recommend such a marketing strategy to the reader (especially since it is based on deception). However, think about what feelings of the people these scammers used to stimulate the charitable activities of passersby. Couldn't that be harnessed? Alternatively, you are negotiating with a client, and your competitor appears who is so much worse than you in all respects that your advantages are especially noticeable (though you will have to share them with the "competitor" later).

Part 2.
Results of Some
Sociological Research
in Ukraine

15. Interethnic Relations in Ukraine (1994–2023)

Now that the reader has already got a certain idea of some sociological concepts, we will give examples of their application to the study of specific social processes in Ukraine. The first such example is interethnic relations.

The level of ethnic intolerance is one of the most important indicators of potential instability in particular regions of the world. From time to time, interethnic conflicts arise in certain regions (Rwanda, Nagorno-Karabakh). Therefore, monitoring the state of interethnic relations is very relevant.

Since 1994, KIIS has been conducting a study of the attitudes of the Ukrainian population toward certain ethnic groups. This research is conducted on the scale by American sociologist Emory Bogardus (adapted by N. Panina). For each ethnic group from the list, respondents have to answer how close relations they are ready to accept with representatives of each group. This is called social distance. The minimum social distance is 1 (agree to allow as a family member), and the maximum is 7 (would not allow in Ukraine). Often, the level of social distance is interpreted as the level of prejudice toward one or another group.

I agree to allow representatives of the national group named in the line..... (see *figure 3,* where they are listed in alphabetical order)

As members of your family	1
As close friends	2
As neighbors	3
As coworkers	4
As residents of Ukraine	5
As guests of Ukraine	6
Would not **let into Ukraine**	7

Several answers are possible for each national group.

160 SOCIOLOGY IN JOKES

Figure 3.

	Members of your family	Close friends	Neighbors	Coworkers	Residents Ukraine	Guests Ukraine	I would not let into Ukraine
Americans	1	2	3	4	5	6	7
Belarusians	1	2	3	4	5	6	7
Jews	1	2	3	4	5	6	7
Canadians	1	2	3	4	5	6	7
Africans	1	2	3	4	5	6	7

Etc., list of groups in the appendix

Below are the results of a survey conducted by the Kyiv International Institute of Sociology (KIIS) from September 29 to October 9, 2023.

A total of 1010 respondents were interviewed using CATI based on a random sample of cell phone numbers. The survey was conducted with adult (aged 18 years and older) citizens of Ukraine who, at the time of the survey, resided in the territory of Ukraine (within the limits controlled by the Ukrainian authorities until February 24, 2022). The sample did not include residents of the territories that were not temporarily controlled by the Ukrainian authorities until February 24, 2022 (Crimea, Sevastopol, and certain districts of Donetsk and Luhansk regions).

In the studies of previous years up to 2020, personal F2F interviews, rather than telephone surveys, were used, and about 2000 respondents were interviewed in each survey wave. Here are the results of these studies.

Hierarchy of social distances

Figure 4 shows the social distance (average index obtained using the Bogardus scale) from the Ukrainian population to certain ethnic groups.

Figure 4. Social distance from the adult population of Ukraine to some ethnic groups (the Bogardus scale), October 2023

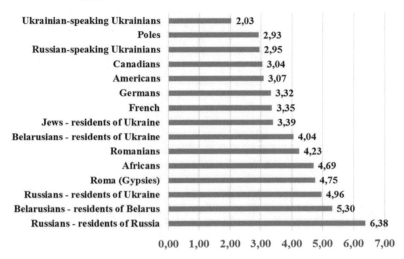

The smallest social distance is to Ukrainian-speaking Ukrainians (index 2.03), followed by Poles and Russian-speaking Ukrainians (index is almost the same — 2.93 and 2.95), respectively. The majority of respondents are ready to admit representatives of these groups as members of their family and close friends. Then come Canadians and Americans (indices are also practically the same — 3.04 and 3.07), and Germans, French and Jewish residents of Ukraine (indices from 3.32 to 3.39; the difference is statistically insignificant). The greatest social distance is to Africans (4.69), Roma (4.75), Russians — residents of Ukraine (4.96), and Belarusians — residents of Belarus (5.30). The last place with the greatest social distance is naturally occupied by Russians — residents of Russia (6.38). The overwhelming majority (80%) would not allow Russians even as tourists.

However, this situation was not always the case. From 1994 until Russia seized Crimea, 90% of the Ukrainian population had a positive attitude toward Russia and an even higher percentage toward Russians. They ranked second in the hierarchy on the

162   SOCIOLOGY IN JOKES

Bogardus scale after Ukrainians themselves. Figure 2 shows a comparison of the results of the survey in 2023 with 2013.

Figure 5.   Comparison of social distance from the adult population of Ukraine to some ethnic groups from September 2013 to October 2023.

	2013			2023 oct.
Ukrainian speaking Ukrainians	2.03		Ukrainian speaking Ukrainians	2.03
Russian speaking Ukrainians	2.25		Poles	2.93
Russians	2.70		Russian speaking Ukrainians	2.95
Belarusians	3.29		Canadians	3.04
Poles	4.05		Americans	3.07
Jews	4.24		German	3.32
German	4.55		French	3.35
French	4.59		Jews	3.39
Romanians	4.61		Romanians	4.23
Americans	4.63		Belarusians	4.67
Canadians	4.64		Africans	4.69
Africans	5.21		Roma (Gypsies)	4.75
Roma (Gypsies)	5.53		Russians	5.67

As we can see, in 2013, the attitude of Ukrainians to Russians and Belarusians was better than to all other ethnic groups. Note that it was the best during the entire period of observation, more than 25 years. Even after 2013, the social distance between Russians and Belarusians was the smallest after Ukrainians; they ranked 2nd and 3rd in social distance after Ukrainians. The situation changed dramatically only after Russia's full-scale invasion of Ukraine on February 24, 2022. We can see from Diagram 2 that Russians and Belarusians moved from the beginning of the list to its end, the attitude toward Poles, Americans and Canadians improved significantly, and other ethnic groups changed their place in the hierarchy by no more than 1–2 positions.

Dynamics of xenophobia

Figure 6 shows the dynamics of the xenophobia index, which is calculated as an average social distance to 13 ethnic and linguistic-ethnic groups (all groups except Crimean Tatars). The name of the index is conditional, and I do not consider it an exact measure of xenophobia. I consider this index as an indicator that is related to the level of xenophobia (in general, xenophobia is a complex multidimensional phenomenon and cannot be characterized by one indicator). At the same time, this index provides an opportunity to study the dynamics of xenophobia.

Figure 6. Dynamics of xenophobia level in Ukraine from 1994 to 2023 (average value of social distance for 13 ethnic groups according to Bogardus scale).

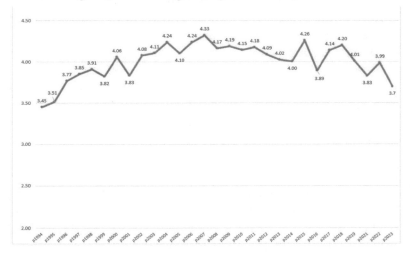

As we can see, the level of xenophobia in Ukraine grew with some fluctuations from 1994 to 2007; it increased from 3.5 to 4.3 points during this period. The growth of the xenophobia level from 1994 to 2000 may be related to the growth of the poverty level (see section "Dynamics of poverty level in Ukraine"). Researchers of xenophobia have obtained some empirical evidence of the scapegoat theory. As the general situation worsens, people look for a scapegoat, and often national minorities become them. The second factor explaining further changes in the level of xenophobia may be interethnic conflicts taking place outside the country, wars and conflicts in other regions of the world, which are widely covered in the media and become media events (the war in Chechnya, Afghanistan, the Balkans, and Iraq, which were taking place at the same time). International conflicts increase the level of fear and distrust toward members of other ethnic groups. From 2008 to 2013, the index decreased to a score of 4.0.

Further, the xenophobia index fluctuates around this value; in October 2022, it was actually equal to 4 (3.99 to be exact), and now it has slightly decreased to 3.7. This level is not high, and it shows that for the majority of ethnic groups, the population of Ukraine maintains a distance of 3, 4 or 5 (i.e., they would not like representatives of these ethnic groups to be their family members and close friends, but are ready to see them as neighbors, work colleagues and residents of Ukraine). Despite the war, the level of xenophobia in Ukraine remains stable.

Among Ukrainians, a tolerant attitude toward Jews has persisted for many years (in addition to the fact that most Ukrainians now support Israel in the conflict with Palestine, a level of support greater than in the US or the UK. This dispels myths about Ukraine as a state with widespread anti-Semitism.

I will not review the factors influencing the level of xenophobia in detail here but refer the reader to the relevant press release. In brief, the level of xenophobia is most influenced by such factors as education (the higher the education, the lower the level of xenophobia), type of settlement (a higher level of xenophobia in rural areas than in cities), region of residence, financial status (the higher the level of wealth, the lower the level of xenophobia) and age (the level of xenophobia increases with age).

Appendix. Figure 7. Distribution of answers regarding ethnic groups, October 2023, %

Ethnic or linguistic-ethnic group	Willing to allow representatives of this group as								
	Members of their family (score 1)	Close friends (score 2)	Neigh-bors (score 3)	Work col-leagues (score 4)	Residents of Ukraine (score 5)	Guests of Ukraine (score 6)	Would not let in Ukraine (Score 7)	Total	xeno-phobia index
Americans	31.7%	24.9%	7.8%	5.8%	3.7%	21.9%	4.3%	100%	3.72
Africans	15.4%	1.9%	5.9%	5.5%	3.9%	35.2%	23.1%	100%	4.84
Belarusians—residents of Ukraine	25.2%	9.2%	12.3%	2.2%	14.2%	14.4%	22.5%	100%	4.37
Belarusians	12.4%	4.8%	8.6%	2.9%	3.1%	22.5%	45.8%	100%	5.34
Jews—inhabitants of Ukraine	33.4%	11.8%	10.0%	3.9%	18.7%	13.5%	8.8%	100%	3.8
Canadians	33.9%	22.4%	8.7%	4.0%	7.5%	19.8%	3.8%	100%	3.51
Germans	29.4%	20.7%	8.4%	6.3%	6.6%	22.6%	5.9%	100%	4.05
Poles	34.4%	23.6%	11.3%	3.2%	5.5%	17.5%	4.6%	100%	2.95
Roma	13.9%	8.7%	9.8%	3.2%	14.8%	19.7%	29.9%	100%	5.08
Russians—residents of Ukraine	18.4%	5.4%	5.5%	2.2%	12.7%	12.0%	43.8%	100%	5.03
Russians	4.6%	2.2%	2.3%	1.2%	1.6%	7.9%	80.2%	100%	6.39
Romanians	20.0%	11.1%	11.8%	4.5%	5.9%	29.4%	17.3%	100%	4.49
Ukrainian speakers	68.4%	7.5%	2.7%	1.6%	14.8%	4.4%	0.7%	100%	2.22
Russian-speaking Ukrainians	45.4%	11.6%	5.7%	3.1%	16.9%	8.1%	9.1%	100%	2.74

166   SOCIOLOGY IN JOKES

First, a few anecdotes with stereotypes about Jews

For centuries, Jews have been seeking an audience with the pope, but something always got in the way. Sometimes, it was the Crusades ("we don't accept Jews"), sometimes religious wars, or something else. Closer to our time, Pope John Paul, a peacemaker, says: *"It is inconvenient. They have been asking for so many years, let's accept them!"*
Pontifical Council, sitting in the Vatican, two Jews come in, and one of them is carrying a scroll under his arm. One of the Jews points to the famous painting "The Last Supper" hanging on the wall and asks, *"Papa, are these your people?"* The pope turned green at the insolence and said: *"Can't you see who is depicted? Here is Jesus Christ, our father; here are the apostles Peter and Paul, and here is Judas, now he will betray Christ."*
— *"No need for details, you tell me: are these your people or not?"*
Papa: *"Of course, they are ours!"*
The first Jew: *"Fima, bring it out!"*
The second Jew unrolls the scroll: *"The dinner hasn't been paid for!"*

* * *

A priest, a mullah and a rabbi got together. They began to discuss who would keep how much of the donation.
The priest: *"I'll draw a circle, then throw the money up. What inside the circle is mine. Whatever is outside the circle, I give to the church ..."*
Mullah: *"I'll also draw a circle. I'll throw the money up, too. What goes inside the circle, I leave in the mosque and I'll take the rest for myself."*
Rabbi: *"I'll also throw the money up and shout, 'Lord, take as much as you need!' And what falls to the ground I keep."*

* * *

An airplane flies from Tel Aviv to New York. On the plane, 50 rabbis are flying to participate in a conference. The steward knows that rabbis are not *poor* people, and in anticipation of a generous tip, he does his best: he runs around, jokes, smiles, brings coke to some, recommends ice cream to some, and tucks a blanket for others. The airplane lands in New York, and the first rabbi comes out and says to the steward: *"Thank you very much. It was a wonderful flight. I have never flown so comfortably"* — shakes his hand and leaves. The second rabbi, same story. The third, fifth, twentieth, forty-ninth — the same. The steward gets more and more upset with each rabbi and loses hope, realizing that he was left without any tips at all for the flight. Then the last rabbi comes out with a diplomat and starts thanking him, too, saying the flight was wonderful, etc. *"We"*, he says, *"have consulted our rabbinical friends and decided (so as not to humiliate you, and each rabbi does not give you a small tip) to all pitch in and here you are your 5000 dollars."* The steward was stunned, sat down on a folding chair and said: *"I don't know whether you Jews crucified Christ or not, but you certainly took his soul out of him."*

* * *

A Jew, having reached home in a cab, gets out of the car in silence and starts searching his pockets, and under his breath, he mutters: *"Shit, I think I dropped my wallet in the car."* Hearing this, the cab driver presses on the gas and speeds off. The Jew, looking at the taxi driver, says: *"Rabinovich is not lying. It really works ..."*

* * *

After twenty years of playing the violin, a person automatically becomes a Jew.

* * *

— *"Are you Rabinovich, Moses Solomonovich?"*
— *"Hello!"*
— *"I'm so glad to meet you finally! I've been told so much about you!"*
— *"Ha! Let them try to prove it!"*

* * *

Semyon Katz, an accountant at the Odesa port, and Gavrila Kandyba, a longshoreman, often drank together at lunchtime and talked about philosophical topics. One day, they were sitting drinking, and there were two cucumbers left — a big one and a small one. Semyon reached out and took the big cucumber. *"And didn't I tell you, Semyon Iz-railevich,"* said Kandyba, *"that it's not without reason your nation isn't liked. Is that why you took the big cucumber?"*
— *"Tell me, Gavrila Stepanovich, but if you were the first to take, which cucumber would you choose?"*
— *"Of course, it's small!"*
— *"Well, you got it! What's your problem?"*

168   SOCIOLOGY IN JOKES

* * *

> The ancient Kirghiz knew nothing about the existence of Jews, so they explained all their troubles as the action of dark forces of nature.

As Jews have been forced to flee their historic homeland and have settled in many countries around the world, anti-Semitism has become probably one of the most widespread types of xenophobia in the world and one of the most researched. A host of studies have shown that the causes of anti-Semitism (like the causes of other prejudices) are not related to the actual characteristics of Jews (or any other ethnic group) but are determined by the history of relationships, the degree of hostility, the degree of competition, and the level of wealth.

> "For a long period of European history, Jews epitomized commodity-money relations in the depths of the subsistence economy. The development of commodity-money relations was an objective regularity that did not depend on anyone's evil or good will. But this process was very painful. Indebtedness and ruin were easily associated in the backward consciousness with the image of a Jew usurer or a Jew merchant, who thus became a symbol of all sorts of troubles".[31]

That is why, very often, Jews appear in anecdotes as people who are rich, cunning, and eager to deceive you. Igor Kohn's article is wonderfully written; I read it when I was in my second year of study at the faculty of mathematics of the university, and it largely determined my desire to become a sociologist.

* * *

> — "Uncle Stefan, Uncle Stefan! What are you doing? Why are you cutting the birch tree? It's so slender, young, so sweet to the eye with green leaves, and you're cutting it down!"
>
> — "Oh, neighbor, don't even mention it, my heart bleeds, but I have to do it — because the Russians will come, see the birch tree, and say: 'Oh, this is truly a Russian landscape!'"

---

31   Igor Kohn. The Psychology of Prejudice. On the social-psychological roots of ethnic prejudice. "Novy Mir", M, 1966, No. 9 http://evartist.narod.ru/text9/15.htm.

This anecdote appeared in 1991 after the creation of the independent state of Ukraine. The formation of national consciousness implied the creation of a negative image of the Russian chauvinist and repulsion from the "friendship of peoples" proclaimed in the Soviet Union. I had to delete other anecdotes on this topic, as it is impossible to translate them. In this anecdote, the main humorous effect was that the whole text was in Ukrainian. Then, the hero of the anecdote switches to Russian and parodies Russian speech and stereotypes of the Russian landscape (birch trees): "Oh, this is a truly Russian landscape". In turn, Russian anecdotes also demonstrated negative stereotypes of Ukrainians. For example:

* * *

A Ukrainian and two Black students are traveling in the same compartment. The Ukrainian takes out bread and lard. The Black students take out some bananas. Ukrainian: *"What's yours?"*
— *"Bananas."*
— *"Can I try it?"*
They gave him a banana. The Ukrainians tried it and liked it. The Black students, in turn, ask: *"What about you?"*
— *"Lard."*
— *"Let me try."*
— *"What's there to taste? Lard is just lard! ..."*

It is interesting that to have a negative attitude toward one or another ethnic group, it is not necessary to have any negative experience of acquaintance with representatives of this group. We once inserted Assyrians into the list for the Bogardus scale, and the attitude of the Ukrainian population was negative. In surveys in the USA experiments were also conducted with fictional ethnic groups — the same result. Here are some anecdotes about chukchas. Well, who and when in Ukraine has seen chukchas? Meanwhile, in the anecdotes, the Chukcha looks naive and stupid.

* * *

Two Chukchas on the subway platform. One Chukcha asks the subway driver: *"Tell me, will this train take me to Khreshchatyk, though?"*

170   SOCIOLOGY IN JOKES

– *"Yes, it will."*
The second Chukcha asks: *"What about me?"*

* * *

A Chukcha guide and a geologist are sitting by the fire. The Chukcha stares silently at the fire for a long time and then asks the geologist: *"Please tell me, geologist, is a white woman white everywhere, front and back?"*
– *"Uh, yeah, sure."*
– *"Is a Black woman all black from front to back?"*
– *"Of course, why do you ask?"*
The Chukcha again looks long and sadly at the fire, sighs heavily and says: *"So it was a penguin."*

I have come across three anecdotes in which the Chukcha looks quite different from the others.

* * *

A Chukcha is sitting on the ocean shore, catching fish. Suddenly, a submarine floats up, the hatch opens, and a young sailor sticks out and asks: *"Hey, Chukcha, we're having trouble with our navigation equipment. What direction is the Bering Strait from here?"*
– *"Zui-Zuid West"*, replies the Chukcha.
– *"Don't be clever, Chukcha."* The sailor took offense. *"Show me with your hand!"*

* * *

A big white man came to the north to hunt bears. A tourist company organized a meeting with a Chukchi gamekeeper, gave him skis, and brought him to the Chukchi's chum. Chukcha asks him: *"Do you shoot well?"*.
The big white man replies: *"Sure! I hunted lions on safari!"*
Chukcha asks, *"Can you ski?"*
The big white man says, *"Can't you see? How would I have got to you if I hadn't skied?"*
"All right," said the Chukcha, *"but obey me in everything!"*
In the morning they went hunting. They walked three kilometers. When they came to the den, the Chukcha said: *"Now I will annoy the bear, he will jump out, and we will run away from him. But don't shoot, shoot only on my command!"*

The Chukcha started throwing sticks and branches, woke up the bear, and the bear came out of the den and chased them. They were running, running, and the Chukcha did not give the command to shoot. Finally, the big white man could not stand it, turned around and started shooting at the bear. He killed the bear. The Chukcha came up, looked, twirled his finger at his head and said to the big white man: *"Very bad, however! You run badly, shoot badly — you have ruined the whole skin! And the head is completely gone — now take this bear and drag it three kilometers to the lodge!"*

* * *

A Chukcha is helping a geologist collect stones on the ocean shore. Suddenly, they see a polar bear running toward them. Chukcha grabs his skis and starts putting them on. Geologist: *"It's no use. You can't run faster than the bear anyway."*
— *"I don't need to run faster than a bear. I need to run faster than you!"*

These anecdotes make the Chukchi look much smarter than the "white man". Dissemination of such jokes to combat "anti-Chukchism" is much more effective than calls for tolerance. Perhaps, to fight xenophobia, it would make sense to open a unit in the SBU that would compose and distribute anecdotes that would compensate for anecdotes with negative images of discriminated groups.

* * *

An airplane on the Moscow-Paris route is waiting for its departure at the airport. All passengers are in their seats except for one blonde woman who, instead of her seat in economy class, sat on a seat in business class. The flight attendants and passengers unanimously persuaded the woman to change seats, but she was adamant — she had to fly in business class. After 20 minutes, the pilot came out of his cabin. He approached the woman, whispered something in her ear, and then she promptly moved to her seat in economy class. The passengers, flight attendants, and, most importantly, the co-pilot were surprised. The co-pilot asked: *"What did you say to her that made her go back to her seat in a flash?"* The captain smiled and said, *"I told her that business class would not fly to Paris."*

Stereotypes and prejudices do not only exist on ethnic grounds but can arise from any other differences between people and lead to

172 Sociology in Jokes

discrimination. There is discrimination based on age (against young and old), gender (feminists have been fighting this since the late 19th century), and skin color. This anecdote supports a stereotype based on hair color.

* * *

A blonde and a male lawyer are sitting in adjacent seats on an airplane. The flight is long and boring, and the lawyer suggests: *"Let's play a game: I ask you a question, and if you don't know the answer you give me five dollars. Then you ask me a question, and if I don't know the answer, I pay you $500."*
The woman agrees. Lawyer: *"What is the distance from the moon to the earth?"*
The woman silently hands him five dollars.
Woman: *"Who goes up a mountain on three legs and comes down on four?"*
A couple of hours go by. The lawyer has called all his friends and scoured the Internet, and can't find an answer. He gives the blonde 500 dollars and asks: *"Well, who is it?"*
The blonde silently hands him the five dollars and turns away to the porthole.

And this is another anecdote useful for fighting stereotypes. A woman fooled a lawyer who thought he was much smarter than her.

* * *

Moscow. Tatiana Petrovna, returning home, says to her husband:
"I was riding in the subway. Can you imagine a carload full of Tajiks? I was watching with all my eyes to make sure they didn't steal my bag." Mitsuko from the Tokyo Symphony Orchestra, which is on tour in Moscow, writes on Facebook: *"Today we visited the Moscow subway in its entirety. In the carriage, one woman looked at us very sternly: apparently, our performance of Rachmaninoff's Second Symphony was far from ideal."*

I once had a meeting with a representative of the Japanese embassy and discussed attacks on Asians. One of the problems was that, according to surveys, the attitude toward the Japanese in Ukraine was better than toward the Vietnamese or Tajiks. However, xenophobes did not distinguish some Asians from others (as in the famous

INTERETHNIC RELATIONS IN UKRAINE   173

anecdote, "Sarah! We have Jews being beaten up in the street! Calm down, Abram, you're a Russian by passport! They don't beat them on their passports. They beat them by their faces). Another aspect that is played out in this anecdote is our interpretation of other people's behavior. The formation of the human community depended on the ability to understand what other people think about you, how they will behave and how they will behave toward each other; the need to keep a multitude of connections in mind stimulated the development of human intelligence. Of course, it is more difficult for representatives of different social groups with different norms and values to understand the motives of each other's behavior than for representatives of the same social group.

* * *

Monya Rabinovich comes home from school in tears: *"Mom, they called me a Jew face!"*
— *"Get used to it, son; you'll be a Jew's face at school, in the institute, in graduate school. But when you win the Nobel Prize, you will be called a great Russian scientist!"*

Different nations have oriented themselves to the creation of a political nation to varying degrees. For example, Germany from 1933 to 1945 focused on nationality; a German is primarily an ethnic German. An American, on the other hand, is people of different ethnic groups who are citizens of the United States. If all residents, regardless of gender, age, ethnic group or language, feel like full citizens, it creates many benefits for the country. The level of patriotism and cohesion increases, people do not feel alienated, work more actively and the level of happiness of the population as a whole increases. The US has benefited a lot from the emigration of Jews and some other groups of people persecuted by the Germans from Europe to the US (for example, 40% of Nobel Prize winners since its inception are from the US, and 35% of them are emigrants from other countries, including Jews). For Ukraine, in my opinion, it is also very important to form exactly a Ukrainian political nation. This is not obvious; representatives of ethnic nationalism insist on preferential treatment for the titular nation and do not consider non-Ukrainians

174   SOCIOLOGY IN JOKES

or Russian-speaking Ukrainians as fully-fledged citizens. However, the parties representing this point of view are marginal. In the last elections (2019), they gained less than 3% and did not get into the parliament.

"The great Russian painter Levitan was born into a poor Jewish family."

It's the same thing we were just discussing. During the quarantine period, everyone was actively sending each other all sorts of funny sayings, drawings, and videos. I was sent phrases from schoolchildren's essays, where among all sorts of nonsense (like "Mikhail Lermontov died in the Caucasus, but that is not why he loved it!" "Girls like Olga have long since bored Onegin, and Pushkin too") was this phrase. And why, in fact? The phrase is absolutely correct. Just like for example, "The outstanding Ukrainian and American pianist Vladimir Horowitz was born into a well-to-do Jewish family". It is simply a test for the degree of formation of a political nation. So far, this kind of phrase seems strange — a political nation has not been formed.

* * *

— *"Mikola, tell me honestly, do you like Jews?"*
— *"No, I don't."*
— *"Oh, so you're anti-Semitic?"*
— *"I'm not anti-Semitic. I like Jewish women."*

Question for you — can Mikola be considered an anti-Semite?

16. Attitudes of the Population of Ukraine Toward Russia and of the Population of Russia Toward Ukraine (2008–2022)

The results presented below were obtained from a joint project of the Kyiv International Institute of Sociology (KIIS) and the Russian public opinion research center Yuri Levada Analytical Center (the Levada Center[32]). The project started in 2008. KIIS) and the Levada Center had been studying the attitude of citizens toward their neighbors even before 2008, but in 2008, I proposed to Alexei Grazhdankin[33] to make these questions completely identical and synchronize our polls. He supported this idea, and since 2008, approximately every three months, KIIS introduced questions about the attitude of Ukrainians toward Russia into its omnibus and the Levada Center about the attitude of Russians toward Ukraine. A total of 37 polls were conducted in each country. About 2000 Ukrainians and about 1600 Russians were interviewed in each wave (over 70,000 Ukrainians and almost 60,000 Russians were interviewed in total during the project). The data are representative of the population of each country aged 18 and older. In Ukraine after 2014, the surveys were conducted only in the territory controlled by the Ukrainian government.

The attitude of Ukrainians toward Russia from 2008 (and perhaps earlier) until May 2014 can be called unrequited love (see figure 8).

---

32 The sociological organization Levada Center has been forcibly entered in the register of non-profit organizations in Russia that perform the functions of a foreign agent.

33 Alexei Ivanovich Grazhdankin (10.10.1959 – 07.07.2017) was a well-known Russian sociologist, and deputy director of the Levada Center

Figure 8. Dynamics of a good attitude of the Ukrainian population toward Russia and the Russian population toward Ukraine (2008–2021)

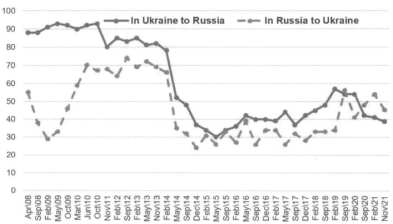

During this period, in different years, 80 to 90% of Ukrainians had a positive attitude toward Russia, while the share of Russians who favored Ukraine ranged from 30 to 70%. For example, after the Russo-Georgian war in August 2008, Russians' attitudes toward Ukraine deteriorated significantly; by January 2009, only 29% of Russians had a positive attitude toward Ukraine (62% were negative, 10% found it difficult to answer), while 90% of Ukrainians continued to have a positive attitude toward Russia.

What could it have to do with? I can only make hypotheses. The positive attitude of Ukrainians toward Russia from 2008 (and most likely earlier) until 2013 can be explained by a natural attitude toward a brotherly (in a good sense of the word[34]) nation, which in the historical life experience of most Ukrainians was still a nation of the same country. During this period, 15–20% of the Ukrainian population wanted to unite with Russia into one state, while the rest supported the independence of Ukraine, but 70% wanted special relations with Russia without visas and customs. In 2008, different political forces in Ukraine took different positions on the

---

[34] Nowadays, the word brotherly in relation to Russians has a negative connotation for Ukrainians (especially, 'elder brother').

Russian-Georgian war, and media owned by different oligarchs gave different assessments of the events, so the Ukrainian population as a whole did not change its positive attitude toward Russia.

Hypotheses in relation to the population of Russia are more difficult for me to formulate; they are based on consultations with my Moscow and St. Petersburg colleagues and consist of the following. Unlike Ukrainians, for Russians, for various reasons, belonging to the Great Country is valuable. Ukraine should be a part of this country; the process of the collapse of the USSR and the formation of independent states is not seen, in particular, as the creation of independent states—Ukraine and Russia—but as the separation of Ukraine from Russia. Since Ukrainians separated from Russia, they are in the minds of most Russians to some extent traitors. Hence, the attitude toward them since 1991 is worse than the attitude of Ukrainians toward Russians (and the attitude toward citizens, as will be seen below, dominates the attitude toward the country).

The second reason for the 'unrequited love' may be the purposeful work of the mass media, primarily television, which for Russians (as well as for Ukrainians) was the main source of information at that time. Opposition television channels were almost absent from the daily television viewing of the vast majority of Russians. In contrast, the remaining channels are controlled by a single center on many issues (including geopolitical ones). The well-known Russian journalist Yevgeny Kisilev, who worked in Russia until 2009 (he was the general director of NTV), said that the main principle of presenting news about Ukraine resembled the principle of talking about the dead ("one should talk about the dead either well or not at all"), but only in reverse: about Ukraine either badly or nothing.

The collapse of Ukrainians' positive attitude toward Russia began after Russia annexed Crimea and continued after the outbreak of war in Donbas; by March 2015, only 30% of Ukrainians had a positive attitude toward Russia. However, after the end of active hostilities, the positive attitude of Ukrainians toward Russia gradually recovered. At the same time, Russians' attitude toward

Ukraine after the annexation of Crimea also deteriorated (the minimum was 24%).

However, the most radical change in the attitude of Ukrainians toward Russia and Russians occurred after the outbreak of the full-scale war on February 24, 2022.

Figure 9. Dynamics of good and bad attitudes of the Ukrainian population toward Russia (2008–2022)

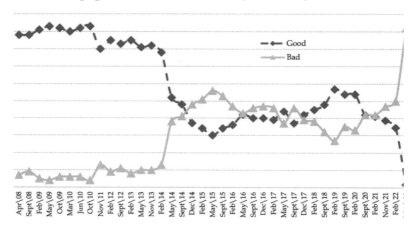

Figure 9 shows the same line of good attitude toward Russia as figure 8 (the percentage of Ukrainians who have a positive attitude toward Russia) but without the attitude of Russians toward Ukraine. In addition, the line of bad attitude toward Russia is added and two more points in February 2022 (we finished the survey a week before the war started) and May 2022. As we can see, the percentage of those who sympathize with Russia fell from 35% to 2%, and the percentage of those who have a negative attitude toward Russia increased from 50% to 92%.

Thus, the attitude of Ukrainians toward Russia changed from unshared love (90% of the population had a positive attitude toward Russia) to hatred (92% had a negative attitude). The first sharp drop occurred in 2014 after Russia seized Crimea and part of Donbas, and the second after the beginning of a full-scale war in 2022. Relations between the two nations have suffered irreparable damage that will affect the lives of both countries for decades to come.

Russia's attack on Ukraine was such a shock that it still does not fit well in the mind. Felix Krivin's miniature "Cain" comes to mind.[35]

* * *

Already at the dawn of history, half of humanity was destroyed: Cain killed Abel. Then, the days were peaceful. Cain proved to be a good steward: he quickly developed the land and populated it with abundant offspring. And to his children, who could not appreciate it all, Cain said many times: *"Cherish, children, this world for which your uncle died!"*

It is also surprising that the overwhelming majority of Russian citizens supported Russia's attack on Ukraine. How could it happen that a huge country, a multitude of intellectuals and cultural figures found themselves in 'united ranks'? It turns out that you do not have to have an "aggressive majority" to form full control over information, as was the case in the Soviet Union, not necessarily jam foreign radio or ban the Internet. It is enough to control the main sources of information, in particular television, to prevent competition in elections (Putin has been in power for 24 years) and kill the most active opposition journalists (e.g., Politkovskaya and Shchekochikhin). All candidates who could compete significantly with Putin were not allowed to run and were imprisoned (like Khodorkovsky and Navalny) or killed (like Nemtsov).

The war unleashed by Russia only adds to Putin's popularity. Chart 1 shows data from the Levada Center on approval of Putin's performance.

---

35   Krivin F. World History in Anecdotes. Uzhgorod: Bokor, 1993.

180 Sociology in Jokes

Figure 10. Approval of Putin's activity 1999–2022, %.

After a peak of 86%, which was during Russia's attack on Georgia in 2008, approval of Putin's activities gradually decreased. In November 2013, it dropped to 61% (i.e. by 25 percentage points). However, after Russia seized Crimea and the war in Donbas, it rose to 88%. After a while, the potential for "Crimean euphoria" dried up, and approval of activities dropped to about 60%. However, after the war started on February 24, 2022, it jumped again to 83%. Putin's regime is purposefully promoting a "revival of national pride" and Russia's great-power ambitions (63% of Russians have a favorable view of Stalin, one of humanity's greatest tyrants). One can argue about the real reasons for the war (the ones Putin cites do not stand up to any criticism), but one of the most compelling reasons is his desire to stay in power.

What about Russian anecdotes? What sentiments dominate them in connection with the war against Ukraine? Two periods can be distinguished: from 2014 to February 2022 (after the seizure of Crimea and the war in Donbas) and after the outbreak of full-scale war.

Anecdotes 2014–February 2022

> — *"Maria Ivanovna, what does your neighbor Lyusya do?"*
> — *"I see she doesn't seem to work anywhere, and she's always at home. Someone comes to her all the time: a Kazakh, a Russian, a Latvian, a Georgian."*
> — *"Oh, so she's a sex worker!"*
> — *"Sex workers ruined our country! And the poor girl collects as much as she can."*

Here it is, the idea of rebuilding a great country, taking hold of the masses.

* * *

I can't remember what was shown on the 'News' before the events in Ukraine.

* * *

A TV turned off is a better reflection of reality than a TV turned on.

* * *

Can ORT's information be trusted? Only when they transmit precise time signals.

* * *

— *"Direct line with President Putin. Thank you for your reply, Vladimir Vladimirovich!"*
— *"You haven't asked anything yet!"*
— *"We don't even have to ask! Just as you say now, that's what we thought!"*

* * *

— *"Direct line with President Putin Vladimir Vladimirovich! This is Nina Egorovna, 65 years old, from Kostroma! We have no hot water, the toilet is in the street, I pay half of my pension for housing and utilities, the hospital has been closed, and the ambulance has not come to us. It is difficult for us, but we are holding on. I have a question: why is Zelensky not contributing to the implementation of the Minsk agreements? Thank you, God bless you!"*

These anecdotes show that Ukraine occupies a large place in the propaganda work of the Russian leadership with its population; supporting the negative image of Ukraine requires constant work. These anecdotes about the media mainly play on two themes: the overpopulation of information about Ukraine and lies on TV.

Many anecdotes have to do with inflation, sanctions, and the economic situation.

* * *

182 SOCIOLOGY IN JOKES

The prime minister said he keeps his savings in rubles. Well, we hadn't overestimated him before, either ...

* * *

According to Russian intelligence, the US is to blame for the collapse of the ruble. Why doesn't Russia respond adequately and collapse the dollar? Why this nobility?

* * *

In this difficult time for Russia, I would like to write about love ... Love is also becoming more expensive ...

* * *

The worst payback for sins is when you are paid back in rubles.

* * *

With each passing day, the outgoing year gets better and better than the coming year.

Anecdotes after February 24, 2022

> *– "We've prepared troops, ammunition, reconnaissance ..."*
> *– "So, why don't you invade?"*
> *– "We can't figure out why it's necessary ..."*

The goals of the Special Military Operation (SMO), as Russia called the invasion of Ukraine, were unclear and constantly changing. It was about helping the Russian-speaking population of Donbas, then about denazification (ridding Ukraine of Nazis), then about demilitarization, then about fighting NATO in order to prevent Ukraine from joining NATO. Before 2014, as shown above, 80 to 90% of Ukrainians had a positive attitude toward Russia. Putin was more popular than any Ukrainian politician (for example, in 2009, 60% of the Ukrainian population had a positive attitude toward Putin, while only about 30% had a positive attitude toward the most popular Ukrainian politicians, Yulia Tymoshenko and Viktor Yanukovych). As for NATO, only 16% were in favor of joining

NATO; few Ukrainian politicians dared to insert such an unpopular item into their election program. However, after Russia seized Crimea, the number of NATO supporters rose to 48%, and after the start of the war in 2022 to 90%. Thus, Ukraine had no serious plans to join NATO; these plans emerged only after the Russian attack.

* * *

George Orwell came to Putin in a dream and asked: *"Well, did my warnings help you?"*
— *"What warnings? Weren't they manuals?"*

Putin congratulated Macron on France once again becoming the largest country by territory in Europe! Ukraine has an area of 603,628 km² and is the largest country in Europe. The next largest country in Europe is France, with a European territory of 547,030 km². By March 2022, Russia had captured 27% of Ukraine's territory, i.e., about 163,000 km². This is equal to the area of Hungary and Austria combined. The part of Ukraine's territory controlled by the Ukrainian government has become smaller than the area of France. In 2023, Ukraine managed to regain a significant part of its territory, but still, Russia occupies 18% of Ukraine's territory (108,600 km²) at the moment (May 2024).

* * *

If a cat is given a worming enema by a doctor, it is a special military operation for the doctor, a war for the worms, and cleansing for the cat.

Russian propaganda has managed to indoctrinate the majority of its population that Russia has the right to consider a neighboring country, whose independence it has officially recognized, as its sphere of influence and treat it like a master treats a cat.

The war, however, has become increasingly dominated by the Russians' view that the "cat" is already so infected that it is subject to destruction rather than cure.

* * *

> Putin is asked at a press conference: *"Tell me, why did the president of France receive you so warmly, talk to you a lot and see you off warmly, but the prime minister of Great Britain did not even give his hand?"*
> — *"Well, probably because Russian troops have never entered London before."*

Once, on a tourist bus in Spain before 2014, I found myself next to someone from Moscow. We got to talking ("What kind of outrage is going on there in your country? In Ukraine!"). They were very proud of the fact that Russia could destroy the entire world with nuclear weapons. "Fear is respect!" In this one, it was unexpected for a seemingly intelligent man with a college education to hear a speech imbued with imperial consciousness and pride. The dissemination of anecdotes such as the one above should make the patriot proud and nourish imperial feelings.

Roskomnadzor demanded that Russian mass media use the term SWO (special war operation) instead of the word war. On March 4, 2022, Russia passed a law establishing criminal liability for disseminating "obviously false information about the use of the Armed Forces of the Russian Federation, as well as for discrediting the Russian army". In exact accordance with George Orwell's world, war was forbidden to be called war, but only SWO. Violation of the law is punishable by serious prison terms.

* * *

> — *"What happened to you?"*
> — *"Can you imagine, I bought an apartment with Smart Home technology. While I was at work, the apartment moved out of Russia."*

After the war began, at least a million people left Russia (many because of disagreement with the policies of the country's leadership and many because of fear of mobilization).

* * *

> Russian soldier from captivity calls home. *"Mom! I'm a prisoner!"*
> — *"Where?"*
> — *"In Ukraine!"*
> — *"In Ukraine? Buy dollars!"*

ATTITUDES OF THE POPULATION   185

* * *

A Russian soldier calls his mother from Ukraine: "Mom, I'm in Ukraine. There's shooting, it's scary, I'm hiding in a house, there's a real meat grinder here."
— "Don't take a meat grinder, take a blender instead!"

There are many testimonies of how, in occupied towns and villages, Russian soldiers looted houses and took televisions, household appliances, and even toilet bowls.

17. Dynamics of the Level of Happiness and Its Determinants in Ukraine (2001–2017)

This section is co-authored with Julia Sakhno and Alisa Piaskovskaya.

The section considers the dynamics of subjective feelings of happiness by the population of Ukraine from 2001 to 2017. The factors affecting the level of happiness of the entire population aged 18 years and older are considered.

Measurements of happiness levels.

Sociologists and economists, who are increasingly interested in the concept of happiness, also use similar concepts — subjective wellbeing and life satisfaction. These are understood as emotional reactions to events, as well as judgments about the satisfaction and contentment of life. Subjective wellbeing is a broad concept that includes experiencing pleasant emotions, low levels of negative moods, and high life satisfaction. Although sociologists write about different understandings of happiness and its various aspects (see, for example, the interview "Sociology and Happiness" by sociologist and social philosopher Zygmunt Bauman, one of the best contemporary social thinkers[36]), we believe that the subjective feeling of happiness is one of the most adequate measures of subjective wellbeing. We agree with the definition by the American researcher Richard Layer, who understands happiness as "the feeling that you feel good, that you are happy with life and want to keep this feeling."

I prove the validity of this approach in my book *The Quality of Sociological Information*. We can consider all sociological attributes

---

36   "I have never found a better answer than to repeat Johann Wolfgang Goethe's answer to the question of whether he had a "happy life." As you probably now know, he answered that he had a happy life, although he could not recall a single happy week. The message in this statement is as easy to read as it is crucial to our understanding of the nature of happiness: namely, that happiness does not consist in freedom from trouble, but in facing trouble, fighting it, and overcoming it... " [2, c. 93]

188   SOCIOLOGY IN JOKES

from the point of view of what indicator (what information) can be the ultimate evidence of the validity of a sociological measurement. The analysis showed that from this point of view, there are five types of sociological attributes, and for measuring the level of satisfaction and the level of happiness, the most valid method is the respondent's self-assessment. "No objective indicators — both physiological (pulse, breathing, etc.) and social (high salary, good housing conditions, etc.) — testify, from the researcher's point of view, the complete wellbeing of the respondent, no observations and judgments of other people are the basis for asserting that a given person is satisfied if he or she denies it"[37]. The most valid information about respondent satisfaction is when it comes from the respondent, not when it is derived by researchers using other indicators in the process of analysis. Therefore, to measure happiness, we use the direct question "Do you consider yourself a happy person?" with answers "yes," "more likely yes than no," "both yes and no," "more likely no than yes," and "no."

To assess satisfaction with certain aspects of life, we use a question with a similar scale (e.g., "How satisfied or dissatisfied are you with your job?", "completely satisfied", "more satisfied than not", "as much as satisfied, as much dissatisfied", "more dissatisfied than satisfied", and "completely dissatisfied").

Data.

Since 2001, KIIS has been monitoring the feeling of happiness of the Ukrainian population, which allows us not only to track changes, but also to identify the factors affecting happiness. We use the data from our annual omnibus surveys (except for 2004) to describe the dynamics of the happiness level of the Ukrainian population (17 surveys). In each survey from 2001 to February 2014, 2000 respondents aged 18 and older living in 110 villages, urban-type settlements and cities in all regions of Ukraine and Crimea, as well as in Kyiv, were interviewed using a four-stage stochastic at each stage sampling method.

---

37   V.I.Paniotto. Quality of sociological information (methods of assessment and procedures for ensuring)- K.: Nauk. dumka, 1986. — 205 c

Data from 2001 through February 2014 are representative of the entire adult population of Ukraine. Surveys conducted since February 2014 are representative of the adult (18+) population of Ukraine, but without the occupied territories (without Crimea and parts of Donetsk and Luhansk oblasts that are not under Ukrainian control). The surveys after February 24, 2022, are also representative of the adult population of Ukraine, but without the territories occupied by Russia (in addition to Crimea and parts of Donetsk and Lugansk regions, other territories were added, some of which Ukraine has returned; as of May 2023, about 18% of Ukraine's territory is occupied).

As in many other surveys conducted in Ukraine after the annexation of Crimea and the occupation of part of Donbas, part of the dynamics of the results of sociological surveys is related to changes in people's views, thoughts and orientations, and part is related to changes in the territory of Ukraine, which is available for sociological surveys. For example, according to our polling data, the number of supporters of Ukraine's accession to the EU increased from 37 to 46%, i.e., by nine percentage points, from February 2013 (polling on the whole territory of Ukraine) to September 2016 (polling without occupied territories). However, if we compare comparable territories, i.e., if we remove Crimea and the occupied part of Donbas from the 2013 data, the growth for this period will be only six percentage points (from 42 to 48%). Thus, we can say that two-thirds of the dynamics are related to changes "in people's heads" and one-third to changes in the territory controlled by Ukraine. However, separating the components of the dynamics each time requires a separate analysis.

Dynamics of the level of happiness in Ukraine

The lower figure describes the dynamics of the level of happiness (percentage of respondents who said they were happy or completely happy).

Figure 11. Dynamics of the level of happiness of the Ukrainian population (2001-2023). A positive answer to the question of whether you consider yourself a happy person, in %.

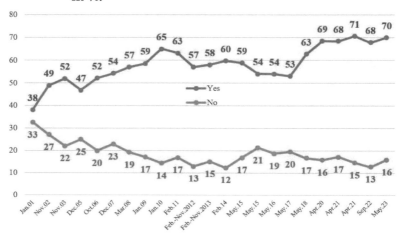

As we can see, the level of happiness (the number of happy people) increased from 2001 to 2010 from 38 to 65%. A possible reason for such a significant increase in the level of happiness could be the economic growth in Ukraine, which lasted from 2002 until the global economic crisis in 2008. Of course, this factor alone cannot explain the rise and fall of the level of happiness; economic difficulties in 2008 not only did not lead to a drop in the level of happiness but even to its growth up to 65% in 2010. Happiness levels are particularly paradoxical after the outbreak of the full-scale war in February 2022. Ukraine suffered and continues to suffer terrible losses. Tens of thousands of people were killed, and a third of the population was forced to abandon their homes and move to other parts of Ukraine and abroad (in May 2024, there were about six million refugees from Ukraine in Europe). People's incomes fell, and unemployment rose. In these conditions, we were even afraid to include a question about happiness in our questionnaire so as not to cause indignation among respondents—"What happiness are you talking about when there is a war?" However, it turned out that the indicator of happiness has not changed much. Before the war, 71% were happy. After the beginning of the war, 68%, in the second year of the war, 70%. Ukrainians, despite the sea of difficulties and challenges, find ways to adapt to the difficult reality and move forward. The results of our study seem surprising. How can people be happy when there is a terrible war going on? There are a few thoughts on this subject.

First, the mechanism of happiness formation is not simple and linear. For example, an increase in abundance does not always lead to an increase in the level of happiness. In the United States, from 1985 to 2005, the real income of the population doubled, but the level of happiness did not change. The point is that conditionally, the level of happiness can be represented as a fraction, in the numerator of which there is the level of achievements in the broad sense (the level of material security, creative work, favorite person, etc.), and in the denominator the level of claims (for example, what level of material security a person considers sufficient).

$$\text{Happiness} = \frac{\text{level of achievements}}{\text{level of aspirations (claims)}}$$

The level of claims is formed depending on the level of achievements of the respondent's reference group. As Layard, an American researcher of happiness, wrote, people do not become happier when their whole society becomes richer; people become happier when they become richer than their neighbors. In conditions of war, when millions of people suffer, the level of claims (the denominator of the happiness formula) is significantly reduced, and this compensates for the problems that people experience. For example, in 2021, when asked how much money per month you need to live normally, people, on average, stated 385 dollars, but after the war started, it was 240 dollars. Understandably, those in war zones become unhappy, but they are only a few percent of the total population. Decreasing the level of pretension (decreasing the denominator of the fraction) leads to increased satisfaction with what one has now. If your home is not destroyed, you and your family are safe, and your loved ones are with you, you are already happy.

192 SOCIOLOGY IN JOKES

Second, the level of happiness is influenced by many factors, such as children's behavior, intimate relationships, relationships with friends, etc. Although material living conditions have deteriorated significantly and many people suffer from separation from their families, some factors increase the level of happiness. The cohesion of society has significantly increased, regional divisions have decreased, the value of the state for the population of Ukraine has increased, mutual support has increased, and the socio-psychological climate has improved. All this increases the level of happiness of Ukrainians.

Factors of happiness in Ukraine

We study two types of factors affecting the level of happiness: first of all, factors related to reality, such as socio-demographic factors and the level of wellbeing. However, people's behavior is influenced not only by reality but also by their perception of that reality. For example, Vladimir Gimpelson and Daniel Treisman show that the perception of inequality is more important than inequality itself. Therefore, we also study the influence of the perception of the situation, in particular, the strength of the influence of satisfaction with different aspects of life (satisfaction with family, job, level of security, etc.) on the level of happiness.

A comparison of the situation before the annexation of Crimea and the war in Donbas with the current situation shows that the main factors positively affecting happiness are quite stable (except for the occupied territories). We present the results of a dependency analysis based on aggregated data from three surveys between 2015–2016 (Ukraine without occupied territories), a total of 5952 interviews.

Gender

Figure 12. Wellbeing and level of happiness (% of those who are happy and rather happy than unhappy)

	% happy/more likely to be happy
Men	57
Women	55
Total	56

Men are somewhat happier than women, but this is largely due to the fact that women in Ukraine live about ten years longer than men, and with age, the level of happiness in Ukraine decreases. In addition, due to longer life expectancy, there are more single people among older women, which also negatively affects the level of happiness.

Age

As can be seen from figure 13, the dependence of the level of happiness on age is almost linear and inversely proportional: the higher the age, the lower the level of happiness.

Figure 13. Age and level of happiness (% of those who are happy and more happy than unhappy)

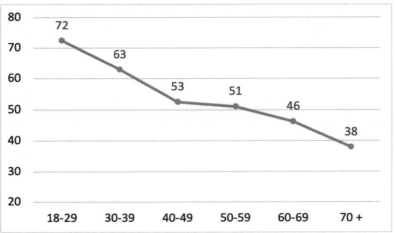

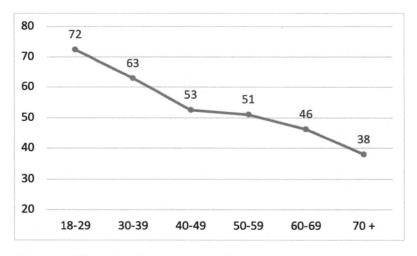

Ukraine differs significantly from the USA and many European countries in this respect. As Seppo Laaksonen writes, "Many studies have shown that the relationship between age and happiness is U-shaped in such a way that there is a minimum between 40 and 50 years. Young people are happier, then the stresses and problems of life increase, but after 50-60 years, when the mortgages for housing are paid, children are educated and health is not yet a concern, people enjoy life more and more. These dependencies are far from those characteristic of Ukraine. In Ukraine, the relationship between happiness and age is linear — the older the age, the lower the level of happiness, with each year of life reducing the level of happiness.

Education

The higher the education, the higher the level of happiness (a higher level of education also increases the material level and makes labor more creative).

Marital status

Married people are happier across all age groups, but especially those over 30.

Welfare

The higher the level of wealth, the higher the level of happiness; the relationship is almost linear.

Figure 14. Wellbeing and level of happiness (% of those who are happy and more happy than unhappy)

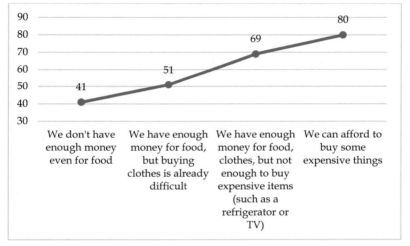

Health

Figure 15. Health and level of happiness (% of those who are happy and more happy than unhappy)

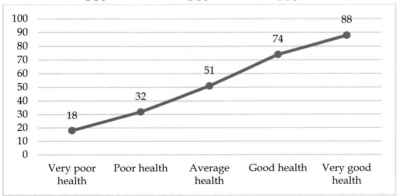

196   SOCIOLOGY IN JOKES

The level of happiness also depends on the level of health almost linearly; the higher the level of health, the higher the level of happiness. By the way, self-assessments of health and the level of material wellbeing are also closely related to each other (according to May 2017 data, the correlation coefficient is 0.395), which casts doubt on the theory that "no money can buy health". Rather, according to our data we can say that it is better to be rich and healthy than poor and sick.

Factors of happiness and value orientations of the population

As it has already been said, the level of happiness is influenced not only by the real situation but also by its perception; not only the level of material security or housing conditions is important, but also their perception as good or bad, i.e., satisfaction with them. We asked about respondents' satisfaction with various aspects of their life. Figure 16 shows the so-called regression coefficients, which show the impact of satisfaction with these or those aspects of life on the level of happiness (data from the KIIS survey conducted in May 2017, 2040 people aged 18 and older on the territory controlled by Ukraine were interviewed using the same methodology described in the "Data" section). All coefficients are significant at the 1% level.

Figure 16.   Relationship between satisfaction with different aspects of life and the level of happiness of respondents (May 2017)

How satisfied are you with the following aspects of your life (abbreviations for graphs in parentheses)	Regression co-efficient Beta*
Your personal (intimate) life? (Intimate life)	0,327
Your level of financial security? (Money)	0,288
Existing opportunity to influence what happens to you?	0,274
An opportunity to realize your abilities?	0,267
Existing opportunity to be independent (ouch)?	0,257
Your family (everyone you include in your family)? (Family)	0,246
Degree of Confidence in the Future? (Stability)	0,243

WAS ONLY ASKED OF PEOPLE WHO WORK: Is your job? (Work)	0,234
Existing opportunity for community involvement?	0,226
How do the people around you feel about you? (Society)	0,205
Your knowledge, experience, and skills?	0,190
Your behavior toward the people around you? (Social Behavior)	0,188
ASKED ONLY TO THOSE WHO HAVE CHILDREN: Behavior of your children, development of their personal qualities? (Children)	0,182
Your housing conditions? (Conditions)	0,170
Ensuring Ukraine's security? (Security)	0,131
Economic situation in Ukraine? (Economy)	0,114
State of the natural environment in the city (town), village? (Ecology)	0,045

As we can see, the two most significant factors of happiness of the Ukrainian population are satisfaction with sexual life (0.327) and the level of material security (0.288). Note that the relationship between self-assessment of one's financial situation ("what is not enough money") and the level of happiness is slightly lower (0.237), and between income (reported income) and the level of happiness is even lower (0.134). The next factors are the perception of freedom (the ability to control one's own life, realize one's abilities and be independent), family, degree of confidence in the future and work. It is surprising that children, which, according to existing stereotypes, should be one of the main factors of happiness, occupy only 13th place out of 17 factors. Perhaps children bring not only happiness but also worries and unhappiness.

Common methods of studying values (for example, the Schwartz methodology used in the European Social Survey) stipulate that the respondent should evaluate a set of values and say for each of them how important it is for them. The validity of such a measurement is questionable. First, respondents may answer these questions by choosing socially desirable and approved factors, and second, they may not realize what is important to them because of defense mechanisms. For example, a person who values money most of all but cannot get a job with a high level of payment will convince themselves that the most important thing is not money but the creative nature of labor and answer the questions in this way.

That is why KIIS uses Valery Khmelko's methodology in its research. Khmelko proves that the more time a person devotes to one or another activity (regardless of whether they like or dislike this activity), the more changes in satisfaction with this activity bring changes in life satisfaction. The greater the contribution of a particular aspect of life to life satisfaction in general, the more valuable that aspect of life is to the person. The methodology of values measurement developed by them provides for measuring satisfaction with individual aspects of life and life in general and calculating the relationship (paired regression coefficients) between the aspects of life and satisfaction with life in general (the level of happiness can also be used as an indicator of life satisfaction). This technique looks more valid than techniques based on self-assessments, but it can be calculated only for a certain population, a certain group of people, not for individuals. Interestingly, from this point of view, the hierarchy of factors influencing the level of happiness can be considered as the value structure of the social group under study.

* * *

A recent sociological survey by VTsIOM showed that three-quarters of Russians feel happy. And the rest do not drink.

* * *

At a doctor's appointment. *"What are you complaining about?"*
— *"Doctor, I feel awful. I don't feel like getting up in the morning, no mood all day, and I feel completely miserable."*
— *"Do you drink?"*
— *"No, I don't drink!"*
— *"My dear, so what do you want?"*

* * *

DYNAMICS OF THE LEVEL OF HAPPINESS   199

— "Fedya, what's the matter with you, you're thinking so deeply? What are you thinking about?"
— "Yes, Andrew, I think about the meaning of life, about happiness."
— "You're a good philosopher. I live my life without thinking. What do you think about happiness?"
— "Have you noticed how transient it is? You know, it's such a strange thing. You feel good, you feel perfectly happy, and you think you'll always be that way. But happiness is fleeting. It has a way of ending quickly."
— "Oh, my God, you're so right! I've noticed that, too. So what do we do?"
— "I think you should always have one more bottle than you planned!"

These three anecdotes speak to another happiness factor that was not in our surveys.

The parable of the clown

Yesterday, a sad man came to the psychologist's office and, sinking hopelessly into the reception chair, covered his face with his hands and cried. *"Doctor"*, he said, *"I seem to have lost the meaning of life. Nothing pleases me. I am constantly sad, lonely and often afraid. Friends and loved ones no longer give light to my soul as they used to. I feel bad, doctor ... And I can't even explain why. Maybe you can help me. I've heard you're the best doctor in this town."*
— "Alas, this kind of depression is a typical phenomenon of our century. With very high stress and a fast pace of life, our organism was formed in other conditions. You know, nowadays, of course, there are good tranquilizers. I could prescribe you a course. However, they are all chemicals. Let's try it without drugs first. Get some rest, a little wine, and some light reading. And one more thing", the doctor continued with a smile. *"You know, a circus has come to our town. It spreads its tent on the central square of the city and every evening gives performances. So, in the middle of the evening, a funny red-haired clown comes on stage. He has a gift! Looking at him, people start laughing, and their sorrows and griefs go away. All troubles disappear somewhere, and offenses are forgotten. He gives people laughter and happiness. Go to the circus tonight, and you will see that everything bad, everything that is eating you, will be swept away with a hand."*
— "That's very good, doctor," the sad man smiled sadly. *"But you know what the problem is ... That red-haired clown ... That's me."*

The level of a population's happiness is sometimes tried to be determined with the help of indirect characteristics. In my book *Quality of Sociological Information*, I try to prove that no objective

200 Sociology in Jokes

characteristics give adequate estimates. A millionaire's child who has everything, from our point of view, may suddenly commit suicide. The most adequate (valid, as sociologists say) assessment is only the assessment of the person. In July 2011, the UN General Assembly adopted a resolution calling on UN member countries to assess the happiness of their people and use it as a benchmark in the state policy. From time to time the "World Happiness Report" is published, where countries are ranked according to the Happiness Index. The index consists of six factors: GDP per capita, social support, life expectancy, freedom of citizens to make their own vital decisions, generosity and attitude to corruption. In the 2017 report, Russia ranked 49th in terms of happiness, and Ukraine only 132nd (while in response to the question "Do you consider yourself a happy person?" The percentage of happy people both here and there did not differ so radically). What is the reason for such a difference? The difference between Russia and Ukraine was largely determined by two factors: GDP per capita, which was 40% higher in Russia, and freedom of citizens, which was three times higher in Russia! If a country does not change its president, there are no opposition TV channels, and the main oppositionists are in jail, it is much easier to explain to people that they are free. "I know of no other country where man breathes so freely," as they sang in Stalin's time. The happiness index itself is interesting, but if we talk about the feeling of happiness in the generally accepted meaning, people's self-assessment is more adequate.

* * *

> — "Misha, why are you so glum and disgruntled? What's good? I heard you got a nice inheritance from your aunt two weeks ago, a house, a car."
> — "Well, I got it."
> — "And last week, they said you had a distant relative in America who died and left a lot of things behind. Is that true?"
> — "I mean, really."
> — "So, what are you unhappy about?"
> — "Well, this week, it's just like I've been cut off!"

As I have already said, happiness can be considered as a fraction, in the numerator of which is security, the degree of satisfaction of certain needs, and in the denominator is the level of claims, i.e., the idea of what you should have for a normal life. Having moved into a new apartment, a person is at first happy and feels completely satisfied with their new dwelling. Over time, they get used to it, and their friends also move to better housing and then their satisfaction drops. There must be some positive dynamics.

* * *

It is inherent in human beings to feel unhappy that there is someone happier.

* * *

Ivan's house burned down. You'd think I'd care! But it's still nice...

* * *

A person needs very little to be happy: to have someone they love and for their friend not to have one.

* * *

In my opinion, the greatest happiness for someone is to marry the person they want to marry. No, the greatest happiness is to marry the person the other one wanted to marry!

* * *

How much does someone need for complete happiness? Not much! But only so that others have even less.

* * *

St. Nicholas appeared to the peasant and told them that for their diligence in faith, he would give the peasant anything he wished. A manor, a herd, money, ask for whatever your soul desires. But there is one condition, the miracle worker added: *"I will give your neighbor twice as much!"*
"St. Nicholas", the peasant knelt down: *"Do me a favor and poke out my eye!"*

202   SOCIOLOGY IN JOKES

All these anecdotes and stories — albeit in an exaggerated form — describe the mechanism of forming the feeling of happiness. What friends and neighbors have creates an idea of what is normal and desirable forms the level of claim. And people are happy or not, depending on whether they get or do not get from life what corresponds to their level of claim.

A few more anecdotes about happiness that are understandable without commentary

* * *

For a horseshoe to bring happiness, you have to work like a horse!

* * *

If you've found a horseshoe for good luck, it means someone else has hoofed it.

* * *

What is Jewish happiness?
It is the brief interval between Jewish misfortunes.

* * *

"Aunt Mary!" the little niece exclaims as she runs to greet the guest. *"It's so great that you've come. Now we'll have complete happiness."*
— *"Why do you say that?"* Aunt Mary asks, *"Because when Dad found out you were coming, he said, 'The only thing we're missing for complete happiness is her!'"*

* * *

Happiness is the talent of appreciating what you have rather than what you don't have.

* * *

— *"Money is evil. It's not the money that makes you happy. He who is strong in spirit is rich ... "*
— *"What else can I do to make myself feel better before I get my paycheck?"*

DYNAMICS OF THE LEVEL OF HAPPINESS   203

* * *

I don't want to say happiness is about money, but at the moment, it could solve 90% of my problems .....

* * *

Interview with a billionaire: *"What is the greatest happiness that money has brought you?"*
– *"I guess my wife stopped cooking."*

* * *

Happiness is for wimps.

* * *

When you seek happiness, you gain experience. Sometimes you think this is happiness! But no, it's experience again.

* * *

A Russian, a French man and an American once argued about what happiness is.
American: *"Happiness is when you sit on the veranda of your villa, sip whiskey leisurely, look at the ocean and admire your yacht."*
French man: *"No, happiness when you are sitting in a cool restaurant, drinking Clicquot, there is one woman on your left, another on your right, soon you will all go up to the hotel room, and another woman is waiting for you."*
Russian: *"Yeah, well, is that really happiness? Happiness is when you leave your mansion in the morning, walk to the pool, and then suddenly two buses arrive: from one, riot police spill out, and from the other, tax officials. They surround you, throw you to the ground, and ask: Is this 8 Lesnaya Street? And you reply: No, it's 12."*

18. Self-Assessment of Health Status by the Population of Ukraine

The following is data from surveys that KIIS conducted from 1995 to 2023. Self-rated health is closely related to actual health and is a good indicator of the health status of a population. See, for example, Development and validation of the WHO self-assessment tool for health promotion in hospitals: results of a study in 38 hospitals in eight countries | Health Promotion International | Oxford Academic (oup.com)[38]. In addition, wellness also makes sense as a self-value, it is a component of quality of life, and it affects people's level of happiness. Kyiv International Institute of Sociology has been tracking the dynamics of self-assessment of health status by the Ukrainian population since 1995. The question we use is as follows:

How would you rate your health?

Very good	1
Good	2
Mediocre (neither good nor bad)	3
Bad	4
Very bad	5
HESITATE TO SAY / REFUSE TO ANSWER	6

Survey data show that from 1995 to 2002, about 20% (plus or minus 3%) thought they were in good health. Over the next few years, health improved. From 2005 to 2011, 31–36% thought they were in good health. From 2011 to 2014, health continued to improve, with a high of 45% in 2014. However, after Russia's attack on Ukraine and the outbreak of war in Donbas, the health of Ukrainians deteriorated, and the war resulted in many deaths and injuries, as well as displacement, which had a negative impact on people's physical and mental health. After the end of active warfare, health improved somewhat and reached 40% (this is the number of people considered to be in good health). However, then COVID-19 and the

---

38   https://academic.oup.com/heapro/article/25/2/221/561629

beginning of the large-scale war with Russia reduced the number of people with good health (according to their self-assessment) to 30%.

Figure 17. Dynamics of self-assessment of Ukrainians' health status, 1995–2023.

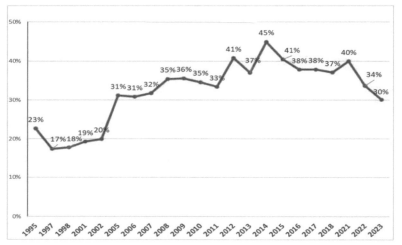

Theoretically, health status can be influenced by various factors, such as age, gender, wealth, place of residence or other factors.

We conducted a correlation analysis on a total sample of all surveys for all years (approximately 50,000 respondents). The correlation coefficient is an indicator that varies from -1 to +1 and shows how attribute B changes when attribute A changes. If attribute B (e.g., health) also increases when attribute A increases (e.g., age), the coefficient is positive and the closer it is to +1, the closer the relationship. The maximum connection +1 means that by knowing the value of attribute A in a person, we can accurately say the value of attribute B. In sociology, such connections practically do not happen. If the increase of attribute A leads to a decrease of attribute B, then the relationship is negative (for example, the more smokers, the lower the number of healthy people. The results of the correlation analysis showed that the most essential factor influencing the health of Ukrainians (at least, the self-assessment of health) is age). The correlation coefficient is -0.45 (the higher the age, the worse the health). The second place is occupied by financial status, and the correlation coefficient is 0.25 (the higher the income, the better the health). The influence of gender is much lower; men are healthier than women, and the coefficient is 0.15. Finally, the level of education also has some influence (a coefficient of 0.13), but this is because people with higher education are better paid.

Figure 18. The effect of age on self-assessed health of Ukrainians, 1995–2023.

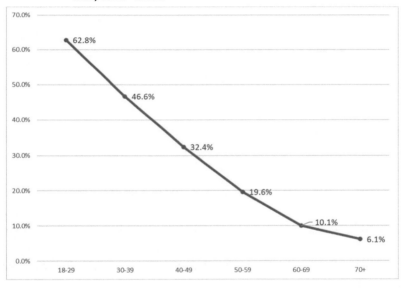

As we can see, the dependence is almost linear; the higher the age, the worse the health. Among young people, 63% had good health; among people over 70 years old, only 6%.

Figure 19. Impact of the level of wellbeing on Ukrainians' self-assessments of health, 1995–2023.

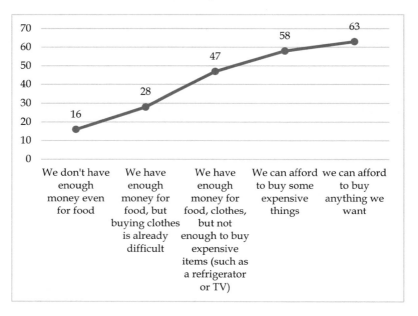

The dependence of health on the level of income is also almost linear; the higher the income, the better the health. Among people living in poverty, 16% had good health, among the rich, 63%. There is a proverb: "It is better to be rich and healthy than poor and sick". It turns out that it is closely related, and the rich are usually healthier than the poor.

Among men, 41% are in good health, while among women, 26%, i.e. 15 percentage points less. This is partly due to the fact that women in Ukraine live ten years longer than men. In 2019, for example, the average life expectancy for men was 67 years and for women 77 years. So there are more people over 70 among women, who, as we have seen, have poorer health. However, even if we consider the population under 60 years of age, this correlation remains.

* * *

In the doctor's office, a man sits, swaying and quietly praying: *"God, if only I turn out to be sick, if only I turn out to be sick."*
The woman sitting next to him was surprised. *"What do you mean, you want the doctors to find a disease? What good is that?"*
— *"You see, I feel so bad, so bad. If it turns out that I am sick, there is hope to be cured, but if I am healthy, there is no hope."*

Feeling well is important not only as an indicator of level of health but also in and of itself.

* * *

— *"Doctor, I understand everything. I know that no money can buy health."*
— *"Who told you such a stupid thing?"*

Of course, in this case, the doctor's statement was intended to incentivize the client to pay the doctor. However, as we have seen, higher salaries also lead to better health (healthier diet, lifestyle, higher treatment costs, etc.).

* * *

Usually, you get sick with one disease and are treated for one that the doctor knows well.

* * *

A woman is sleeping, and she dreams of Paris, where she is on a summer excursion. Everyone went to the opera, and she went for a walk through the evening streets and suddenly got lost and found herself in an unfamiliar part of the city. It's deserted. There's no one to ask for directions. Suddenly, she hears someone following her. She turned around to see a young man. She is frightened and quickens her step. So did he. She ran. He followed her. She skidded into a back alley, he followed her, and she went further. There is a grate; there is nowhere else to run. She turns around, and a young man runs up to her. The girl's heart sank: *"What do you want from me?"*
— *"Me? Madam, you want something from me, it's your dream."*

Apparently, the anecdote was invented in a country where Freud is firmly embedded in the culture. In our country, for many decades Freud was either banned altogether or was not in the mainstream

210   SOCIOLOGY IN JOKES

of medical tradition. I was once at a conference in St. Petersburg, Florida. I was looking for medicine in a pharmacy and asked the pharmacist some questions. My accent immediately gave me away, and she recognized me as a former compatriot. We got talking. It turned out that she was from Vinnytsia and worked as a psychologist, and there she retrained as a pharmacist. "You see, to work as a psychologist in the US, you need to know children's books; they are all built on Freud and his followers. Now that my daughter is five years old, I have read everything, but when I arrived, I didn't know anything.

* * *

A patient walks into a doctor's office and complains: *"Doctor, I have some very strange disease – I'm ignored by everyone."*
The doctor gets up, goes to the door, opens it and says: *"Next!"*

* * *

The worst consequence of a serious illness is the attitude of those around you.

* * *

You go to the doctor to hear what a disease is called and then read about it on the Internet.

* * *

Masha moved into a new apartment and, a few weeks later, invited a friend to visit her. They were walking through the courtyard, and two grandmothers were sitting on a bench in the courtyard. They passed by the women, and then one woman said to the other:
– *"There's the new neighbor. She's dressed up like a prostitute!"*
A friend overhears and says: *"Did you hear what she said? How can you let this happen? Let's go back and tell her what we think!"*
– *"Quiet, shut up! Let them say what they want, as long as they don't find out I'm a therapist!"*

On the one hand, doctors take the Hippocratic Oath and should help people. On the other hand, the Soviet system of free medicine had taught the older generation that a doctor's time was worthless. Older ladies would simply torture Masha with constant complaints and requests to look, listen, and give advice.

* * *

— *"Doctor, I'm so sick. I'd sell my soul to the devil to get rid of this damned disease!"*
— *"Well, father, why such heavy thoughts? We'll help you for free, and you can give it to God in peace."*

The Soviet system of free medicine is, in many ways, characteristic of modern Ukraine. Mikhail Zhvanetsky brilliantly described the difference between official and real norms:

* * *

You're out of luck. The specialist who is treating you is away, but there is a second one who is just as good.
It's better to arrange it in person, though you can also come with a referral.
We only have passes, but you can get through anyway.
The treatment is expensive, but you don't have to pay.
Nannies and nurses are usually paid, but they will still take care of you without money.
So I advise you to wait for the specialist, arrange things with the nanny, and pay.
But you don't have to do that if you're not interested in the result.
(Михаил Жванецкий. Мой портфель. Издательство Махаон-Україна, 2004. – 384 с.)

* * *

— *"You know, Syoma, the doctor, managed to cure me of sclerosis. He's just a magician, Syoma! I highly recommend him."*
— *"Thank you, Haim, but what's your doctor's name?"*
— *"What's the name? Um, what's the name ... Uh ... What's the name of the flower, the red flower with thorns? Rose. Yes, yes, that's right, Rosa! ... Rosa, my dear"*, Sema turns to his wife; *"what is the name of my doctor?"*

* * *

212   SOCIOLOGY IN JOKES

Pharmacy.
Customer: *"Do you have a pill for everything?"*
— *"Yes, here's a placebo."*
— *"Come on! 3000 hryvnia! It's so fucking expensive!"*
— *"But if it's cheap, everyone will recover, so how can I make money later?"*

* * *

Doctor to patient: *"What can I tell you? The situation is that you have a new life inside of you."*
— *"Doctor, what are you saying? How can it be? I'm a man!"*
— *"And worms don't give a shit if you're a man or a woman!"*

19. Dynamics of the Poverty Rate in Ukraine (1994–2020)

What poverty is and how to measure it is a topic about which many books are written. There are different concepts of poverty[39] and different ways of measuring it. We will consider only one approach, which is often used by the World Bank, where absolute and relative poverty are distinguished.

Relative poverty is when a person or family receives money substantially less than the median income in this country.

Absolute poverty is when a person lives on the edge of survival. This limit is determined as follows. First, medical experts calculate how many calories a person needs to live normally. Then, they select a basket of products typical for a given country (for example, for Ukraine, it does not include bananas but includes potatoes, buckwheat, chicken meat, lard, sugar and other common products).

The value of this 'consumer basket' is then calculated. People whose income is less than this value are considered poor[40]. Absolutely poor people are people who do not have enough money for food and basic necessities.

To determine how many poor people there are in Ukraine, representative surveys are conducted, and people's expenditures are determined. They also ask about income, but this is a sensitive question, and people do not answer it sincerely. But when they are asked several hundred questions about expenses (for example, "Did you buy cereals during the last two weeks? What kind? How much? At what price? And so on), they have less control over the amount they are told about. In 1995, KIIS, commissioned by the World

---

39 Kharchenko N. "Diversity of poverty aspects: an attempt of sociological analysis." *Scientific Notes of the National Academy of Sciences of Ukraine*: Political Science. Sociology. 1999. 38-49.

40 To be more precise, it is also added the minimum mandatory non-food expenses — payment for an apartment, electricity, communication, detergents, etc. In order to determine this minimum, they study how much money is spent on non-food expenses by those who have incomes at the level of the food basket — they certainly buy only the most necessary things.

Bank, conducted such a study and found that, on average, people's expenditures were about twice as much as the income they reported. However, such a study takes a lot of time, and the questionnaire lists hundreds of possible items. Therefore, KIIS uses a rough estimate of whether a person or household has enough money for food.

In general, all people lack money, but it is important what they lack money for. Some people do not have enough for food, and others cannot buy a TV channel or a factory in Odesa. People experiencing poverty spend more than 60% of their income on food. The higher this percentage, the poorer the person is. The lower this percentage, the wealthier the person is (by the way, the UN also assesses the poverty level of countries: a country where the share of food expenses in the total structure of expenditures is 60% or more is considered extremely poor, 50–60% — with a low standard of living, 40–50% — below average, 30–40% — average, 20–30% — above average and 20% or less, high).

Since 1994, KIIS has regularly asked in its surveys, "Which of these statements most closely matches your family's financial situation?" with possible options:

1. We don't even have enough money for food.
2. We have enough money for food, but it is already difficult to buy clothes.
3. We have enough money for food and clothes and can save some, but not enough to buy expensive things (like a refrigerator or TV).
4. We can afford to buy some expensive things (like a TV or refrigerator).
5. We can afford to buy anything we want to buy.

Experiments have shown that the answers to this question are correlated with more sophisticated techniques for assessing the well-being of the population; this question yields results close to the World Bank estimates.

During this time, KIIS has conducted hundreds of studies that have asked this question. Below is a figure showing the data from these surveys (as a rule, several such surveys were conducted during a year; the figure for each year shows the average percentage of those who do not have enough to eat for all the surveys conducted in that year). All these surveys in recent years were conducted by face-to-face interviews. In each of them, we interviewed 2000 respondents. The results are representative of the Ukrainian population aged 18+. The error does not exceed 3.2%. Since 2015, no surveys have been conducted in the occupied territories.

Figure 20. Percentage of people who answered that they do not have enough for food.

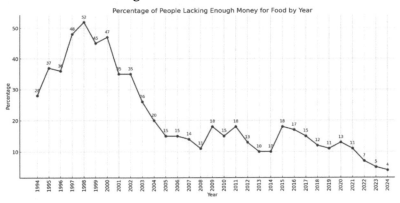

As can be seen from the figure, in the first years of Ukraine's independence the poverty rate was increasing. This may be due to the difficulties of transition to a market economy and the severing of economic ties with former Soviet countries. We recorded the maximum level of poverty in 1998 when 52% of the population said that they did not have enough even for food. During this period, many people (including highly qualified specialists — scientists, engineers, doctors) worked on their own and other people's homestead plots to provide themselves with food. In 10 years, from 1998 to 2008, the poverty rate fell from 52% to 11%, and this is one of the important achievements of Ukraine, which, for some reason, few people pay attention to. In 2008, after the onset of the global crisis, the poverty rate rose and then fell to 9%. After the start of the military conflict with Russia in 2014, there was again an increase in the poverty rate. Between 2014 and 2015, it almost doubled, but then in

216   SOCIOLOGY IN JOKES

2016, the situation stabilized. Until 2019, there was a decrease in the poverty rate to 11% (this is a high figure, but in all the years of Ukraine's existence as an independent state, it was lower only in 2008 before the financial crisis, in 2013 and in early 2014). Unfortunately, due to the pandemic, this level started to rise again, and in 2020 it was around 13%. Since mid-March 2020, a quarantine has been introduced in Ukraine, which, according to experts, politicians, and ordinary citizens, could affect the employment of the population and their incomes.

Most surprising is the dynamics of the poverty rate after the outbreak of a full-scale war with Russia. About 70% of the population experienced a decrease in income, and about 30% were unemployed. According to the World Bank, during the first two years of the war, the poverty rate increased from 5% to 24%. Objectively, the situation has deteriorated a lot. Meanwhile, subjective assessments of the level of prosperity, in particular the percentage of people who said that they do not have enough even for food, decreased from 11% to 4%. What is the reason for this? The situation here is the same as with happiness. Before the war, subjective estimates of poverty were higher than the World Bank's objective estimates because people said they did not have enough to eat, not when they experienced frequent hunger, but when they could not eat the way they used to. After the outbreak of the war, the level of claims decreased dramatically. People began to be satisfied with the food that was available to them and were happy that this food was available despite the war.

* * *

A married couple who are both teachers are discussing their budget. They barely have enough to eat but would like to save a little to save money for clothes and shoes. The wife thinks out loud: *"Seryozha, what if we borrow a little money every month and save it?"*

A very pathetic anecdote. The family is absolutely poor according to the World Bank's classification; there is not enough money even for food. To buy something expensive, such as furniture, a coat, or a car, is out of the question. The poor teacher who wants to borrow a little money is somehow very pitiful. I realize that this is just an anecdote, but it did not come from nothing.

* * *

Wife to husband: *"What kind of life is this? Work, lunch, laundry, I'm running around like a fool on a wheel."*
— *"You mean like a hamster on a wheel!"*
— *"No, I mean a fool on a wheel, at least a hamster has a fur coat!"*

* * *

Two former classmates met at the store.
— *"Petyka, is that you? I haven't seen you for a long time! Ten years, probably."*
— *"Hi, Seryoga. Yeah, probably all 15. What are you doing in our neighborhood?"*
— *"I'm on my way to buy some cognac. Do you live here?"*
— *"Yeah, two houses down. My wife gave me a list. I bought milk, cheese, bread, sausage. By the way, everything's gone up in price. You've noticed everything's going up. And rent, electricity, and transportation, absolutely everything is getting more expensive."*
— *"Well, don't exaggerate. Some things are getting cheaper."*
— *"Yeah? Well, what's getting cheaper? Name one thing."*
— *"Yachts have become cheaper this year."*

This is an anecdote on the same theme as the folk proverb -"To some, the soup is liquid, and to some, the pearls are small". Everyone lacks money, but what matters is what exactly they lack money for. We considered in the section on happiness and the mechanisms of its formation. Happiness is the ratio of the level of wellbeing to the level of claims, and it does not stand still but changes depending on its level and the level reached by friends and the nearest social environment.

This is not an anecdote but a story about an acquaintance of mine. Her name is Natasha. She married Carlos and went to Colombia. Once, on her next visit to Kyiv, we met, and she told me about life in Colombia. By the way, she told me that Carlos was poor. "How so," I said, surprised. "You told me what kind of house you have, even an estate, and you have servants; Carlos has a good job; he even helps his relatives. Why do you say he's poor?" She

218   SOCIOLOGY IN JOKES

answered: "If he were rich, he wouldn't have to work. As it is, he has to work for a living."

Now in our family, we sometimes remember poor Carlos and think how poor we are!

* * *

If everyone is poor, then who are the authorities stealing from?

* * *

The government has long known that it is easier to take money not from the rich, but from the poor. Of course, the poor have little money, but there are a lot of them.

The last two anecdotes explain why, in some countries with low incomes, there is such a large disparity between rich and poor. Conflictionist theories of inequality, particularly Marxism, prove that the ruling classes live off the enslaved majority. Capitalism itself has changed a lot since then, and the theories have moved away from simplification and become more complex. But often, in poorer countries, the rulers are particularly defiant because the mechanisms of democracy do not work. Moreover, this is the reason why the countries are poor.[41]

I once listened to an interview with one of our business people who was also a politician. The journalist asked why the government taxes small and medium-sized businesses and sets surprisingly low taxes for big businesses (unlike in many developed countries). They looked at the journalist as if they were a small child: "Do you want the cat not to catch mice? The deputies who came to power are nominated and supported by big business, their TV channels and direct funding. They form a government that protects the interests of the oligarchs; this government won't even look in the direction of big business when it comes to taxes! They take money wherever they can."

---

41   Acemoglu, D., Robinson, J. A. (2012). Why Nations Fail: The Origins of Power, Prosperity, and Poverty. New York: Random House.

DYNAMICS OF THE POVERTY RATE   219

* * *

– *"Vasya, did you marry Olga?"*
– *"No, she said I was poor."*
– *"But you have a rich uncle. Why didn't you tell her that?"*
– *"I did."*
– *"So what?"*
– *"She's my aunt now."*

* * *

According to the economic definition of poverty, if half or more of your real income is spent on food, you are poor. So what do you do? How do you get out of poverty? Eat less, obviously.

* * *

– *"All your life, you have had very modest earnings. How did you manage to build such a luxurious house?"*
– *"I did three years in prison for that."*

* * *

The rich and the poor are similar in that they lack money but differ in that the rich lack more.

* * *

–*"I can buy myself anything, absolutely anything I want!"*
– *"Are you that rich?"*
– *"No. I just don't want much."*

* * *

In other countries, whoever works is not poor. But here, only the poor work.

* * *

If you approach the fight against poverty with intelligence, you can not weakly get rich.

Incidentally, I was once at a conference on poverty studies held in Portoroz, Slovenia, in a five-star hotel by the sea. The conference

220 SOCIOLOGY IN JOKES

participants made a lot of jokes about this topic during dinner, that their research subject would never disappear and about the place the organizers had chosen for the poverty studies conference.

* * *

At the counter, a wealthy customer chooses: *"White wine to go with the salmon, red wine to go with venison on a spit, and cognac for Brazilian coffee."* When they were finally finished, the customer standing behind demanded with fury: *"And half a liter of vodka for the capelin in tomato!"*

Moiva in tomato—some of the cheapest canned food, was popular among alcoholics. However, the hero of the anecdote is not quite down yet. They have pride and a desire to show their exquisite taste.

* * *

A few signs that you are living below the poverty line.
1. You don't go on vacations; you go for walks.
2. You make your own mayonnaise.
3. You notice that salt has become more expensive.
4. Salt has become terribly expensive! 5. It's horrifying how much salt has become more expensive!
6. You know 50 recipes for dishes made from bread and sausage.
7. You have decided to give away your family table.
8. Your hamster is eating you out of house and home.
9. Fashion for your everyday clothes goes away and then comes back again.

In 2000, the Kyiv International Institute of Sociology participated in a study of allowances in Dnipropetrovsk Oblast. The idea was to make allowances targeted. Our study showed that allowances were given on formal grounds without taking into account family structure and real income. As a result, 55% of people with low incomes and 45% of the non-poor received benefits, i.e., 10% targeting. If it had been possible to increase targeting and to give benefits only to people experiencing poverty, their amounts would have increased significantly, and the fight against poverty would have been more successful. We had to find criteria by which the social worker could make a more accurate assessment of the family's situation through interviews and home visits. For this purpose, we developed a regression model that predicted the level of poverty according to the World Bank criteria. Interestingly, one of the most significant factors indicating poverty was the presence of a working sewing machine in the house.

* * *

December 31. Russia. A remote province. An ordinary average family, tormented by the financial crisis, is preparing for the New Year. The children are decorating the Christmas tree, and the mother is busy in the kitchen. The father is wary. *"Kids, do you hear that? There's some noise in the yard."*
— *"No, we don't."*
— *"I'm gonna go check it out."*
Dad takes a shotgun off the wall, goes out on the porch and shoots it in the air a couple times. He goes into the house and announces loudly: *"Children, someone was working there. I thought it was robbers, but it turned out to be a sleigh with Santa Claus and the Snow Maiden. As soon as I saw them, I started shouting that it was an accident and that I would not shoot again, but they turned the sleigh around and ran away. Sorry, but there will be no presents this year!"*

* * *

— *"Rabbi, I opened a factory. How much should I pay my workers?"*
— *"Exactly enough for them to go to work, not rallies."*

* * *

— *"Yesterday I bought new shoes, I spent my whole paycheck!"*
— *"Wow! What kind of shoes are those? Amedeo Testoni? Stefano Bemer? Louis Vuitton?"*
— *"No, the shoes are just regular, it's the paycheck that's like that!"*

Actually, people experiencing poverty spend most of their paychecks on food. The percentage of paychecks that is spent on food can even be a criterion for poverty. So it was a brave, courageous act.

20. Political Orientations of Cat and Dog Owners (2005)

I want to cite here our rather old press release from 2005 because it describes an important pattern in studying the influence of some social factors on others. I regularly use this example in lectures to students. But first, the press release.

On the eve of the Year of the Dog, our institute decided to find out how many dog owners live in Ukraine and whether they differ from other people, for example, from the owners of the original enemies of dogs — cats. In particular, what are the political orientations of dog owners and whether they differ from those of cat owners? The results turned out to be quite interesting (see the table):

Do you keep dogs or cats at home?

	%
Yeah, just the dogs	11
Yeah, just cats	17
Yeah, and cats and dogs	37
I'm not holding anyone back	35
Total	100.0

The first surprise is that there are a lot of dogs. As we can see, almost half of the Ukrainian population (11% + 37% = 48%) keeps dogs at home. If we take into account the adult population of Ukraine (about 38 million as of 2005) and the average family size (one dog is the property of all family members), it means that there are at least 13 million dogs at home. Dogs from Ukraine could easily populate a small European country — Switzerland, Greece or Denmark. And there are even more cats, at least 14 million.

The second surprise related to the relationship between dogs and cats. It is sometimes said that cats and dogs are class enemies. There is a perception that dog owners dislike cats and vice versa — cat owners dislike dogs. Our data do not give an estimate of the relationship between dogs and cats. Maybe there really is antagonism here. But as for owners, the situation is different.

It turns out that about 77% of dog owners also have cats! The first thing that comes to mind is that such a high percentage is due

224 SOCIOLOGY IN JOKES

to the villagers, they have both dogs and cats and chickens. Indeed, among rural residents, 81% of dog owners also have cats. However, it turns out that even among city dwellers, this proportion is 65%. So, cat and dog owners are, in most cases, the same people. And if most Ukrainian dogs live in the same family as cats, it is unlikely that there is strong antagonism between them. They are forced to establish if not friendly, then at least diplomatic relations with each other.

Let us consider the socio-political orientations of dog owners. We cannot say that they are radically different from the orientations of the general population or from the orientations of cat owners. However, there are still some statistically significant differences. Looking at party ratings (the percentage of those who are now ready to vote for these parties), the main trends remain. We see that there are significantly fewer supporters of the Party of Regions (V. Yanukovych) among dog owners than among cat owners. Dog owners are slightly more supportive of the Yulia Tymoshenko Bloc (BYuT) than cat owners and slightly less supportive of the Communists and Socialists, but this difference is insignificant. Not a single dog owner supports the Ukrainian People's Bloc (Kostenko-Plyushch), but this bloc has virtually no support from cat owners and the general population.

Rating	Which of these types of pets do you keep at home?		
	dogs	cats	Difference
Party of Regions of Ukraine (V. Yanukovych)	28.6	34.5	-5.9*
Yulia Tymoshenko Bloc	15.9	12.9	2.9
Yushchenko's 'Our Ukraine' bloc	12.3	12.9	-0.6
Volodymyr Lytvyn's People's Bloc	3.1	3.3	-0.2
Communist Party of Ukraine (Symonenko)	1.8	5.1	-3.3*
Socialist Party of Ukraine (Moroz)	1.8	3.9	-2.1
Civic Party "PORA" (V.Kaskiv)	0.9	1.2	-0.3
Social Democratic Party of Ukraine (United) (V. Medvedchuk)	0.4	0.9	-0.5
Ukrainian People's Bloc Kostenko-Plyushcha	0.0	0.6	-0.6

(*) Significant differences at the 5% level (i.e., differences exist with a probability of 0.95).

If we consider the degree of trust in political leaders, the pattern is similar — dog owners have less trust in Yanukovych and more trust in Tymoshenko than cat owners.

	Percentage of those who fully trust politicians among owners		
	dogs	cats	variance
Yanukovych	19.1	26.4	-7.3*
Yushchenko	16.4	17.1	-0.7
Timoshenko	21.7	15.3	6.4*
Simonenko	9.3	8.5	0.8
Frosty	9.3	9.9	-0.6

And why, exactly, are the orientations of dog owners different from cat owners or from the general population? There are no calls to keep cats at home in the program of Yanukovych's party, and Tymoshenko does not urge her followers to buy dogs. Even less likely is the hypothesis that cats harbor an inclination toward the Party of Regions and do campaigning work among their owners.

To answer this question, first consider the following table:

Ukraine as a whole			
Nationality	No dogs	There's a dog	Total
Ukrainian	48.2%	51.8%	100.0%
Russian	68.2%	31.8%	100.0%

As we can see, Ukrainians have more dogs than Russians. The difference is 20%. What can this be connected with? Maybe with the Ukrainian mentality? Most likely, no. The fact is that among Ukrainians, the share of rural residents is much higher. Therefore, the above differences can be explained by the fact that, as we already know, more dogs live in the village than in the city. To test this hypothesis, let us calculate the same table, only for the population of a large city.

Big City			
Nationality	No dog	There's a dog	Total
Ukrainian	74.8%	25.2%	100.0%
Russian	73.9%	26.1%	100.0%

226 SOCIOLOGY IN JOKES

As we can see, all differences have practically disappeared. The same situation with the political orientations of cat and dog owners. It is more difficult to keep dogs in the city than cats, so there are more rural residents among dog owners and more urban residents among cat owners.

Do you keep at home...	City	Village	
Dogs	43.4	56.6	100
Cats	51.4	48.6	100

When we talk about the differences between dog and cat owners, we are actually talking about the differences between rural and urban dwellers.

At the same time, very many differences between Ukrainians and Russians, which are found in our institute's studies, become insignificant when controlling for settlement type and region, i.e., when we compare people living in the same type of settlement or in the same region (more ethnic Ukrainians live in the west than in the east of Ukraine). Therefore, one should be very cautious about the results concerning the psychology or mentality of certain population groups — very often, all differences are explained by regional or settlement differentiation rather than by differences "in the heads" of people (in orientations, values, and culture). For once, the anecdotes below have nothing to do with the concept of false addiction outlined in this press release. I mention them simply because I like dogs and cats (I've had a cat in my house almost all my life; my wife and I wanted a dog, but we never made up our minds), and I also like anecdotes about these animals.

* * *

An inspector stops a car driven by a dog. *"Are you crazy?"* He shouts to the man sitting next to the driver to put a dog behind the wheel! *"How could you think of such a thing? That's the last thing we need on the highway! You're risking people's lives! You should have your license taken away for that!"*

"Let me get a word in edgewise", says the man calmly. *"This dog is not mine, and the car is not mine either. I was hitchhiking, and it stopped. What claims are against me?"*

POLITICAL ORIENTATIONS OF CAT AND DOG OWNERS 227

* * *

— *"Rabinovich, what's wrong with you? What is it? Are you crazy? Why did you bring that dog into the synagogue? Are dogs allowed in the synagogue?"*
— *"Rebbe, this is an unusual dog. You don't know how it sings! Listen to it for a few minutes."*
The Rebbe listened and was completely shocked.
— *"So yes, you're right, it's an amazing dog! He could be a cantor at our synagogue!"*
— *"That's what I told him. But he was adamant and said, 'No, I only want to be a dental technician!'"*

* * *

A man decided to get rid of his wife's cat, put it in a bag and drove it 10 km away. When he comes home, the cat is sitting contentedly on the porch. Next time, the man took the cat 15 km away, and again the same story. The man got angry, took the cat, sat in the car, and drove 15 km straight, 10 km left, and 12 km to the right. An hour later, the man calls his wife: *"Hello, the cat home?"*
— *"Yes, what's the matter?"*
— *"Put the bastard on the phone, I'm lost!"*

* * *

— *"Professor, what is childhood?"*
— *"Childhood, young man, is when your cat is older than you."*

* * *

The husband came home from fishing and rang the doorbell. His wife opens the door; he doesn't go in and asks in a whisper: *"Is the cat in the house?"*
— *"Don't worry, come on in. I ran to the store and got some fish, just in case."*

* * *

A call to the vet.
— *"Sergei Stepanovich, help! My cat is having problems again!"*
— *"Did he tear his ear again?"*
— *"No, no, it's fine, thank you very much. His ear isn't bothering him. But he's got fleas!"*

228 SOCIOLOGY IN JOKES

— "Listen, my dear, you got yourself a cat, and the cat got itself fleas. It's only fair! The freedom of choice of animals should be respected!"

* * *

Sanatorium, a lady on the phone: *"You are my favorite, the best. I miss you so much. I'll be there soon, don't miss me."*
On the next bench, a husband to his wife: *"What tenderness, what words, what words, you do not remember when you called me shafta."*
— "Yeah, dream on! She is probably telling her cat on the phone, and the husband holds the phone near the cat's ear."

* * *

At the vet's office: *"Does your cat have a good pedigree."*
— "She does? If she could talk, she wouldn't talk to you or me."

And on the same topic.

— "Neighbor, I'm in great distress! My cat ran away from me!"
— "Strange, when your wife left, I don't think you were that upset!"
— "But my wife didn't have three medals from the international exhibition!"

* * *

— "Comrade policeman! My wife left the house for a walk the day before yesterday and has not returned."
— "Describe her; how was she dressed? Well. A woman ... medium height ... wearing a dress. Yeah, she had a dog with her!
— "What dog? A Pomeranian Spitz, 5'4" at the withers, color red. Tail on the back. Round, small, dark eyes. Ears like a kitty cat, pointy. The breast is white, and on the back, there is a black strip of hair. The collar is brown leather."

* * *

My best friend is a cat. He'll never say, "Why do you eat at night?" He'll sit next to you and eat with you!

* * *

A cat walks into a cafe and orders coffee and a pastry. The waiter stands with his mouth open.
Cat: *"What?"*

– "Uh … You're a cat!"
– "Yeah". (chuckles).
– "And you're talking?!"
– "What news! Are you going to bring my order or not?"
– "Oh, I'm sorry, please, of course I will. I've just never seen it before."
– "I've never been here before. I'm looking for a job, I had an interview, so I thought I'd grab a coffee."
The waiter returns with the order and sees the cat scribbling something on a laptop keyboard.
– "Here's your coffee. I've been thinking … You're looking for a job, aren't you? It's just that my uncle is the circus director and he'd love to have you on a great salary!"
– "Circus?" Says the cat. *"Is that with the arena, the dome, the orchestra?"*
– "Yes!" (Laughs).
– "Clowns, acrobats, elephants?"
– "Yes!" (Laughs).
– "Cotton candy, popcorn, lollipops on a stick?"
– "Yeah, yeah, yeah, yeah!"
– "Sounds like fun! Why do they need a programmer?"

Application

Anecdotes That Say Something Not Only About Sociology but About Psychology, Philosophy, and More

Two anecdotes from S.B. Krymsky

I will not claim that the following two anecdotes are relevant to philosophy[42]. However, they are definitely relevant to philosophers since I heard them from Sergiy Borisovych Krymsky (1930–2010), one of the best Ukrainian philosophers. I say this not unsubstantiated, but on the basis of a survey of philosophers. One of the oldest educational institutions in Ukraine was the Kyiv-Mohyla Academy, which existed from 1701 to 1817. It was founded on the basis of the Kyiv Brotherhood School at Kyiv Brotherhood Epiphany Monastery, so its foundation is sometimes attributed to 1615.

In 1992, the Kyiv-Mohyla Academy was revived as a national university. The main initiator of its creation was Vyacheslav Bryukhovetsky, who became the first president of the National University, the Kyiv-Mohyla Academy." I and my friend Valeriy Khmelko (who, unfortunately, is no longer here) were also involved in the creation of the university. We created the Department of Sociology, and Valeriy Khmelko was the head of the department. Now (October 2024) I am still working as a professor of this department in parallel with my work at the Kyiv International Institute of Sociology. In 1992, Valeriy Khmelko and I helped Vyacheslav Bryukhovetsky to select teachers for this university and by snowball method, we conducted a survey: who is the best in Ukraine in six specialties, including philosophy. We addressed philosophers and asked who was the best, then we addressed those whom they

---

42 I highly recommend this book: Dan Klein, Thomas Cathcart. Plato once walked into a bar...Understanding philosophy through jokes. Alpina Publishers, 2017. 236.

232   SOCIOLOGY IN JOKES

named, etc. In the end, we polled about 50 philosophers, and the first three places, far ahead of the others, went to Miroslav Popovich, Sergei Krymsky, and Vilen Gorsky. I worked with Krymsky for about 20 years. He often came to our department and told us many things, including anecdotes. Here are two of them. I tried to find where he took them from in order to specify the surnames of the historical persons/heroes of the anecdotes and I couldn't. Therefore, the surnames are on my conscience.

* * *

France in the 17th century. A famous physician, Charles Bouvard, was visited by a noblewoman who was about to give birth. She gave birth to a boy and paid the physician a huge sum to keep the boy and bring him up properly. It happened that the next day, a noble courtier was brought to the physician in a semi-conscious state and with a swollen abdomen. The physician decided that it was a blockage of intestines, performed an operation, and when the patient regained consciousness — showed him the child. So and so, you were pregnant. The nobleman was horrified and begged the physician to keep the child, paying him a fabulous sum. Bouvard brought up the child as his son and, when he came of age, told him that he was the son of this nobleman and advised him to go to him: "*Little wonder, maybe he will be able to give you some patronage, set you up with someone at court.*"
The boy obtained a meeting with the nobleman, reminded him of all the circumstances and said: "*I decided to meet you because you are my father.*"
"*My son,*" replied the nobleman, "*I am not your father, but your unhappy mother! And your father is King Louis XIII.*"

* * *

In the time of Napoleon III, one of the most brilliant women of the era was the famous courtesan Countess Castiglione[43]. She was the dream

---

43   Countess Virginia Oldoini, known as Countess Castiglione (1837–1899), was one of the most prominent figures of the Napoleonic III era. Originally from Italy, she gained fame as a courtesan and had a significant influence on the social and political life of Paris. Using her beauty and charm, she established connections with powerful individuals, including Napoleon III, which allowed her to participate in political intrigues. She was also one of the first women to actively collaborate with photographers, creating striking images. The

of many. And so once the soldiers of the 3 Hussar Regiment, before going to war, discounted one franc each, collected many francs and cast lots. The lucky one got 1000 francs and managed to negotiate with the eccentric courtesan. He spent a delightful night. In the morning, talking to the soldier, the courtesan learned that he was a very poor man and that he was soon going to war. The story of a thousand soldiers who dreamed of her and the poor guy touched her. She jumped up, ran to the next room where the money was kept, came back and said: *"I will never take money from a man who goes to war and risks his life for his country. I'm giving you your money back."* And she solemnly returned one franc to the soldier.

A person's self-image, which is described by the concept of self-image or self-concept, usually agrees with the norms of decent, socially approved behavior available in society; negative characteristics are driven into the subconscious and are not realized. In their demonstrative behavior to others and in their own eyes, a person should look honest, kind, noble, etc. When they have a dodgy mind and use considerable intellectual effort to build such a system of coordinates in which their behavior always looks worthy, they find justification for any of their actions.

* * *

Krymsky also had a joking theory that some anecdotes could be told to men but could not be told to women. The fact is, explained Sergei Borisovich, that women have a too rich imagination, and what men say without thinking, women will imagine, so the joke becomes indecent. And here is an example of an anecdote that is decent for men and indecent for women. "A boy goes to his parents' bedroom in the morning, but the door is locked, and strange noises are coming from there. He looks through the keyhole for a while, then, shaking his head, returns to himself: And these people forbid me to pick my nose!"

---

photographs of Countess Castiglione, taken by Pierre-Louis Pierson, are considered important examples of early artistic photography and a symbol of the style of that time.

234   SOCIOLOGY IN JOKES

* * *

— *"Believe me, all troubles end someday."*
— *"Oh, you're an optimist!"*
— *"No, I'm a cemetery keeper."*

Don't you think that's a philosophical anecdote? Another philosophical anecdote is about the meaning of life.

* * *

A man dies and goes to heaven. He is met by the Apostle Peter.
Man: *"Sorry to bother you, but I have one question for you."*
Apostle: *"I'm listening."*
Man: *"I've lived quite a long life, but I never realized one thing. Tell me, what was the meaning of my life?"*
Apostle: *"Why do you need to know?"*
Man: *"You see, everything in the world is so interconnected that the life of each person is intertwined with the lives of other people and understanding the life of one person does not give anything for understanding the life of humanity as a whole. But I am still interested in the meaning of my life."*
Apostle: *"Alright. Do you remember in 1987, you were sent on a business trip to Odesa?"*
Man: *"Well, I remember, it was a year after Chornobyl."*
Apostle: *"And you also met fellow travelers."*
Man: *"I vaguely remember."*
Apostle: *"And you went together to wagon-restaurant."*
Man: *"Yes, I think so."*
Apostle: *"And at the next table sat a pretty woman."*
Man: *"Perhaps."*
Apostle: *"And she asked you to pass her the salt."*
Man: *"I don't remember that. So, what, I gave her salt?"*
Apostle: *"Yes, you gave it to her."*
Man: *"So?"*
Apostle: *"So there you go. That was the meaning of your life!"*

Ray Bradbury wrote a short story called *And Then There Was Thunder* (published in 1952). Time travelers went to the Mesozoic era. They were strictly warned that they should move on a special path. Any changes in the past can lead to unpredictable consequences in the future. The death of one cave dweller can lead to the death of a billion of their descendants. Crush a mouse with your foot, and you

APPLICATION 235

crush the pyramids. Maybe Rome will not appear on the seven hills, and Europe will remain a forest. One of the travelers accidentally crushed a butterfly. When they returned, they found that the spelling had changed, the composition of the air had changed, and a dictator had come to power. Because of this story, scientists studying complex systems have called it the "butterfly effect," one of the properties of complex, chaotic systems when a small impact on the system can have large and unpredictable consequences.

And this is on the verge of sociology and psychology — social psychology. The Abilene paradox is the idea that a group of people can make a decision contrary to the possible choices of any one member of the group due to each individual believing that their goals are contrary to those of the group and, therefore, not objecting.

The paradox was described by management science expert Jerry Harvey in The Abilene Paradox and other Meditations on Management[44]. The paradox is named after the anecdote described in this article:

* * *

One hot Texas evening, a certain family played dominoes on the porch until the father-in-law suggested a trip to Abilene for dinner. The wife said: "*Sounds good.*"
The husband, even though the trip promised to be long and hot, thought it would be a good idea to fit in with the others and pronounced: "*Sounds good to me; I hope your mom won't say no.*"
The mother-in-law replied, "*Sure, let's go! I haven't been to Abilene for a long time.*"
The road was hot, dusty and long. When they finally arrived at the cafeteria, the food was unpalatable. Four hours later, exhausted, they returned home. One of them said disingenuously, "*That wasn't a bad trip, was it?*".
The mother-in-law responded by saying that, in fact, she would have rather stayed home but went since the other three were enthusiastic.
The husband said: "*I would have been happy not to go anywhere. I only*

---

44 https://ru.wikipedia.org/wiki/%D0%9F%D0%B0%D1%80%D0%B0%D0%B4
%D0%BE%D0%BA%D1%81_%D0%90%D0%B1%D0%B8%D0%BB%D0%B8%
D0%BD%D0%B0#cite_note-1

236   Sociology in Jokes

went to give the others a treat."
The wife pronounced: *"And I went counting on the joy of the others. You'd have to be crazy to voluntarily go on that trip."*
The father-in-law replied that he had only suggested it because he thought the others were bored. So they sat there, stunned that they had gone on a trip that none of them wanted. Each of them would rather enjoy that day in peace.

* * *

An older woman selling radishes near the subway for 10 UAH per bundle was approached every day by the same young man who left her a tenner but did not take the radishes. And one day, when he once again left 10 UAH, she grabbed him by the hand.
Young man: *"I understand you are interested in why I leave you money but do not take anything?"*
— *"No, I'm not interested in that at all. It's just that from today, a radish costs 15 hryvnias."*

It seems to me that this anecdote tells us the truth about human nature. For some reason, I remembered in connection with this anecdote a saying about gratitude: If you helped a friend in trouble, they will surely remember you when they are in trouble again.[45]

And next anecdote relevant to pedagogy and psychology.

A boy at a store in the toy department asks his dad to buy a big and very expensive car to sit in. Dad tries to explain to him that they don't have that kind of money and there is no place to keep it in their apartment. And he's going to buy him this nice little car that looks so much like a real one. But the boy threw a tantrum, crying and screaming, and it was impossible to quiet him. A man came up to the father and said: *"If you would allow me, I could talk to him. I am a psychologist and have experience with children."*
— *"Yes, of course you can try it, thank you."*
The man came up to the boy, took him by the shoulder and said something quietly in his ear. The boy immediately quieted down and told his father that he was quite happy with the small car. The astonished dad rushed after the departing man.
— *"For God's sake, how did you do it? What did you say to him?"*

---

45   Arthur Bloch. Murphy's Laws. Chates' Rule.

APPLICATION   237

— *"Well, I don't think it would suit you to use it systematically."*
— *"Still, please, my wife and I are having a hard time with him."*
— *"I told him that if he squeaked one more time and kept demanding that car, I'd bite his ear off."*

This technique is non-pedagogical but, as it turns out, effective. It is similar to the anecdote about the blonde woman who was told that business class on the airplane does not fly to Miami (after a press release about xenophobia).

* * *

Odessa. A Jewish boy is brought to enroll in school. At the interview, he does well with counting and can already read. The principal decided to find out his general erudition. Asked if he knows any poems, he tells them. *"Does he know any songs?"* He sang. Then, the principal asks him how many seasons he knows. He thinks for a moment and confidently says: *"Six!"*
Director: *"And if you think about it?"*
— *"Well, think".* The child hangs back again for a moment — and says: *"I honestly don't remember anymore. Six!"*
The principal looks expressively at the boy's scarred mom, coughs, and sends them out the door. There, the distraught mom asks the boy: *"Well, Semochka, how could it be? What was that?! Don't you know how many seasons there are?"*
— *"Mommy ..."* — the son replies with tears in his eyes, — *"but I really only remember six 'Seasons'. 'Seasons' by Vivaldi, Haydn, Piazzola, Lussier, Tchaikovsky and Glazunov! ..... "*

This is not only an anecdote about pedagogy but about tests in general. In this case, after the question about songs, the boy thought that the questions about music were going on while the principal went on to another topic. Often, test questions and tasks are formulated in such a way that they allow different interpretations, and it is not known what the authors of the test meant. We teach sociology students to imagine different audiences when formulating survey questions, for example, a university professor, a janitor, and an older person from a village, and to think about whether they would understand the question in the same way.

Does anyone teach the test makers?

On the psychology of the terrorist.

> Gerasimus, turning to the captain of the Titanic: *"Can you give the doggie a ride?"*

If we ignore the fact that the deaf-mute Germasim spoke, there are two interpretations. One is that he, having a sensitive disposition and unable to bear the sight of the animal's suffering, simply took advantage of the circumstances to solve his problem painlessly. Another, and more severe, is that Gerasim contributed to the Titanic's destruction (he broke the radio, for example, or planted a bomb). Then Germasim has the psychology of a terrorist who plants a bomb on an airplane with 250 passengers in order to take out one of them.

* * *

> A woman comes to the tattoo parlor and says: *"I have a tattoo of Misha on my arm right here. Could you take it off, please?"*
> — *"Show me. Unfortunately, we can't."*
> — *"All right, well, put 'Misha the jerk' in there."*

A sad story that makes you wonder how many steps there are from love to hate. Sociology raises many questions about tattoos, such as why they are done at all, the social functions of tattoos, what types of tattoo cultures exist, whether prisoners' tattoos are different from teenagers' tattoos, etc. There are dissertations, books and articles written on the sociology of tattoos. For example, Lee Barron's *Tattoo Culture: Theory and Contemporary Contexts*[46]. Miliann Kang and Katherine Jones: *Why do People get Tattoos? Contexts,*[47] Baldaev's Tattoos of Prisoners[48]. Vorobyeva: Tattooing as an object of sociological research. Theoretical and methodological aspects[49]. Hambly's History of Tattooing. Marks on the body: rituals, beliefs, taboos[50].

---

46 Rowman & Littlefield International Limited, 2017 — Social Science — 189 pages
47 Vol. 6, Number 1, pps 42-47. ISSN 1536-5042, electronic ISSN 1537-6052. © 2007 by the American Sociological Association.
48 Moscow: Limbus Press, 2006
49 Dissertation for the degree of candidate of sociological sciences. 2018.
50 Moscow: Litres, 2015.

APPLICATION   239

* * *

> The mother comes home and complains to her daughter: *"You know, I've never been self-conscious about my age. But this time, I felt a bit offended. As I was walking through the yard, Petyka, the son of our neighbors, came running up to me and asked, 'Anna Dmitrievna, please tell me, when Lenin died, did you cry?'"*
> — *"Well, what about you?"*
> — *"What what?"*
> — *"Well, have you been crying?"*

It's about the psychology of time perception. Ten years of your life is a lot, especially when you are young. There is a big difference between a ten-year-old and a 20-year-old. But everything that was before we were born seems so old that it is much more difficult to figure out which events your parents can remember and which they cannot. For example, I remember when Stalin died (I was six years old at the time; there was mourning music playing all day long, and many people wore black armbands, which made an eerie impression). Why wouldn't I remember when Lenin died? But it was 30 years earlier, and I have to be 106 years old to remember it. There is a very interesting book by Eugene Golovakha and Alexander Kronik, *"Psychological Time of the Personality,"*[51] which explores various forms of experiencing the past, present and future, psychological age, and mechanisms of temporal self-regulation of the personality.

Here is another anecdote about the perception of age.

> "I went to the dentist, a nice older woman and her face seemed familiar. While she was treating me, I kept trying to remember where I had seen her before. Then I noticed a certificate on the wall — Elena Vasilievna Kuznetsova. Could she be my old classmate, Lenka Kuznetsova? But she looks so much older. When she finished, I cautiously asked:
> — *'Excuse me, but which school did you graduate from?'*
> — *'The 33rd Kyiv school.'*
> — *'In 1987?'*

---

51   Ripol Classic, 1984: 207.

240 Sociology in Jokes

> – *'Yes, how do you know?'*
> – *'You were in my class!'*
> – *'Sorry, I don't recognize you. What did you teach us?'"*

We age gradually, seeing ourselves in the mirror every day, and we only notice the changes through old photographs. When we see classmates we haven't met in many years, they seem older to us than we do to ourselves. By the way, about photographs. I enjoy taking portraits of my friends. When there are several people in a photo, everyone says, "Oh, everyone looks great except me." So I usually tell my subjects, "Photographs are like wine. They need to age. With time, photographs get better. Look at this photo in a few years—you'll see how it improves."

* * *

> – *"I don't get it, Lyusya. Why is my bottle of cognac half empty?!"*
> – *"Because you, Borya, are a pessimist!"*

The wife skillfully defended herself against the accusation. By the way, although we all know the definition of an optimist and a pessimist as a person who sees a glass as half full or half empty, respectively, this definition has not become an idiom. In Ukraine, for example, they do not say "a person for whom the glass is half-empty". In contrast, Americans say a glass-half-empty person or glass-half-full person instead of pessimist and optimist, maybe because the American expression is shorter.

Anecdotes about rabbis

Many Jewish anecdotes are a combination of philosophy, psychology and worldly wisdom. It is said that humor helped Jews to survive under difficult conditions of persecution by the authorities and anti-Semitism of the population of the countries where they lived. This may be true. It is also possible that these jokes were not composed by Jews but that they reflect stereotypes of Jews existing in society. For example, English humor is clearly not anecdotes created in Britain, but our anecdotes reflect our stereotypes of the British, for example.

London. The turn of the century. Her Majesty's Lord is sitting by the fireplace in the drawing room of his mansion, reading a newspaper and smoking an afternoon cigar. A servant announces the arrival of a guest, a good acquaintance of their family, and also an English lord. There is a ceremonious bowing, and then the new arrival asks: *"Pardon me, sir, is your wife at home?"*
— *"Yes, sir, of course, please!"*
The guest disappears into the depths of the mansion and reappears an hour later to bow and take his leave: *"You know, sir, your wife was colder today than ever before!"*
The master of the house, melancholically folding his newspaper: *"Yes, sir, she wasn't very temperamental when she was alive either!"*

The first hypothesis, that anecdotes about Jews are composed by Jews themselves, seems more plausible to me. Be that as it may, here are a few classic anecdotes that I believe are an integral part of our multinational culture.

* * *

A Jew comes to the Rabbe and says: *"Rebbe, my life is so hard. I have five kids, and we all live in a one-room apartment, no money, the house is filthy, kids are yelling and pushing, wet diapers are drying everywhere ... nightmare ..... Life is just unbearable. What am I supposed to do?"*
— *"All right"*, says the Rebbe, *"I'll help you, but you must do exactly as I tell you."*
— *"Sure, Rabbe, I'll do anything."*
— *"Take this money I'm lending you and buy yourself a goat."*
— *"What, a goat? Why? I can't take it to my apartment!"*
— *"Do you want to get better? Do as I say."*
He thought and thought and went and got a goat. Brought it home. A week later, he comes to the Rabbi with a complaint.
— *"Rebbe, I believed you, and what happened? Life got even worse! This goat in a one-room apartment with five kids shits everywhere, breaks everything, the kids ride on it, run amok, the stench is everywhere, it's just horrible!"*
— *"Everything is going great"*, said the Rebbe, *"now sell the goat."*
A week later, the Jew came to the Rebbe again, returned the borrowed money and thanked him for a long time.
— *"Oh my goodness, Rebbe, you saved me, I feel so good right now!"*

The goat method can be useful in many situations. It can be used in psychotherapy less straightforwardly. The psychologist can

242 SOCIOLOGY IN JOKES

describe imaginary situations and show that the situation is not as bad as the patient thinks but could be much worse. Unfortunately, this method is also adopted by bad people (and even governments), who first create problems for you and then help you solve the problems they created (not for free, of course).

* * *

Once upon a time, there was a Jew. And he had two chickens, one black and one white. It was Sunday, and he was expecting guests. So the Jew wondered which chicken he should slaughter. He went to the Rabbi. *"Hello, Rabbi. I have two chickens, one black and one white. I have guests coming tomorrow. Which chicken should I slaughter? If I kill the white one, then the black one will be bored."*
— *"Then, slaughter the black one."*
— *"But the white one will be bored."*
— *"Yes"*, said the smart Rebbe, *"your problem is more complicated than I thought, I need to think about it, come back tomorrow."*
The next day, the Jew came, and the Rebbe said to him: *"I've solved your problem. Cut the white chicken."*
— *"But then the black hen would be bored!"*
— *"To hell with her, let her!"*

* * *

Two Jews came to the Rabbi with a very difficult problem.
— *"What is the complexity of your problem?* — the Rabbi asked.
— *"As you know, Rabbi, a bathhouse is being built in our place. And, imagine, it's almost built. All that's left is to lay the floor. But there was a disagreement. The village is divided into two groups. One group believes that the floor boards should be planed; otherwise, you can splinter your foot. The other group thinks you can't gouge the floorboards, or you'll slip. People cannot agree among themselves, quarrels arise even within the same family, and disagreements can grow into serious conflict. So, what should we do — cut the boards or not cut them."*
— *"Yes, the problem is serious"*, said the Rabbi. *"Let me think about it."*
He sat for a while, pondering, and then he raised his finger and said solemnly. *"Here it is, the right solution: plane the boards, but lay them planed side down!"*

On the one hand, the anecdote can be seen as Jewish self-irony, like the anecdote about the white and black chicken, a self-mockery,

APPLICATION 243

where the 'wise' Rabbi appears as a man with a clever look who proclaims truisms or outright nonsense. However, the anecdote has another interpretation. The locality is threatened by conflict; people are pitted against each other, and a decision in favor of one side or the other could create displeasure on the other side rather than resolve the conflict. The Rabbi offered a Solomonic solution, a compromise that recognized both sides as right, and everyone won (except for the convenience of the bathhouse, of course).

* * *

A disciple came to the Rabbi.
— *"Rebbe! I have a desire to live forever! What should I do?"*
— *"Get married!"*
— *"So what? Will I live forever?"*
— *"No! But the desire will soon pass."*

* * *

A millionaire died, and relatives came to the Rebbe to solve a difficult problem they were facing: *"You see, Rebbe, our uncle, willed us to sell his bank and houses and bury all his savings with him. We did, but the money won't fit in the coffin. What should we do? Bury it separately?"*
— *"You idiots split the money and write him a check!"*

* * *

— *"Rabbi, my chickens are dying. What do I do?"*
— *"How do you feed them?"*
— *"Just the usual — I spread the grain, and they peck."*
— *"Oh, like this? No, that's wrong. Draw a circle about a meter in diameter and throw grain into it from the circle."*
The Jew drew a circle and began to throw grain into it, but the chickens still died. Then he again came to the Rebbe.
— *"What to do? Strange. Draw a square inside the circle and throw the grain exactly into that square."*
The Jew drew a square and began to throw grain into it, but the chickens still died. And he went again to the Rebbe.
— *"What to do, Rebbe."*
— *"Didn't the square help? Erase the square and draw a triangle inside the circle. Throw the grain only inside the triangle."*
The Jew never came to the Rebbe again, but a week later, he met him

by chance in the street.
— *"So, how are you doing with the chickens?"*
— *"Bad Rebbe, all the chickens are dead."*
— *"Oh, my God, what a shame! And I had so many more ideas!"*

This is a very useful anecdote that I often remember myself and, sometimes, remind my employees in different situations. For example, when there is a tight deadline, and there is no time to test ideas by trial and error.

* * *

Two Jews meet on the street.
— *"Oy vey! Are you, by any chance, Aron Rabinovich's son?"*
— *"Yes, I am. But it's the first time I've heard that by chance."*

* * *

In a small Ukrainian village, old Rabinovich fell ill and invited a rabbi to discuss his will just in case. He bequeaths his entire fortune to his two sons. He leaves just the tavern to the intelligent and hardworking Iza and everything else to the dissolute and perpetually drunk Yasha. Rebbe tries to instruct him on the path of wisdom: *"Of course, it's none of my business. It's your money and your sons. But Yasha will drink all your wealth in six months!"*
— *"Right! But where will he drink it if there's only one tavern in town?!"*

* * *

A large factory owner comes to the Rabbi.
— *"Rabbi, I have a problem. The factory brings only losses, there is no discipline, productivity is at zero, debts are growing, and taxes are so high. What to do?"*
— *"Take the Talmud, put it under your armpit and go around the factory twice a day."*
A month later, the joyful factory owner comes to the rabbi and says: *"Great, stealing at work has stopped, idlers have been fired, productivity has increased, debts are over! What's the secret?"*
— *"A manager must constantly be in his factory and look into everything that is going on."*
— *"I understand that. What's the Talmud for?"*
— *"For solidity."*

* * *

An Israeli newspaper conducted a poll: *What is the difference between politicians and thieves?*

One answer caught the attention of the editorial board: "*Dear Editorial Board, I have thought a lot about your question and have come to the conclusion that the difference between politicians and thieves is that we choose the former, and the latter choose us.*"

To which the editorial board replied: "*Dear reader, we decided to reward you with a year's subscription to our newspaper for your brilliant answer. Because you were the only one who found the difference between politicians and thieves*".

* * *

— "*You have an ad here for kosher condoms. Can you tell me how they differ from regular condoms?*"

— "*They're circumcised.*"

* * *

Two Jews came to the rabbi to settle a dispute. Rebbe said to one of them," *I lent money to my neighbor, and yesterday was the due date, and he won't pay me back. I demand that he pay me back immediately. Am I right?*"

— "*Yes, you are right,*" said the Rebbe.

— "*But listen, Rabbi, I borrowed the money to grow the crops. I need to hire workers to harvest them quickly and sell them; otherwise, everything will be lost. I need another week to do all this and pay back the money. He's a wealthy man, he doesn't need the money now, he's demanding it out of principle. If I give him the money now, I'll be broke. I only have to wait a week. Am I wrong?*"

— "*Yes, you are right,*" said the Rebbe.

The Rebbe's wife heard all this and looked at him in surprise. "*Look, these people are saying completely opposite things. You told both of them he's right and the other, that's wrong!*"

— "*And you're right too,*" the Rebbe answered her.

Interestingly, this anecdote is also recalled by the real-life Rabbi Adin Steinzaltz when answering Michael Gorelik's questions. Here is the beginning of this dialogue, in which Adin Steinzaltz explains that one does not necessarily need to know the truth in order to solve a problem.

246 SOCIOLOGY IN JOKES

* * *

> The Talmud tells a story like this: *Two men and a woman come to court. The first man claims that the woman is his wife, and the second man is his servant. The second man accuses the first man of lying. He claims that the woman is his wife and the (lying) man is his servant. The woman says that both men are lying: in fact, they are both her servants, and she is not married at all.*

So, how to investigate? Unfortunately, it is impossible, because both witnesses and documents are missing. King Solomon conducted an investigative experiment in such cases, and Daniel caught false witnesses in contradictions. They had an opportunity to establish the truth—our history does not have such an opportunity. The example of this situation discusses the general problem of whether anything can be done when the truth is fundamentally inaccessible. The sages of the Talmud answer this question in the affirmative. The judge makes a decision based on the assumption that each of the three is telling the truth. How can you assume this when their testimony contradicts each other? Assume, as you know, you can assume anything. In mathematics, there is a way of proving when some assumption is made.

Does the first man have a wife and a servant? The court believes him and requires him to let the servant go free and grant a divorce to the wife. The same is true of the second man. Does the unmarried woman have two servants? The court believes her, confirms her status as an unmarried woman, and demands that the servants be set free. Everyone is free. No one owes anyone anything. If I ask the judge where the truth lies, they say, "I don't know, and probably never will. I don't have the tools to find out, but you don't have to know the truth to solve the problem." Yes, but if anyone involved in this litigation tells the truth, they suffer because of an unjust judgment: the woman loses her servant, and the man loses his wife and servant. Of course, with this decision, someone may suffer (if all three are lying, no one will suffer), but with another decision, someone may suffer much more.

Minimization of damage. An example from game theory. You know, it reminds me of an old joke. Two disputants come to the

Rabbi. The first one states his opinion. The Rabbi says, "You're right. The second one states an opinion inconsistent with the first one. The Rabbi says, "You're right. Then the third one says: How can it be so? It's impossible! They can't be right! The Rabbi says: and you are right, too.

This anecdote has Talmudic roots, but there is a big difference between our story and this anecdote. It's not like the judge tells anyone that they are right. The judge doesn't know the truth, doesn't hope to know it, and doesn't set such a goal. They say "suppose", and the assumption that everyone is right is conditional and instrumental; the task is pragmatic and utilitarian: what to do? Can this question be answered without knowing the truth? The judge believes that not only can but must[52].

---

52 See http://www.judaicaru.org/navigator/steinsaltz_interviews_frame.html

Independent Work

Home Task for Readers

I've been working on the book for a few years now whenever I get some free time. Below are some more anecdotes that interested me and that I was going to comment on. But the work on the book has already been delayed, so I decided to leave these anecdotes to the readers to decide for themselves where there is philosophy, psychology or life wisdom. And, perhaps, you are already tired of these comments, then you can see what anecdotes I like—maybe you will like them too.

* * *

Boss meets a new chauffeur:
— *"What is your last name?"*
— *"My name is Lyosha."*
— *"I asked for your surname. I can't stand palibracy. I'm used to addressing chauffeurs by their family name!"*
— *"I think that you will be uncomfortable with my last name."*
The boss started to get angry and said:
— *"I'm not interested in what you think!"*
— *"All right, my last name is Darling."*
A confused pause.
— *"Okay, Lyosha, let's go!"*

* * *

A politician speaks at a rally: *"If I become president, I guarantee you that in five years, we will live better than most in Europe!"*
A shout from the crowd: *"What will happen to them?"*

* * *

— *"Lonya, remember when you were sick, I made you some soup?"*
— *"No, Raya, you made soup first, and then I felt bad!"*

* * *

— *"Seryoga, you never got married?"*
— *"For what? I have two sisters to care for me, feed me, and cater to me."*
— *"But I hope you don't sleep with them, that's a big sin."*

252   SOCIOLOGY IN JOKES

— *"What does sin have to do with it? They're not my sisters!"*

* * *

The groom meets his future father-in-law.
— *"So tell me how you envision your life together and whether you can provide for yourselves."*
— *"I have good prospects. I graduated from school with a gold medal and university with a red diploma, and I am used to doing everything to the best of my ability. I have only been working for a year, but I have already been promoted. I don't drink, I don't smoke, I don't look at women."*
— *"That's it, you're not marrying my daughter, don't dream of it."*
— *"How, why, what's wrong?"*
— *"Look, I've got enough problems with my wife. I don't need her making an example of you!"*

* * *

Before the wedding, a mom gives her daughter some final instructions. *"Olga, listen carefully, I won't repeat myself. It is very important to follow your husband's mood and try to prevent possible quarrels. If he is in a bad mood, try to be especially sensitive and affectionate. If there is a quarrel never tell me anything!"*
— *"Why, Mom, what if I need advice?"*
— *"No way! You see, you'll forgive him later, but I'll never forgive him!"*

* * *

Vitya and Nadya sent their names to a compatibility test, and they got a negative answer. They decided to divorce, although their children, grandchildren and great-grandchildren dissuaded them.

* * *

— *"When my wife left me, there was a tremendous feeling of emptiness in the house."*
— *"What was it like with her?"*
— *"Well, we had some furniture in the apartment."*

* * *

This was back in the days when there were still landlines but no cell phones. A husband felt sick and didn't go to work. The phone rang. He picked up the phone, listened for a while and said: *"Thanks, but*

HOME TASK FOR READERS   253

I'm not going anywhere today. What about tomorrow? But they hung up on me."
Wife: "Who was it?"
— "A weatherman, I guess. He said everything was fine, the horizon was clear, and you could leave! I asked about tomorrow, and he hung up. What kind of service is this, I wonder?"

* * *

Teacher: "Vovochka, I'm warning you for the last time. If you disrupt my lesson again, I'll tell your parents that you have a great talent for music!"

* * *

— "My wife left me for my best friend."
— "May I? But it's me, isn't it, your best friend?"
— "He is now."

* * *

Conscription. Out of three friends, two have entered a university, they are not taken away, and the third has not entered, he is working and has received a summons. And these two are discussing the situation.
— "It's a pity that Andryukha didn't get in. Now he's in the army. And he is having an affair with Galya. We don't know whether she'll wait for him or not."
— "I don't think she will."
— "Why is that?"
— "She didn't always wait for him to come home from work!"

* * *

An elderly gentleman tells me. "It took me forty years to realize I had no talent."
— "And what did you do?"
— "It was too late to do anything. By then, I had already become a famous artist."

And a similar anecdote

A guy is learning to play the guitar. After a few lessons, he disappears and never shows up. Six months passed, and the teacher ran into him on the street.

250 SOCIOLOGY IN JOKES

— *"Master, it's so good to see you! I'm sorry I've been away. I'm going through a difficult time in my life."*
— *"Why'd you drop out, you didn't like it?"*
— *"What a teacher you are, I owe you everything I know, I really need lessons! But there's no time at all — concerts, tours, and studio recordings. I'm only here for two days. I'm leaving again tomorrow ..."*

* * *

A male director, old and famous, is about to marry a young actor. They captivate him with their purity, innocence and freshness. He asks:
— *"Am I the first person you've ever loved?"*
— *"Of course, you're the first! Why do men always ask the same thing?"*

* * *

— *"You know, there's probably no other idiot like me. I lost my cell phone, so I turned on the flashlight on my phone and spent half an hour looking for it, looking in every crevice and under the sofa."*
— *"Well, where was it?"*

* * *

The daughter came home, and her father immediately talks to her. *"I want to have a serious talk with you. I saw you having sex with someone in the car. Explain to me what this is all about. Are you in a serious relationship? Who was it?"*
— *"Dad, where was it, and what color was the car?"*

* * *

I contend that no — literally no — moral satisfaction compares to immoral satisfaction.

* * *

One girlfriend tells the other. *"My husband went to take a shower and I decided to check his phone in the meantime. I found a 'Free Sex' contact. Can you believe it?"*
— *"No way! What did you say to him?"*
— *"I decided to call the number first. I dialed the phone, my cell phone rang, and I almost fell off my chair. What a parasite."*

HOME TASK FOR READERS 255

* * *

— *"Are you straight or gay?"*
— *"What?"*
— *"Well, are you in the sexual majority or sexual minority?"*
— *"I am a sexual loneliness."*

* * *

— *"Can you tell me how to get to the center?"*
— *"Easy! Drive behind any empty tow truck!"*

* * *

Two cops call homicide: *"Homicide, hello, this is Sergeant Smith and Staff Sergeant Martynov."*
— *"What have you got?"*
— *"Murder, a 38-year-old man, his wife stabbed him six times for stepping on a wet, freshly mopped floor."*
— *"You apprehend his wife?"*
— *"No, the floor is still wet ..."*

* * *

A gynecologist is a pediatrician looking into the future.

* * *

As a child, I heard many fables, but only now do I realize the essence of the fable "The Crow and the Fox." Only by losing the cheese can you gain freedom of speech.

* * *

— *"Doctor, my God, is it true? Am I barren?"*
— *"Unfortunately, there's no doubt about it. Moreover, it is congenital infertility."*
— *"Medicine is powerless! How awful! And how am I going to tell my wife that both our children are not mine?"*

The following two anecdotes are about electoral sociology.

Elections, polling station. *"I'm sorry. Could you please see if my wife has already voted?"*
— *"What's your last name? Nechiporenko."*

256 SOCIOLOGY IN JOKES

— *"Let me see. Yes, she voted. Here's the signature. You live with her, why don't you know?"*
— *"You see, my wife died 12 years ago, but she still comes to vote. And I can't meet her."*

* * *

A week before the local council elections, a tough candidate for deputy comes to the village in a jeep. They organize a meeting with the villagers for him so that he can help them in some way. The candidate stood up and approached the podium.

— *"Dear residents of Malye Lokhvitsy village! I have come to listen to you and solve some of your problems even before the elections, the rest I will solve if I am elected as the head of the OTG. So, what are your problems?"*
— *"Let me begin, said the township council member presiding over the meeting. We have two main problems. The first one is that our polyclinic has an acute shortage of doctors. There is absolutely no one left, only paramedics and nurses. The second problem ..."*
— *"Wait, I'm used to solving problems right away. Hold on a second, please!"*

The candidate stepped back a few meters, pulled out his cell phone and started talking vigorously. After a few minutes, he returned to the podium.

— *"Your problem is solved; there's an election next Sunday, and a wonderful internist with 30 years of experience is coming to your workplace on Monday. What's the other problem?"*

The second problem is the total lack of cell phone service, no operator, and absolutely no connectivity.

Here is an anecdote from the wonderful book Intellectual Anecdotes Collected and Commented[53]:

A lord comes to visit a baron, and the baron allows him to hunt pheasants on his property. The lord walks through the forest, sees a pheasant, raises his rifle, and then the baron's servant whispers to him: *"Don't shoot, it's Alexander! The Baron never shoots Alexander!"*

They go on, and they see another pheasant. Again, the servant whispers: *"Don't shoot, it's Delia! The Baroness's favorite pheasant. The Baron never shoots Delia!"*

They go further and see a third pheasant. The lord didn't even raise his rifle, but the servant said: *"You can shoot, it's Victor! Mr. Baron always shoots at Victor."*

---

53 By Boris Akunin. Moscow: Zakharov, 2021.

UKRAINIAN VOICES

Collected by Andreas Umland

1 *Mychailo Wynnyckyj*
Ukraine's Maidan, Russia's War
A Chronicle and Analysis of the Revolution of Dignity
With a foreword by Serhii Plokhy
ISBN 978-3-8382-1327-9

2 *Olexander Hryb*
Understanding Contemporary Ukrainian and Russian Nationalism
The Post-Soviet Cossack Revival and Ukraine's National Security
With a foreword by Vitali Vitaliev
ISBN 978-3-8382-1377-4

3 *Marko Bojcun*
Towards a Political Economy of Ukraine
Selected Essays 1990–2015
With a foreword by John-Paul Himka
ISBN 978-3-8382-1368-2

4 *Volodymyr Yermolenko (ed.)*
Ukraine in Histories and Stories
Essays by Ukrainian Intellectuals
With a preface by Peter Pomerantsev
ISBN 978-3-8382-1456-6

5 *Mykola Riabchuk*
At the Fence of Metternich's Garden
Essays on Europe, Ukraine, and Europeanization
ISBN 978-3-8382-1484-9

6 *Marta Dyczok*
Ukraine Calling
A Kaleidoscope from Hromadske Radio 2016–2019
With a foreword by Andriy Kulykov
ISBN 978-3-8382-1472-6

7 *Olexander Scherba*
Ukraine vs. Darkness
Undiplomatic Thoughts
With a foreword by Adrian Karatnycky
ISBN 978-3-8382-1501-3

8 *Olesya Yaremchuk*
Our Others
Stories of Ukrainian Diversity
With a foreword by Ostap Slyvynsky
Translated from the Ukrainian by Zenia Tompkins and Hanna Leliv
ISBN 978-3-8382-1475-7

9 *Nataliya Gumenyuk*
Die verlorene Insel
Geschichten von der besetzten Krim
Mit einem Vorwort von Alice Bota
Aus dem Ukrainischen übersetzt von Johann Zajaczkowski
ISBN 978-3-8382-1499-3

10 *Olena Stiazhkina*
Zero Point Ukraine
Four Essays on World War II
Translated from the Ukrainian by Svitlana Kulinska
ISBN 978-3-8382-1550-1

11 *Oleksii Sinchenko, Dmytro Stus, Leonid Finberg (compilers)*
Ukrainian Dissidents
An Anthology of Texts
ISBN 978-3-8382-1551-8

12 *John-Paul Himka*
Ukrainian Nationalists and the Holocaust
OUN and UPA's Participation in the Destruction of Ukrainian Jewry, 1941–1944
ISBN 978-3-8382-1548-8

13 *Andrey Demartino*
False Mirrors
The Weaponization of Social Media in Russia's Operation to Annex Crimea
With a foreword by Oleksiy Danilov
ISBN 978-3-8382-1533-4

14 *Svitlana Biedarieva (ed.)*
Contemporary Ukrainian and Baltic Art
Political and Social Perspectives, 1991–2021
ISBN 978-3-8382-1526-6

15 *Olesya Khromeychuk*
A Loss
The Story of a Dead Soldier Told by His Sister
With a foreword by Andrey Kurkov
ISBN 978-3-8382-1570-9

16 *Marieluise Beck (Hg.)*
Ukraine verstehen
Auf den Spuren von Terror und Gewalt
Mit einem Vorwort von Dmytro Kuleba
ISBN 978-3-8382-1653-9

17 *Stanislav Aseyev*
Heller Weg
Geschichte eines Konzentrationslagers im Donbass 2017–2019
Aus dem Russischen übersetzt von Martina Steis und Charis Haska
ISBN 978-3-8382-1620-1

18 *Mykola Davydiuk*
Wie funktioniert Putins Propaganda?
Anmerkungen zum Informationskrieg des Kremls
Aus dem Ukrainischen übersetzt von Christian Weise
ISBN 978-3-8382-1628-7

19 *Olesya Yaremchuk*
Unsere Anderen
Geschichten ukrainischer Vielfalt
Aus dem Ukrainischen übersetzt von Christian Weise
ISBN 978-3-8382-1635-5

20 *Oleksandr Mykhed*
„Dein Blut wird die Kohle tränken"
Über die Ostukraine
Aus dem Ukrainischen übersetzt von Simon Muschick und Dario Planert
ISBN 978-3-8382-1648-5

21 *Vakhtang Kipiani (Hg.)*
Der Zweite Weltkrieg in der Ukraine
Geschichte und Lebensgeschichten
Aus dem Ukrainischen übersetzt von Margarita Grinko
ISBN 978-3-8382-1622-5

22 *Vakhtang Kipiani (ed.)*
World War II, Uncontrived and Unredacted
Testimonies from Ukraine
Translated from the Ukrainian by Zenia Tompkins and Daisy Gibbons
ISBN 978-3-8382-1621-8

23 *Dmytro Stus*
Vasyl Stus
Life in Creativity
Translated from the Ukrainian by
Ludmila Bachurina
ISBN 978-3-8382-1631-7

24 *Vitalii Ogiienko (ed.)*
The Holodomor and the
Origins of the Soviet Man
Reading the Testimony of
Anastasia Lysyvets
With forewords by Natalka
Bilotserkivets and Serhy
Yekelchyk
Translated from the Ukrainian by
Alla Parkhomenko and
Alexander J. Motyl
ISBN 978-3-8382-1616-4

25 *Vladislav Davidzon*
Jewish-Ukrainian Relations
and the Birth of a Political
Nation
Selected Writings 2013-2021
With a foreword by Bernard-
Henri Lévy
ISBN 978-3-8382-1509-9

26 *Serhy Yekelchyk*
Writing the Nation
The Ukrainian Historical
Profession in Independent
Ukraine and the Diaspora
ISBN 978-3-8382-1695-9

27 *Ildi Eperjesi, Oleksandr
Kachura*
Shreds of War
Fates from the Donbas Frontline
2014-2019
With a foreword by Olexiy
Haran
ISBN 978-3-8382-1680-5

28 *Oleksandr Melnyk*
World War II as an Identity
Project
Historicism, Legitimacy
Contests, and the (Re-)Con-
struction of Political Commu-
nities in Ukraine, 1939–1946
With a foreword by David R.
Marples
ISBN 978-3-8382-1704-8

29 *Olesya Khromeychuk*
Ein Verlust
Die Geschichte eines gefallenen
ukrainischen Soldaten, erzählt
von seiner Schwester
Mit einem Vorwort von Andrej
Kurkow
Aus dem Englischen übersetzt
von Lily Sophie
ISBN 978-3-8382-1770-3

30 *Tamara Martsenyuk,
Tetiana Kostiuchenko (eds.)*
Russia's War in Ukraine
During 2022
Personal Experiences of
Ukrainian Scholars
ISBN 978-3-8382-1757-4

31 *Ildikó Eperjesi, Oleksandr
Kachura*
Shreds of War. Vol. 2
Fates from Crimea 2015–2022
With an interview of Oleh
Sentsov
ISBN 978-3-8382-1780-2

32 *Yuriy Lukanov*
The Press
How Russia Destroyed Media
Freedom in Crimea
With a foreword by Taras Kuzio
ISBN 978-3-8382-1784-0

33 *Megan Buskey*
Ukraine Is Not Dead Yet
A Family Story of Exile and
Return
ISBN 978-3-8382-1691-1

34 *Vira Ageyeva*
Behind the Scenes of the
Empire
Essays on Cultural
Relationships between Ukraine
and Russia
With a foreword by Oksana
Zabuzhko
ISBN 978-3-8382-1748-2

35 *Marieluise Beck (ed.)*
Understanding Ukraine
Tracing the Roots of Terror and
Violence
With a foreword by Dmytro
Kuleba
ISBN 978-3-8382-1773-4

36 *Olesya Khromeychuk*
A Loss
The Story of a Dead Soldier Told
by His Sister, 2nd edn.
With a foreword by Philippe
Sands
With a preface by Andrii Kurkov
ISBN 978-3-8382-1870-0

37 *Taras Kuzio, Stefan
Jajecznyk-Kelman*
Fascism and Genocide
Russia's War Against
Ukrainians
ISBN 978-3-8382-1791-8

38 *Alina Nychyk*
Ukraine Vis-à-Vis Russia
and the EU
Misperceptions of Foreign
Challenges in Times of War,
2014–2015
With a foreword by Paul
D'Anieri
ISBN 978-3-8382-1767-3

39 *Sasha Dovzhyk (ed.)*
Ukraine Lab
Global Security, Environment,
and Disinformation Through the
Prism of Ukraine
With a foreword by Rory Finnin
ISBN 978-3-8382-1805-2

40 *Serhiy Kvit*
Media, History, and
Education
Three Ways to Ukrainian
Independence
With a preface by Diane Francis
ISBN 978-3-8382-1807-6

41 *Anna Romandash*
Women of Ukraine
Reportages from the War and
Beyond
ISBN 978-3-8382-1819-9

42 *Dominika Rank*
Matzewe in meinem Garten
Abenteuer eines jüdischen
Heritage-Touristen in der
Ukraine
ISBN 978-3-8382-1810-6

43 *Myroslaw Marynowytsch*
Das Universum hinter dem
Stacheldraht
Memoiren eines sowjet-
ukrainischen Dissidenten
Mit einem Vorwort von Timothy
Snyder und einem Nachwort
von Max Hartmann
ISBN 978-3-8382-1806-9

44 *Konstantin Sigow*
Für Deine und meine
Freiheit
Europäische Revolutions- und
Kriegserfahrungen im heutigen
Kyjiw
Mit einem Vorwort von Karl
Schlögel
Herausgegeben von Regula M.
Zwahlen
ISBN 978-3-8382-1755-0

45 *Kateryna Pylypchuk*
The War that Changed Us
Ukrainian Novellas, Poems, and
Essays from 2022
With a foreword by Victor
Yushchenko
Paperback
ISBN 978-3-8382-1859-5
Hardcover
ISBN 978-3-8382-1860-1

46 *Kyrylo Tkachenko*
Rechte Tür Links
Radikale Linke in Deutschland,
die Revolution und der Krieg in
der Ukraine, 2013-2018
ISBN 978-3-8382-1711-6

47 *Alexander Strashny*
The Ukrainian Mentality
An Ethno-Psychological,
Historical and Comparative
Exploration
With a foreword by Antonina
Lovochkina
Translated from the Ukrainian
by Michael M. Naydan and
Olha Tytarenko
ISBN 978-3-8382-1886-1

48 *Alona Shestopalova*
From Screens to Battlefields
Tracing the Construction of
Enemies on Russian Television
With a foreword by Nina
Jankowicz
ISBN 978-3-8382-1884-7

49 *Iaroslav Petik*
Politics and Society in the
Ukrainian People's Republic
(1917–1921) and
Contemporary Ukraine
(2013–2022)
A Comparative Analysis
With a foreword by Mykola
Doroshko
ISBN 978-3-8382-1817-5

50 *Serhii Plokhy*
Der Mann mit der
Giftpistole
Eine Spionagegeschichte aus dem
Kalten Krieg
ISBN 978-3-8382-1789-5

51 *Vakhtang Kipiani*
Ukrainische Dissidenten
unter der Sowjetmacht
Im Kampf um Wahrheit und
Freiheit
Aus dem Ukrainischen übersetzt
von Christian Weise
ISBN 978-3-8382-1890-8

52 *Dmytro Shestakov*
When Businesses Test
Hypotheses
A Four-Step Approach to Risk
Management for Innovative
Startups
With a foreword by Anthony J.
Tether
ISBN 978-3-8382-1883-0

53 *Larissa Babij*
A Kind of Refugee
The Story of an American Who
Refused to Leave Ukraine
With a foreword by Vladislav
Davidzon
ISBN 978-3-8382-1898-4

54 *Julia Davis*
In Their Own Words
How Russian Propagandists
Reveal Putin's Intentions
With a foreword by Timothy
Snyder
ISBN 978-3-8382-1909-7

55 *Sonya Atlantova, Oleksandr
Klymenko*
Icons on Ammo Boxes
Painting Life on the Remnants of
Russia's War in Donbas, 2014-21
Translated from the Ukrainian by
Anastasya Knyazhytska
ISBN 978-3-8382-1892-2

56 *Leonid Ushkalov*
Catching an Elusive Bird
The Life of Hryhorii Skovoroda
Translated from the Ukrainian
by Natalia Komarova
ISBN 978-3-8382-1894-6

57 *Vakhtang Kipiani*
Ein Land weiblichen
Geschlechts
Ukrainische Frauenschicksale
im 20. und 21. Jahrhundert
Aus dem Ukrainischen übersetzt
von Christian Weise
ISBN 978-3-8382-1891-5

58 *Petro Rychlo*
„Zerrissne Saiten einer
überlauten Harfe ...“
Deutschjüdische Dichter der
Bukowina
ISBN 978-3-8382-1893-9

59 *Volodymyr Paniotto*
Sociology in Jokes
An Entertaining Introduction
ISBN 978-3-8382-1857-1

60 *Josef Wallmannsberger
(ed.)*
Executing Renaissances
The Poetological Nation of
Ukraine
ISBN 978-3-8382-1741-3

61 *Pavlo Kazarin*
The Wild West of Eastern
Europe
A Ukrainian Guide on Breaking
Free from Empire
Translated from the Ukrainian
by Dominique Hoffman
ISBN 978-3-8382-1842-7

62 *Ernest Gyidel*
Ukrainian Public
Nationalism in the General
Government
The Case of Krakivski Visti,
1940–1944
With a foreword by David R.
Marples
ISBN 978-3-8382-1865-6

63 *Olexander Hryb*
Understanding
Contemporary Russian
Militarism
From Revolutionary to New
Generation Warfare
With a foreword by Mark Laity
ISBN 978-3-8382-1927-1

64 *Orysia Hrudka, Bohdan Ben*
Dark Days, Determined
People
Stories from Ukraine under Siege
With a foreword by Myroslav
Marynovych
ISBN 978-3-8382-1958-5

65 *Oleksandr Pankieiev (ed.)*
Narratives of the Russo-
Ukrainian War
A Look Within and Without
With a foreword by Natalia
Khanenko-Friesen
ISBN 978-3-8382-1964-6

66 *Roman Sohn, Ariana Gic
(eds.)*
Unrecognized War
The Fight for Truth about
Russia's War on Ukraine
With a foreword by Viktor
Yushchenko
ISBN 978-3-8382-1947-9

67 *Paul Robert Magocsi*
Ukraina Redux
Schon wieder die Ukraine ...
ISBN 978-3-8382-1942-4

68 *Paul Robert Magocsi*
L'Ucraina Ritrovata
Sullo Stato e l'Identità Nazionale
ISBN 978-3-8382-1982-0

69 *Max Hartmann*
Ein Schrei der Verzweiflung
Aquarelle von Danylo Movchan
zu Russlands Krieg in der
Ukraine
Mit einem Vorwort von Mateusz
Sora
Paperback
ISBN 978-3-8382-2011-6
Hardcover
ISBN 978-3-8382-2012-3

70 *Vakhtang Kebuladze (Hg.)*
Die Zukunft, die wir uns
wünschen
Essays aus der Ukraine
ISBN 978-3-8382-1531-0

71 *Marieluise Beck, Jan Claas Behrends, Gelinada Grinchenko und Oksana Mikheieva (Hgg.)*
Deutsch-ukrainische Geschichten
Bruchstücke aus einer gemeinsamen Vergangenheit
ISBN 978-3-8382-2053-6

72 *Pavlo Kazarin*
Der Wilde Westen Ost-Europas
Der ukrainische Weg aus dem Imperium
Aus dem Ukrainischen übersetzt von Christian Weise
ISBN 978-3-8382-1843-4

73 *Radomyr Mokryk*
Die ukrainischen »Sechziger«
Chronologie einer Revolte
ISBN 978-3-8382-1873-1

74 *Leonid Finberg*
My Ukraine
Rethinking the Past, Building the Present
ISBN 978-3-8382-1974-5

75 *Joseph Zissels*
Consider My Inmost Thoughts
Essays, Lectures, and Interviews on Ukrainian Matters at the Turn of the Century
ISBN 978-3-8382-1975-2

76 *Margarita Yehorchenko, Iryna Berlyand, Ihor Vinokurov (eds.)*
Jewish Addresses in Ukraine
A Guide-Book
With a foreword by Leonid Finberg
ISB 978-3-8382-1976-9

77 *Viktoriia Grivina*
Kharkiv—A War City
A Collection of Essays from 2022–23
ISBN 978-3-8382-1988-2

78 *Hjørdis Clemmensen, Viktoriia Grivina, Vasylysa Shchogoleva*
Kharkiv Is a Dream
Public Art and Activism 2013–2023
With a foreword by Bohdan Volynskyi
ISBN 978-3-8382-2005-5

79 *Olga Khomenko*
The Faraway Sky of Kyiv
Ukrainians in the War
With a foreword by Hiroaki Kuromiya
ISBN 978-3-8382-2006-2

80 *Daria Mattingly, Jonathon Vsetecka (eds.)*
The Holodomor in Global Perspective
How the Famine in Ukraine Shaped the World
ISBN 978-3-8382-1953-0

81 *Olga Khomenko*
Ukrainians beyond Borders
Nine Life Journeys Through the History of Eastern Europe
With a foreword by Zbigniew Wojnowski
With a foreword by Anne Applebaum
ISBN 978-3-8382-2007-9

82 *Mykhailo Minakov*
From Servant to Leader
Chronicles of Ukraine under the Zelensky Presidency, 2019–2024
With a foreword by John Lloyd
ISBN 978-3-8382-2002-4

83 *Volodymyr Hromov (ed.)*
A Ruined Home
Sketches of War, 2022–2023
ISBN 978-3-8382-2008-6

84 Olha Tatokhina (ed.)
Why Do They Kill Our
People?
Russia's War Against Ukraine as
Told by Ukrainians
With a foreword by Volodymyr
Yermolenko
ISBN 978-3-8382-2056-7

Book series "Ukrainian Voices"

Coordinator
Andreas Umland, National University of Kyiv-Mohyla Academy

Editorial Board
Lesia Bidochko, National University of Kyiv-Mohyla Academy
Svitlana Biedarieva, George Washington University, DC, USA
Ivan Gomza, Kyiv School of Economics, Ukraine
Natalie Jaresko, Aspen Institute, Kyiv/Washington
Olena Lennon, University of New Haven, West Haven, USA
Kateryna Yushchenko, First Lady of Ukraine 2005-2010, Kyiv
Oleksandr Zabirko, University of Regensburg, Germany

Advisory Board
Iuliia Bentia, National Academy of Arts of Ukraine, Kyiv
Natalya Belitser, Pylyp Orlyk Institute for Democracy, Kyiv
Oleksandra Bienert, Humboldt University of Berlin, Germany
Sergiy Bilenky, Canadian Institute of Ukrainian Studies, Toronto
Tymofii Brik, Kyiv School of Economics, Ukraine
Olga Brusylovska, Mechnikov National University, Odesa
Mariana Budjeryn, Harvard University, Cambridge, USA
Volodymyr Bugrov, Shevchenko National University, Kyiv
Olga Burlyuk, University of Amsterdam, The Netherlands
Yevhen Bystrytsky, NAS Institute of Philosophy, Kyiv
Andrii Danylenko, Pace University, New York, USA
Vladislav Davidzon, Atlantic Council, Washington/Paris
Mykola Davydiuk, Think Tank "Polityka," Kyiv
Andrii Demartino, National Security and Defense Council, Kyiv
Vadym Denisenko, Ukrainian Institute for the Future, Kyiv
Oleksandr Donii, Center for Political Values Studies, Kyiv
Volodymyr Dubovyk, Mechnikov National University, Odesa
Volodymyr Dubrovskiy, CASE Ukraine, Kyiv
Diana Dutsyk, National University of Kyiv-Mohyla Academy
Marta Dyczok, Western University, Ontario, Canada
Yevhen Fedchenko, National University of Kyiv-Mohyla Academy
Sofiya Filonenko, State Pedagogical University of Berdyansk
Oleksandr Fisun, Karazin National University, Kharkiv
Oksana Forostyna, Webjournal "Ukraina Moderna," Kyiv
Roman Goncharenko, Broadcaster "Deutsche Welle," Bonn
George Grabowicz, Harvard University, Cambridge, USA
Gelinada Grinchenko, Karazin National University, Kharkiv
Kateryna Härtel, Federal Union of European Nationalities, Brussels
Nataliia Hendel, University of Geneva, Switzerland
Anton Herashchenko, Kyiv School of Public Administration
John-Paul Himka, University of Alberta, Edmonton
Ola Hnatiuk, National University of Kyiv-Mohyla Academy
Oleksandr Holubov, Broadcaster "Deutsche Welle," Bonn
Yaroslav Hrytsak, Ukrainian Catholic University, Lviv
Oleksandra Humenna, National University of Kyiv-Mohyla Academy
Tamara Hundorova, NAS Institute of Literature, Kyiv
Oksana Huss, University of Bologna, Italy
Oleksandra Iwaniuk, University of Warsaw, Poland
Mykola Kapitonenko, Shevchenko National University, Kyiv
Georgiy Kasianov, Marie Curie-Skłodowska University, Lublin
Vakhtang Kebuladze, Shevchenko National University, Kyiv
Natalia Khanenko-Friesen, University of Alberta, Edmonton
Victoria Khiterer, Millersville University of Pennsylvania, USA
Oksana Kis, NAS Institute of Ethnology, Lviv
Pavlo Klimkin, Center for National Resilience and Development, Kyiv
Oleksandra Kolomiiets, Center for Economic Strategy, Kyiv

Sergiy Korsunsky, Kobe Gakuin University, Japan
Nadiia Koval, Kyiv School of Economics, Ukraine
Volodymyr Kravchenko, University of Alberta, Edmonton
Oleksiy Kresin, NAS Koretskiy Institute of State and Law, Kyiv
Anatoliy Kruglashov, Fedkovych National University, Chernivtsi
Andrey Kurkov, PEN Ukraine, Kyiv
Ostap Kushnir, Lazarski University, Warsaw
Taras Kuzio, National University of Kyiv-Mohyla Academy
Serhii Kvit, National University of Kyiv-Mohyla Academy
Yuliya Ladygina, The Pennsylvania State University, USA
Yevhen Mahda, Institute of World Policy, Kyiv
Victoria Malko, California State University, Fresno, USA
Yulia Marushevska, Security and Defense Center (SAND), Kyiv
Myroslav Marynovych, Ukrainian Catholic University, Lviv
Oleksandra Matviichuk, Center for Civil Liberties, Kyiv
Mykhailo Minakov, Kennan Institute, Washington, USA
Anton Moiseienko, The Australian National University, Canberra
Alexander Motyl, Rutgers University-Newark, USA
Vlad Mykhnenko, University of Oxford, United Kingdom
Vitalii Ogiienko, Ukrainian Institute of National Remembrance, Kyiv
Olga Onuch, University of Manchester, United Kingdom
Olesya Ostrovska, Museum "Mystetskyi Arsenal," Kyiv
Anna Osypchuk, National University of Kyiv-Mohyla Academy
Oleksandr Pankieiev, University of Alberta, Edmonton
Oleksiy Panych, Publishing House "Dukh i Litera," Kyiv
Valerii Pekar, Kyiv-Mohyla Business School, Ukraine
Yohanan Petrovsky-Shtern, Northwestern University, Chicago
Serhii Plokhy, Harvard University, Cambridge, USA
Andrii Portnov, Viadrina University, Frankfurt-Oder, Germany
Maryna Rabinovych, Kyiv School of Economics, Ukraine
Valentyna Romanova, Institute of Developing Economies, Tokyo
Natalya Ryabinska, Collegium Civitas, Warsaw, Poland

Darya Tsymbalyk, University of Oxford, United Kingdom
Vsevolod Samokhvalov, University of Liege, Belgium
Orest Semotiuk, Franko National University, Lviv
Viktoriya Sereda, NAS Institute of Ethnology, Lviv
Anton Shekhovtsov, University of Vienna, Austria
Andriy Shevchenko, Media Center Ukraine, Kyiv
Oxana Shevel, Tufts University, Medford, USA
Pavlo Shopin, National Pedagogical Dragomanov University, Kyiv
Karina Shyrokykh, Stockholm University, Sweden
Nadja Simon, freelance interpreter, Cologne, Germany
Olena Snigova, NAS Institute for Economics and Forecasting, Kyiv
Ilona Solohub, Analytical Platform "VoxUkraine," Kyiv
Iryna Solonenko, LibMod - Center for Liberal Modernity, Berlin
Galyna Solovei, National University of Kyiv-Mohyla Academy
Sergiy Stelmakh, NAS Institute of World History, Kyiv
Olena Stiazhkina, NAS Institute of the History of Ukraine, Kyiv
Dmitri Stratievski, Osteuropa Zentrum (OEZB), Berlin
Dmytro Stus, National Taras Shevchenko Museum, Kyiv
Frank Sysyn, University of Toronto, Canada
Olha Tokariuk, Center for European Policy Analysis, Washington
Olena Tregub, Independent Anti-Corruption Commission, Kyiv
Hlib Vyshlinsky, Centre for Economic Strategy, Kyiv
Mychailo Wynnyckyj, National University of Kyiv-Mohyla Academy
Yelyzaveta Yasko, NGO "Yellow Blue Strategy," Kyiv
Serhy Yekelchyk, University of Victoria, Canada
Victor Yushchenko, President of Ukraine 2005-2010, Kyiv
Oleksandr Zaitsev, Ukrainian Catholic University, Lviv
Kateryna Zarembo, National University of Kyiv-Mohyla Academy
Yaroslav Zhalilo, National Institute for Strategic Studies, Kyiv
Sergei Zhuk, Ball State University at Muncie, USA
Alina Zubkovych, Nordic Ukraine Forum, Stockholm
Liudmyla Zubrytska, National University of Kyiv-Mohyla Academy

Friends of the Series

Ana Maria Abulescu, University of Bucharest, Romania

Łukasz Adamski, Centrum Mieroszewskiego, Warsaw

Marieluise Beck, LibMod—Center for Liberal Modernity, Berlin

Marc Berensen, King's College London, United Kingdom

Johannes Bohnen, BOHNEN Public Affairs, Berlin

Karsten Brüggemann, University of Tallinn, Estonia

Ulf Brunnbauer, Leibniz Institute (IOS), Regensburg

Martin Dietze, German-Ukrainian Culture Society, Hamburg

Gergana Dimova, Florida State University, Tallahassee/London

Caroline von Gall, Goethe University, Frankfurt-Main

Zaur Gasimov, Rhenish Friedrich Wilhelm University, Bonn

Armand Gosu, University of Bucharest, Romania

Thomas Grant, University of Cambridge, United Kingdom

Gustav Gressel, European Council on Foreign Relations, Berlin

Rebecca Harms, European Centre for Press & Media Freedom, Leipzig

André Härtel, Stiftung Wissenschaft und Politik, Berlin/Brussels

Marcel Van Herpen, The Cicero Foundation, Maastricht

Richard Herzinger, freelance analyst, Berlin

Mieste Hotopp-Riecke, ICATAT, Magdeburg

Nico Lange, Munich Security Conference, Berlin

Martin Malek, freelance analyst, Vienna

Ingo Mannteufel, Broadcaster "Deutsche Welle," Bonn

Carlo Masala, Bundeswehr University, Munich

Wolfgang Mueller, University of Vienna, Austria

Dietmar Neutatz, Albert Ludwigs University, Freiburg

Torsten Oppelland, Friedrich Schiller University, Jena

Niccolò Pianciola, University of Padua, Italy

Gerald Praschl, German-Ukrainian Forum (DUF), Berlin

Felix Riefer, Think Tank Ideenagentur-Ost, Düsseldorf

Stefan Rohdewald, University of Leipzig, Germany

Sebastian Schäffer, Institute for the Danube Region (IDM), Vienna

Felix Schimansky-Geier, Friedrich Schiller University, Jena

Ulrich Schneckener, University of Osnabrück, Germany

Winfried Schneider-Deters, freelance analyst, Heidelberg/Kyiv

Gerhard Simon, University of Cologne, Germany

Kai Struve, Martin Luther University, Halle/Wittenberg

David Stulik, European Values Center for Security Policy, Prague

Andrzej Szeptycki, University of Warsaw, Poland

Philipp Ther, University of Vienna, Austria

Stefan Troebst, University of Leipzig, Germany

[Please send requests for changes in, corrections of, and additions to, this list to andreas.umland@stanforalumni.org.]

ibidem.eu